The Apostles' Creed is chiseled in stone in the chapel of Beeson Divinity School, and every candidate for admission is asked to write an essay on it. Thank you, Michael Bird, for a fresh exposition of this classic expression of our Christian faith. Thank you for reminding us of what too many Protestants, evangelicals no less than liberals, have forgotten: creeds matter!

TIMOTHY GEORGE, founding dean of Beeson Divinity School of Samford University and general editor of the *Reformation Commentary on Scripture*.

You know what I love about Michael? He writes in a colorful, accessible, and engaging way even though he is a scholar of epic proportions; he writes to regular people like me. I'm going to take the staff of Transformation Church through *What Christians Ought to Believe* and I will use it to introduce new Christians to the faith.

DERWIN L. GRAY, Lead Pastor, Transformation Church; author of *The High Definition Leader: Building Multiethnic Churches in a Multiethnic World*.

The genius of this book is the way in which it makes profound truth a pleasure to read. The general reader will be both engaged and richly encouraged by Bird's winsome exploration of the Apostles' Creed. His direct and even chatty style makes you feel as if you are visiting an ancient cathedral in the company of a friendly and yet knowledgeable tour guide. I would commend *What Christians Ought to Believe* to study groups and to individual Christians looking to deepen not just their knowledge of the Christian faith but their knowledge of the triune God.

REV DR. MICHAEL P. JENSEN, St Mark's Anglican Church, Sydney

Michael Bird has done a huge favor for those whose traditions need to be reacquainted with the Apostles' Creed as more than a pedantic statement. He uses the Creed as it was intended to be used—to teach and form Christians in the living way of Jesus! Well-researched and engagingly written, Bird's volume will prove valuable in both church and academy, for those considering Christian faith as well as seasoned saints. His wit, clarity, and scholarship reflect the inherent winsomeness of the theological task and of a creed-contoured faith. I'm already looking for ways to use it.

DON J. PAYNE, Associate Professor of Theology and Christian Formation, Denver Seminary

What Christians Ought to Believe is more than a clear, concise exposition of the essential tenets of faith informed by the very best of biblical and theological scholarship. With deep-rooted evangelical conviction and his trademark wit, Professor Bird also makes a compelling case that even committed biblicists can appreciate the beauty, instructional value, and fidelity to Scripture found in the ancient Creed.

RHYNE R. PUTMAN, Assistant Professor of Theology and Culture, New Orleans Baptist Theological Seminary

We all have a tradition through which we read Scripture, and Michael Bird argues that the Apostles' Creed ought to be that tradition. Far from competing with the Bible, this ancient summary of the faith is an aid in rightly understanding the Bible. Bird approaches the Creed as a syllabus for teaching basic Christian belief, and like the experienced professor that he is, guides his readers through the Creed by highlighting the contours of the narrative and the convictions of the faith. Mike's books have been a constant source of encouragement for me, and in this one the Bird soars high in showing the sweeping narrative of Scripture and the core beliefs that emerge from it. I'm grateful that because of this book many will be able to say with more conviction and clarity: "I believe."

JEREMY TREAT (PhD, Wheaton College), pastor at Reality LA, professor at Biola University; author of *The Crucified King: Atonement and Kingdom in Biblical and Systematic Theology*.

WHAT CHRISTIANS *Ought to* BELIEVE

AN INTRODUCTION TO CHRISTIAN DOCTRINE THROUGH
THE APOSTLES' CREED

Michael F. Bird

ZONDERVAN
ACADEMIC

ZONDERVAN ACADEMIC

What Christians Ought to Believe
Copyright © 2016 by Michael F. Bird

ISBN 978-0-310-52093-1 (ebook)

Requests for information should be addressed to:
Zondervan, 3900 *Sparks Dr. SE, Grand Rapids, Michigan 49546*

Library of Congress Cataloging-in-Publication Data

Names: Bird, Michael F., author.
Title: What Christians ought to believe : an introduction to Christian doctrine through the
    Apostles' Creed / Michael F. Bird.
Description: Grand Rapids : Zondervan, 2016. | Includes index.
Identifiers: LCCN 2015049555 | ISBN 9780310520924 (hardcover)
Subjects: LCSH: Apostles' Creed. | Theology, Doctrinal.
Classification: LCC BT993.3 .B57 2016 | DDC 238/.11--dc23 LC record available at http://lccn
    .loc.gov/2015049555

Cover design: Michelle Lenger
Cover images: Dreamtime, Shutterstock
Interior design: Kait Lamphere

Printed in the United States of America

20 21 22 23 24 25 26 27 28 29 30 /LSC/ 18 17 16 15 14 13 12 11 10 9 8 7 6 5 4

For the Birdlings:
Alexis
Alyssa
Markus
Theodore

I have no greater joy than to hear that my
children are walking in the truth.
(3 John 4)

CONTENTS

CONTENTS
(Detailed)

PREFACE

In recent years, I've enjoyed taking my children through the Apostles' Creed. We've read it together, discussed it, looked up Bible passages, prayed around it, and even memorized it. If you ask me, the Apostles' Creed is probably the best syllabus ever devised for teaching basic Christian beliefs. It is succinct, easy to read, yet immensely profound. The Apostles' Creed is basically a bullet-point summary of what Christians believe about God, Jesus, the church, and the life to come. It is a rudimentary survey of what Christian faith affirms and indeed what all Christians ought to affirm if they are to be called Christians.

Sadly, I know of many churches that make no effort to recite, teach, and confess the Apostles' Creed or any creed for that matter. Indeed, the decision to omit the creeds from worship, preaching, teaching, and Bible study is often quite deliberate. A reticence to employ the creeds as instructive tools is largely borne of a mixture of skepticism toward tradition, a rank biblicism that ignores historical theology, and a certain arrogance that all who came before us were either incomplete or erroneous in their theology. The result is a theological travesty where a treasure trove of riches remains untouched. Even worse, by ignoring the creeds those who consider themselves to be orthodox are effectively sawing off the theological branches upon which they are sitting.

In this book, I have in mind to present the case for why Christians who are not by habit "creedal" in their devotion and discipleship should change their attitude toward the creeds and make use of Christian creeds as part of their statement of belief, worship, preaching, and teaching. I maintain that, as a prime example, embedding the Apostles' Creed in our corporate church life is an excellent way to ensure the integrity and orthodoxy of our faith and also a great means to infusing some ancient wisdom into our spiritual journey.

I have set out in an earlier volume an extensive summary of the evangelical faith—that is, the ancient and apostolic faith of the church as seen through the lens of a modern and missional Protestantism.[1] In this slender book, I have a modest aim to set forth a summary of the basic elements of the Christian faith as outlined in the Apostles' Creed with a view to the theological formation of undergraduate students and keen Christian disciples. Along the way I also hope to demonstrate how the creeds came into being, how they relate to Scripture, and why the creeds remain important for us today. The main effort of this book rests on expositing the Apostles' Creed as a way of summarizing the teaching of Scripture to enable followers of Jesus to "fear the Lord your God" (Deut 10:12), to "know the certainty of the things you have been taught" (Luke 1:4), to "reach unity in the faith and in the knowledge of the Son of God" (Eph 4:13), and "to contend for the faith that was once for all entrusted to God's holy people" (Jude 3).

---

1. Michael F. Bird, *Evangelical Theology: A Biblical and Systematic Introduction* (Grand Rapids: Zondervan, 2013).

The Apostles' Creed[1]

I believe in God, the Father almighty,
creator of heaven and earth.

I believe in Jesus Christ, his only Son, our Lord.
He was conceived by the power of the Holy Spirit
and born of the Virgin Mary.

He suffered under Pontius Pilate,
was crucified, died, and was buried.

He descended to the dead.
On the third day he rose again.
He ascended into heaven,
and is seated at the right hand of the Father.
He will come again to judge the living and the dead.

I believe in the Holy Spirit,
the holy catholic Church,
the communion of saints,
the forgiveness of sins,
the resurrection of the body,
and the life everlasting.
Amen.

---

1. The English text of the Apostles' Creed used in this book is a modern English version used by the worldwide Anglican communion. See http://www.anglicancommunion.org/media/109023/Apostles-Creed.pdf.

CHRISTIAN CREEDS
for BEGINNERS

Who Needs Creeds When
I've Got a Bible?

I used to provide regular supply preaching for a warm and intimate fellowship of Christians in the Free Church tradition. I cheekily smiled to myself whenever I read their bulletin because it always had on it the words, "No creed but Christ, no book but the Bible." The irony, of course, is that those words are not found in the Bible. This delightful group of saints had in fact turned their pious motto into a type of extrabiblical creed. Their genuine concern not to court controversy over creeds led to the formation of their own anticreedal creed as it were.

Hesitation about the value of the ancient creeds for modern Christians is quite understandable. If your only experience of creeds is mindless repetition, if you've been exposed to seemingly esoteric debates about technical theological jargon that does not appear relevant to anything, if you've ever been confused about how the creeds relate to what the Bible actually says, or if you think that the whole process of writing creeds and confessions just becomes divisive, then you may certainly be excused for some misgivings about creeds.

The problem is that it is no good just to say, "We believe the Bible!" Noble as that might sound, it runs into several problems. The fact is that many groups claim to believe the Bible, including Baptists, Episcopalians, Catholics, Methodists, Presbyterians, Jehovah's Witnesses, Oneness Pentecostals, and many more. Yet you cannot help but notice that these groups do not always agree on what the Bible teaches. Most of the time these differences are fairly inconsequential, but other times the differences are absolutely gigantic. Whether we should baptize babies or only believing adults is significant, but is hardly going to shake the foundations of the cosmos. Whether Jesus was an archangel who briefly visited earth or the coequal and coeternal Son of God who was incarnated as a man makes an immense difference, with a whole constellation of things riding on it. If you do believe the Bible, then sooner or later you have to set out what you think the Bible says. What does the Bible—the entire Bible for that matter—say about God, Jesus, salvation, and the life of the age to come? When you set out the biblical teaching in some formal sense, like in a church doctrinal statement, then you are creating a creed. You are saying: this is what we believe the Bible teaches about X, Y, and Z. You are saying: this is the stuff that really matters. You are declaring: this is where the boundaries of the faith need to be drawn. You are suggesting: this is what brings us together in one faith.

Creeds Are Biblical!

Something we need to remember is that creeds are in fact found in the Bible! There are a number of passages in the Old and New Testaments that have a creedal function. In Deuteronomy, we find the Shema, Israel's most concise confession of its faith in one God. Hence the words: "Hear, O Israel: The LORD our God, the LORD is one. Love the LORD your God with all your heart and with all your soul and with all your strength" (Deut 6:4–5). These are the words that faithful Jews across the centuries have confessed daily. It was this belief in one God that distinguished the Israelites from pagan polytheists and even to this day marks out Judaism as a monotheistic religion in contrast to many other world religions. The Shema described the essential elements of Israel's faith in a short and simple summary. The Shema stipulated that Israel's God was the one and only God, the God of creation and covenant, the God of the patriarchs—Abraham, Isaac, and Jacob—who had rescued the Hebrews from slavery in Egypt. Furthermore, the Israelites were to respond to their God principally in love, as love would determine the nature of their faith and obedience to him. As God had loved them, so they in return must love God. No surprise, then, that the Shema was affirmed by both Jesus and Paul and held in tandem with their distinctive beliefs about kingdom, Messiah, and salvation (see Mark 12:29; 1 Cor 8:6). What that means is that Jesus, Paul, and the first Christians were creedal believers simply by virtue of the fact that they were Jewish and lived within the orbit of Jewish beliefs about God, the covenant, and the future.

Given that context, it is perfectly understandable that the early church developed their own creeds to summarize what they believed the God of Israel *had done* and *would yet do* in the Lord Jesus Christ. Jesus's tomb was not long vacated when persons in the early church began to set out summaries of their faith in early creedal statements. Among the first believers were those who composed a short summary of the basic beliefs that were shared by Christians all over the Greco-Roman world.

To begin with, what was arguably the most pervasive of early Christian beliefs was that Jesus died for our sins and rose from the dead:

For we believe that Jesus died and rose again. (1 Thess 4:14)

[Jesus] died for them and was raised again. (2 Cor 5:15)

He was delivered over to death for our sins and was raised to life for our justification. (Rom 4:25)

Christ died and returned to life. (Rom 14:9)

These are the words of him who is the First and the Last, who died and came to life again. (Rev 2:8)

What is striking is that this belief that Jesus was crucified and was raised to life was affirmed in diverse types of material in the New Testament. It is found in liturgical material, apostolic exhortation to congregations, snuggly inserted into theological argumentation, laid out in hymnlike poetry, and even found in New Testament prophecy. It was a belief that was as pervasive as it was popular. Furthermore, this statement was the fulcrum of the church's confession about who Jesus was and what God did through him.

We find more elaborate creedal statements appearing in Paul's letters. During Paul's imprisonment in Rome, he wrote a letter to Timothy in Ephesus, and in this letter Paul referred to what was very probably an early creed:

> *He appeared in the flesh,*
> *   was vindicated by the Spirit,*
> *was seen by angels,*
> *   was preached among the nations,*
> *was believed on in the world,*
> *   was taken up in glory. (1 Tim 3:16)*

This creed gives a basic summary of Jesus's career from incarnation to his exaltation. Each line tells us about some key event in his earthly mission. It is a short summary of the story of Jesus and functions as the touchstone of faith. It doesn't say everything there is to say, but it gives the basic outlines into which other beliefs can be seamlessly added to fill out the picture.

Another important passage is the famous "Christ hymn" found in Philippians 2:5–11. This passage might not be an actual hymn; it could simply be poetic prose or a fragment of an early statement of faith that Paul had received from others. In any case, it is a majestic description of how Jesus went from divine glory to servile humiliation to exaltation to the right hand of God the Father.

In your relationships with one another, have the same mindset as Christ Jesus:

> *Who, being in very nature God,*
> *   did not consider equality with God something*
> *   to be used to his own advantage;*
> *rather, he made himself nothing*
> *   by taking the very nature of a servant,*

being made in human likeness.
And being found in appearance as a man,
he humbled himself
by becoming obedient to death—even death on a cross!
Therefore God exalted him to the highest place
and gave him the name that is above every name,
that at the name of Jesus every knee should bow,
in heaven and on earth and under the earth,
and every tongue acknowledge that Jesus Christ is Lord,
to the glory of God the Father. (Phil 2:5–11)

This wonderful text sets forth the story of Jesus's incarnation, his redemptive death, and his accession to divine glory. Whether sung, read, or recited, it certainly lends itself to a creedal function as it sets out what Christians believe about where Jesus came from, why he died, and why he should be worshipped.

Creeds Carry Biblical Traditions

The creedal-like materials that we find in the New Testament are part of a general pattern of "teachings" or "traditions" that were composed and passed on for the benefit of the churches. We find evidence in the New Testament for a large body of instruction being orally transmitted to the nascent churches by the apostles. In the Pauline churches, this included the story of the gospel (1 Cor 15:3–5), Jesus's final supper with his followers (1 Cor 11:23–26), and a general body of Christian teachings (Rom 6:17). Indeed, Paul tells the Thessalonians that they should "stand firm and hold fast to the teachings we passed on to you, whether by word of mouth or by letter" (2 Thess 2:15). Similarly, the risen Jesus tells the church in Sardis to remember "what you have received and heard" (Rev 3:3). What Jude calls the "faith that was once for all entrusted to God's holy people" refers to the faith taught in the Old Testament Scriptures, the teachings of Jesus, the story of Jesus, and the apostolic instruction in the way of Jesus (Jude 3). The spiritually gifted teachers of the church passed on these teachings—stories and instructions about Jesus—which provided the substance for the later creeds of the church (see Acts 13:1; Rom 12:7; 1 Cor 12:28–29; Eph 4:11; Heb 5:12; Jas 3:1).

We might say that early Christian instruction was the exposition of a "tradition," that is, a collection of teachings that were passed on by Jesus to his apostles, combined with a distinctive way of interpreting the Old Testament that made Jesus the centerpiece of God's promises, a tradition interpreted and augmented in light of their experience of God in life and worship, which was then transmitted and taught among the churches.[1] This "tradition" is what largely generated the New Testament. The Gospels are the traditions of Jesus that were passed on by eyewitnesses, received by early leaders, and written down by the evangelists (see Luke 1:1–4). The New Testament letters use a lot of traditional materials—hymns, creeds, sayings, stories, vice lists, virtue lists, etc.—to instruct congregations in light of the situations they were facing. When leaders in the postapostolic church sought to transmit their faith to other churches through correspondence, they were trying to summarize what they had learned from the Jewish Scriptures and the disciples of the apostles and were attempting to lay out the common consensus of the faith as they understood it. The creeds that were subsequently written were largely the attempt to provide concise statements about the faith that had been received in the church. In other words, early traditions shaped the New Testament, and then the New Testament subsequently shaped the developing traditions of the church, traditions that crystallized into the later creeds. Thus, the creeds are really a summary of the New Testament tradition: the text and its history of interpretation in the churches.

You cannot read the New Testament apart from some tradition. Even the pulpit-pounding fundamentalist who claims that the Bible alone guides him still appeals to an established consensus within his own community to validate his exposition of the Bible as a true and accurate account. This tradition, even if not openly acknowledged, is regarded as an authoritative declaration about what the Bible says in that group. Even the most jiving and thriving of Pentecostal churches has a *normal* way of doing Sunday

---

1. On the importance of "tradition," see Bird, *Evangelical Theology*, 64–70.

morning worship that does not jump directly from the pages of the New Testament. This *normal* way of doing worship, how they organize everything from songs to sermons, is a type of tradition too.

Inasmuch as we all have a "tradition," the creeds arguably provide the best tradition within which to read Scripture. This is because the creeds should be regarded as a biblically generated tradition that meets with the consensus of the universal church about what the main teachings of the Christian faith are. The creeds constitute an attempt to guide our reading of Scripture by setting out in advance the contents and concerns of Scripture itself. The creeds provide a kind of "Idiot's Guide to Christianity" by briefly laying out the story, unity, coherence, and major themes of the Christian faith. In that sense, a creedal faith is crucial for a biblical faith and vice versa!

Creeds in the Cradle of the Early Church

The creeds became particularly important in the second century when the church was faced with many challenges about the integrity of its faith. Various groups, some quite popular for a time, often had vastly different ideas about Jesus, discipleship, and salvation. The Ebionites claimed that an angel or a heavenly Christ figure entered into the body of the man Jesus at his baptism. The Docetists denied that Jesus had a physical body. The Gnostics claimed that a wicked demigod created the world, and Jesus came to save us from this god by releasing our souls from our bodies with the secret knowledge of our primeval origins. In each of these heresies there are vastly different ideas about God, God's relation to creation, the identity of Jesus, the meaning of salvation, and hope for the future.

Most of the creeds were written in response to some heresy or doctrinal controversy. We might say that the creeds are basically the written account of several relationship breakdowns in the early church. While the early church was in many ways diverse and far from monolithic, certain groups on the fringes were advocating a form of belief that exceeded the acceptable limits of diversity and were no longer recognizably Christian. They were espousing a different God who sent a different Jesus to fix a different problem in humanity. The heretics had to be voted off the island because the truth of the gospel and the unity of the church were under threat.

The debates were over no small matters. The bishops and theologians were not arguing over the appropriate length of church candles. For example, the attempt of the Marcionites in the second century to play off the God of creation against the God of redemption was neither convincing nor wholesome. It looked as if Jesus had come to save people from the God of the Old Testament, a totally unacceptable proposition. The efforts of the Arians in the fourth century to insulate Jesus from the divinity of the Father shattered the whole edifice of the gospel. If Jesus was a created being, a supreme angelic creature no less, he could not be our Savior, because one created being cannot eternally save another created being. The heretics were warned, but they didn't listen. So they either left or were shown the door.

The Christians who composed these creeds often did so with a view to distinguishing between authentic and inauthentic expressions of the faith. The creeds attempted to differentiate between a faith rooted in Scripture and one adapted to satisfy the sentiments of popular philosophies of the day. The creeds drew a line between a faith drawn from Scripture and understood in light of apostolic testimony and a different faith emerging from a combination of pagan philosophy and incoherent readings of Scripture. The creeds endeavored to discern the difference between a faith that made sense of their experience of Jesus and one that deliberately obscured things in order to make knowledge of God the possession of an elite few. In sum, the purpose of the creeds was to mark out the boundaries of the faith. The creeds were warnings to the effect that "all who proceed beyond this point do so at the peril of their own souls."

Meet the Ecumenical Creeds

There were many creeds and declarations about doctrine made by leaders in the ancient church. However, the most famous creeds, because they were the most widely utilized, are generally known as the three ecumenical creeds and the Chalcedonian definition. These statements of faith are all upheld by the Western church, that is, the Catholic and Protestant churches.

Creed: Apostles' Creed   **Date:** ca. AD 200

Origins: According to legend the Apostles' Creed, or *Symbolum Apostolorum*, was written by the apostles ten days after the ascension. In reality, however, the Apostles' Creed probably emerged in Rome as an early statement of faith used at the baptism of new converts in the late second or early third century (ca. AD 215). The precise wording of the Apostles' Creed developed over several centuries, and the present form goes back to the eighth century. It is not used in the Eastern churches.

Creed: Niceno-Constantinopolitan Creed   **Date:** AD 325, 381

Origins: Emperor Constantine called for a council of bishops to deal with the controversial teachings of an Alexandrian presbyter named Arius. Arius was a popular preacher who taught that Jesus was a created being *like* God the Father but *not the same as* God the Father. The council took place in AD 325 and its central affirmations were that Jesus was truly God, he was of the same essence as the Father, and he was begotten not made. However, the debate continued for the next fifty years, with the political class committed to an Arian interpretation of the Creed of Nicaea.

Another council was called in Constantinople in AD 381 to deal with the teachings of Apollinaris, who taught that the *Logos* replaced the soul of the man Jesus, thereby injuring his full humanity. In response, the council expanded the Creed of Nicaea to include affirmations about the deity of the Holy Spirit, gave more explicit wording to the incarnation, and referenced the eternal nature of Jesus's kingdom. The Nicene Creed is the creed recited by all Christian churches, East and West, Protestant, Catholic, and Orthodox, as the definitive expression of the Christian faith. The sixth-century Latin-speaking church created controversy when it added the so-called *filioque* (Latin for "and the Son") clause to the Nicene Creed. This addition was made to emphasize that the Holy Spirit proceeds from the Father and the Son. This cosmetic addition ensured the conversion of the Goths from Arianism to Orthodoxy. Yet it was the catalyst for a schism between the Eastern and Western churches in AD 1054 since the Eastern churches did not accept the addition, a rejection that lasts even to this day.

Creed: Chalcedonian Definition   **Date:** AD 451

Origins: While the matter of Jesus's deity was settled by councils held at Nicaea (AD 325) and Constantinople (AD 381), continuing debate surrounded how Jesus's human and divine natures related to each other. A meeting was held at Chalcedon in AD 451 where the council rejected several erroneous views on the relationship between Jesus's two natures. The formula that was agreed on was that Jesus's two natures were distinct yet united without confusion, change, separation, or division.

Creed: Athanasian Creed   **Date:** ca. AD 500

Origins: The Athanasian Creed was not written by Athanasius but was likely named after him; it affirms the central Trinitarian and christological beliefs of the post-Chalcedonian church.

Our focus in this volume will be the Apostles' Creed. Strictly speaking, the Nicene Creed is the most catholic and ecumenically recognized of the creeds as it is recited in both the Western and Eastern churches. However, the Apostles' Creed is profound for its pure simplicity and its concise coverage of the major topics of Christian teaching. The Apostles' Creed is the faith that all professing Christians should know, what all pastors and priests should teach, and what all bishops and theologians should defend. According to the nineteenth-century church historian Philip Schaff:

> As the Lord's Prayer is the Prayer of prayers, the Decalogue the Law of laws, so the Apostles' Creed is the Creed of creeds. It contains all the fundamental articles of the Christian faith necessary to salvation, in the form of fact, in simple Scripture language, and in the most natural order—the order of revelation—from God and the creation down to the resurrection and life everlasting.[2]

---

2. Philip Schaff, *The Creeds of Christendom, Volume 1: The History of Creeds* (Grand Rapids: Baker, 1983), 14–15.

Recommended Reading

Bird, Michael F. "Part One: Prolegomena: Beginning to Talk about God." Pages 27–86 in *Evangelical Theology: A Biblical and Systematic Introduction*. Grand Rapids: Zondervan, 2013.

Jenson, Robert W. *Canon and Creed*. Louisville: Westminster John Knox, 2010.

Johnson, Luke Timothy. *The Creed: What Christians Believe and Why It Matters*. New York: Doubleday, 2003.

Kelly, J. N. D. *Early Christian Creeds*. New York: D. Mackay, 1972.

McGrath, Alister. *Faith and the Creeds*. London: SPCK, 2013.

Trueman, Carl B. *The Creedal Imperative*. Wheaton: Crossway, 2012.

2

WHY YOU NEED *the* CREED

Canon and Creed

Our biblical canon and church creeds go together like peanut butter and jelly or like Vegemite and avocado as we Aussies prefer to say. The formation of the biblical canon and the origin of the early creeds arose out of processes that were concurrent and mutually influential. Beliefs shaped the books that were prized and read, while the books in turn shaped the beliefs that people held and professed. In what follows, we will get a general overview of that complex process and reiterate our contention that the biblical canon and our church creeds naturally belong together.

The Story of the Canon

By the early third century, the churches of the East and West each had their own professions of faith expressed in local creeds. These creeds were based on the Old Testament and Christian writings such as the Gospels and apostolic letters, though without precisely defining which Gospels and which apostolic writings were inspired and authoritative. The formal endorsement of the writings that make up the Old and New Testaments took the best part of four hundred years. Indeed, some Christian writings like the Shepherd of Hermas, 1 Clement, and Didache stood a good chance of being included in the canon, while other writings like Hebrews, 2 Peter, and the book of Revelation were only accepted with some hesitation. The process of the canonization of the New Testament is quite a debated and complex topic, but generally speaking the most important criterion for inclusion in the canon was conformity to the apostolic faith. The consensus that emerged from among the church fathers was that the twenty-seven books that make up our New Testament were the authoritative list of sacred books for the Christian church.[1] The point to note is that the writings that make up our Old and New Testaments shaped the developing creeds, the creeds established the orthodox faith and determined the criteria for books to be included in the biblical canon. In which case, we have to say that there is a symbiotic relationship between creed and canon, as the two entities were mutually creating and mutually reinforcing.

We can picture this process in the diagram below, which shows how canon and creed emerged in the early church.

3. Apostolic Teaching
(instruction, writings, worship)

4. Christian Scriptures
(The Septuagint plus the writings
associated with the apostles)

2. Jesus
(gospel of the kingdom)

5. Rule of Faith
(Irenaeus, Tertullian)

1. Hebrew Old Testament
(Law, Prophets, Writings)

6. Early Creeds

7. Biblical Canon
(Septuagint + New Testament)

---

1. See a variety of perspectives in Arthur G. Patzia, *The Making of the New Testament: Origin, Collection, Text and Canon* (Downers Grove, IL: InterVarsity Press, 1995); Lee Martin McDonald, *The Origin of the Bible: A Guide for the Perplexed* (New York: T&T Clark, 2011); Michael J. Kruger, *Question of Canon: Challenging the Status Quo in the New Testament Debate* (Downers Grove, IL: InterVarsity Press, 2013).

The Hebrew Scriptures

Around the time of Jesus and the apostles, it seems that the religious and scribal leaders of Israel accepted as authoritative three classes of Jewish literature: the Torah (the five books of Moses), the Prophets (the writing prophets), and the Writings (wisdom literature and Jewish histories). As indicative of this trend you can find many references to the "Law" and the "Prophets" in the New Testament (see Matt 5:17; Luke 16:16; John 1:45; Acts 13:15; 24:14; 28:23; Rom 3:21; see 2 Macc 15:9; 4 Macc 18:10). Several other books, which we list among the "Apocrypha" and "Pseudepigrapha," were also venerated to some degree by Jews and Christians, with several books included in a Greek translation of the Hebrew Scriptures called the Septuagint.[2] Jesus's "Bible" was the Hebrew Scriptures and possibly Aramaic paraphrases called targumim, while the Scriptures of the early church were predominantly the Septuagint.

Jesus

Sometime around AD 27, a Galilean prophet named Jesus of Nazareth came onto the scene, preaching the advent of the kingdom of God (Mark 1:14–15). Jesus believed that he was ushering in the kingdom in fulfillment of Israel's hopes for the restoration of the nation (Luke 4:18–21). His death and resurrection was the fulfillment of the prophetic promises and the basis for the mission of the church to the Greco-Roman world (Luke 24:25–27). For the early church, their primary authority was the Jewish Scriptures plus the teachings of Jesus. It was Scripture understood in light of Jesus that authorized their mission, ethics, hopes, and common life together.

---

2. The additional Jewish books included in editions of the Greek Septuagint or inserted into the Latin Apocrypha are Tobit, Judith, a Greek version of Esther, Wisdom of Solomon, Sirach, Baruch, Epistle of Jeremiah, Prayer of Azariah, Susanna, Bel and the Dragon, Prayer of Manasseh, Psalm 151; 1–4 Maccabees, 1 Esdras, 4 Esdras. See further David A. deSilva, *Introducing the Apocrypha: Message, Context, and Significance* (Grand Rapids: Baker, 2002); Timothy Michael Law, *When God Spoke Greek: The Septuagint and the Making of the Christian Bible* (Oxford: Oxford University Press, 2013).

Apostolic Teaching

In the aftermath of Jesus's ascension, the early church naturally looked to Jesus's disciples, the apostles, for leadership and instruction. It was the apostolic teaching about the Scriptures and Jesus that formed the basis of the doctrine of the early church on topics like salvation, hope, and ethics. The apostles and their associates wrote biographies, histories, letters, and an apocalypse that eventually became the basis for the New Testament. In the postapostolic generation, Christians continued to be writing communities who wrote about Jesus, wrote letters to each other, and even copied each other's works. It was among this web of fellowships that Christians shared literature and engaged in mission together.

Christian Scriptures

In the postapostolic generation, we see a few things happening. First, Christians used the Greek translation of the Hebrew Bible, the Septuagint, as their Scriptures. Second, at the same time, Christians began speaking about the Gospels and apostolic letters also as "Scripture." We need to remember that *Scripture* here means "a sacred writing with religious authority." It does not mean *canon* as "an authoritative list of authoritative writings made by divine inspiration, carrying divine authority, and universally recognized." Christians began to call many texts "Scripture," including the Jewish writings we would now consider part of the Apocrypha as well as Christian writings that did not become part of the New Testament. In other words, Christians were beginning to think about which writings they considered authoritative, sacred, and authentic, but without fully delineating the criteria and limitations for inclusion in their register of sacred books.

Rule of Faith

Even though the early church did not have a strictly defined list of Christian writings that served as a theological authority for some time, they did have a definite story that functioned as an authoritative guide. This story was the *regula fidei* or the "rule of faith." In a nutshell, the rule of faith is the narrative generated by the Jewish Scriptures and the Christian Scriptures. It is the story of creation, Jesus's birth, his life, his death and resurrection, the ascension, the beginnings of the church, and the consummation. Irenaeus wrote that even many illiterate barbarians are among those that are

> believing in one God, the Creator of heaven and earth, and all things therein, by means of Christ Jesus, the Son of God; who, because of His surpassing love toward His creation, condescended to be born of the virgin, He Himself uniting man through Himself to God, and having suffered under Pontius Pilate, and rising again, and having been received up in splendour, shall come in glory, the Saviour of those who are saved, and the Judge of those who are judged, and sending into eternal fire those who transform the truth, and despise His Father and His advent. Those who, in the absence of written documents, have believed this faith, are barbarians, so far as regards our language; but as regards doctrine, manner, and tenor of life, they are, because of faith, very wise indeed; and they do please God, ordering their conversation in all righteousness, chastity, and wisdom. If any one were to preach to these men the inventions of the heretics, speaking to them in their own language, they would at once stop their ears, and flee as far off as possible, not enduring even to listen to the blasphemous address. Thus, by means of that ancient tradition of the apostles, they do not suffer their mind to conceive anything of the [doctrines suggested by the] portentous language of these teachers, among whom neither Church nor doctrine has ever been established.[3]

Irenaeus says that what was handed down in the church was not only a collection of written documents but an interpretive framework for understanding them. Even believers among the "barbarians," illiterate and without writings in their own language, assent to the rule of faith because they know it from the first missionaries who preached the gospel to them. In fact, Irenaeus and Tertullian say that the root error of all heresies is studying the Scriptures in isolation from the rule of faith. If you reject the apostolic

---

3. Irenaeus, *Against Heresies* 3.4.1–2 (as found in *The Ante-Nicene Fathers*, ed. A. Roberts and J. Donaldson; 10 vols.; 1885–87; reprint, Peabody, MA: Hendrickson, 1994; hereafter *ANF*).

tradition, then you'll end up with a skewed interpretation of the apostolic writings. Thus, the Scriptures generated the rule of faith, and the rule of faith serves to authorize Scripture.[4]

Creeds

The purpose of the creeds was to take the overarching narrative of the *regula fidei* and translate it into a list of key beliefs to be affirmed. In the case of the Apostles' Creed, this meant affirming the essential narrative moments in the story of God, Jesus, and the church as part of one's formal consent to the apostolic faith before entering baptism. The primary function of the Niceno-Constantinopolitan Creed was to clarify the christological foundation of the church's faith by expounding the precise relation between the Father and Son in terms of their shared essence and distinctive persons. At every point of affirmation, we find that the creeds are simply summarizing what is stated in Scripture or else following the logic of Scripture to explain who God is and what he has done for us in Jesus Christ. The creeds tell us the story of our faith and what parts of the story matter the most. Viewed this way, the creeds are then a type of gold standard by which one can safeguard the fixtures of our faith that are of first importance and warn against falsehood by those who would dangerously fiddle with crucial facets of the faith.

Biblical Canon

The Bible did not fall out of the sky, bound in leather, with the words of Jesus in red, written in *ye auld* Elizabethan English, and complete with Scofield footnotes. The process through which Christian Scriptures became the Christian canon took the best part of four hundred years. There were several impetuses toward the formation of an authoritative list of authoritative books.

---

4. According to Robert W. Wall with Richard B. Steele, *1 & 2 Timothy and Titus*, Two Horizons New Testament Commentary (Grand Rapids: Eerdmans, 2012), 40, "On the basis of this circularity, then, the Rule of Faith should not only regulate the interpreter's critical retrieval of theological goods from the sacred text, it should also supply an apt grammar of theological agreements that arranges those goods into a coherent and unified articulation of God's word across the diverse witnesses that comprise the biblical canon."

The first factor was interest in the person of Jesus and in the teachings of the apostles. This meant that writings that spoke about Jesus and his apostles were naturally prized and venerated. Early collections of the Gospels and apostolic writings, like the Pauline letter collection, emerged out of interest in the story of Jesus and the apostolic testimony to the gospel of Jesus.

Second, when figures like Marcion began to put together their own corpus of writings, many church leaders sought to respond by asserting an alternative list of books for the faithful to utilize in their assemblies. In the case of Marcion, he had a truncated version of Luke (minus all the bits deemed too Jewish), combined with ten epistles of Paul (minus the Pastoral Epistles). He prefaced this collection with a writing of his own composition called the *Antitheses*, which allegedly showed the theological disparities between the Jewish Scriptures and the Christian writings. While Marcion was not the first to make collections of Christian writings, he certainly did cause church leaders to accelerate the process of determining the books that were authoritative and authorized for teaching and use in worship. The Muratorian Canon (ca. AD 180) and Anti-Marcionite Prologues (ca. AD 150–400) provide lists and descriptions of recognized writings and demonstrate that the framework for inclusion of the twenty-seven books that make up our current New Testament was in place by the second half of the second century.

The third factor was also the influence of Roman authorities in forcing Christians to delineate their sacred writings. On the negative side, during the Diocletian persecution (AD 303–13), Christians were forced to hand over their sacred literature to Roman authorities for destruction. Christians were faced with the question as to which writings they regarded as sacred and authoritative. They had to figure out which writings they could happily hand over and which ones they would be prepared to risk death for possessing.[5] Positively, under the imperial patronage of the new Emperor Constantine (AD 313), Christian leaders had to decide which books they would copy, especially when provided with imperial benefaction to pay for the production costs.[6]

---

5. Eusebius, *Ecclesiastical History* 8.2.1–5.

6. Eusebius (*Life of Constantine* 4.36) records that Constantine provided funds for the production of fifty copies of the Christian Scriptures to be used in Constantinople.

Fourth, various catalogues of Christian writings began to circulate in the fourth century. The earliest is by Eusebius who refers to the "enconvenanted" books, that is, the books belonging to the new covenant.[7] According to Eusebius, the books considered for inclusion were categorized as "recognized" (*homologoumena*), "disputed" (*antilegomena*), and "spurious" (*notha*).[8] What guided decisions about which books fell into which category were four basic criteria:

1. Apostolicity: Was it written by an apostle?
2. Orthodoxy: Did it conform to the rule of faith?
3. Antiquity: Could it be dated to the apostolic age?
4. Catholicity: Was it generally accepted in the worship and instruction of the majority of churches?[9]

Fifth, the growing unanimity of the biblical canon that we now possess is reflected in Athanasius's thirty-ninth Festal Letter (AD 367), which gives the listings of the Old and New Testaments as well as other writings that are not part of the canon but remain useful for instruction. In sum, the guidelines for determining which books were canonical were those that accorded with the apostolic gospel found in both the rule of faith and in the church's creeds. Writings by the heretics or writings conducive to their teachings were rejected.

Why Our Churches Need Creeds

I hope my account of the origins of the ancient creeds and their relationship to the biblical canon will make readers sympathetic to the usefulness and value of the creeds. But I suspect that some readers might regard it as still somewhat academic and legitimately ask: Do we need to know, learn, or even recite the creeds to maintain a biblical and orthodox faith? My answer: given that the creeds are great summaries of biblical teaching, they

---

7. Eusebius, *Ecclesiastical History* 6.14.5–7; 6.25.3–14 (author's translation).
8. Eusebius, *Ecclesiastical History* 3.25.1–7.
9. Eusebius, *Ecclesiastical History* 3.24.18; 3.25.4–7; 6.12.1–6.

are undoubtedly useful for cultivating a faith soaked in Scripture. Cyril of Jerusalem (ca. AD 313–96) used an agricultural analogy: "Just as the mustard seed in one small grain contains many branches, so also this Faith has embraced in few words all the knowledge of godliness in the Old and New Testaments."[10] Learning the creeds helps us to grow a truly biblical faith!

The best thing about the creeds is that they conveniently sum up the main truths of the Christian faith and put them into a concise narrative that is meaningful and memorable. Redundant as it sounds, the creeds creedalize biblical propositions and put them into a concise narrative framework. Viewed this way, the creeds are a portable story, a short summary of the scriptural story line that we can carry with us everywhere we go.[11] A creed is not simply a checklist of things I'm supposed to believe, but a synopsis of the entire sweep of redemptive history that narrates a sequence including God, creation, redemption, and consummation. These are the basic acts in the divine drama as Scripture tells it. By its very structure, the creed compels us to see our faith as part of a bigger picture, as part of God's grand purposes, rather than single out one or two pet topics to be myopically treasured. Each line of a creed is also like a travel bag from which we can unpack more scriptural teaching about any given topic. So for instance, the statement, "I believe in the Holy Spirit," not only affirms that there is a Holy Spirit but presupposes a lot of things that we are expected to know and teach about the person and work of the Holy Spirit. So the creeds actually force us to delve deeper into what can be known and learned about a given topic.

If you are still not convinced about the value of the creeds for instruction, then please consider the following story. Baptists have traditionally believed in the Trinity. The 1689 London Baptist Confession and the 2000 Baptist Faith and Message both make reference to the Trinity as the God whom Christians worship as Father, Son, and Holy Spirit. However, it wasn't always that way for Baptists. Among eighteenth-century English Baptist

---

10. Cyril of Jerusalem, *Catechetical Lectures* 5.12 (as found in *The Nicene and Post-Nicene Fathers*, second series; ed. P. Schaff and H. Wace; 14 vols.; reprint, Peabody, MA: Hendrickson, 1996; hereafter *NPNF²*).

11. N. T. Wright, "Reading Paul, Thinking Scripture," in *Scripture's Doctrine and Theology's Bible: How the New Testament Shapes Christian Dogmatics*, ed. M. Bockmuehl and A. J. Torrance (Grand Rapids: Baker, 2008), 62–64.

churches, there arose a hesitation and discomfort with certain doctrines like the Trinity. So much so that the doctrine of the Trinity came to be regarded as a nonessential element of the faith. For some English nonconformists of the day, the Trinity was suspect because it was not explicitly spelled out in Scripture and sounded too philosophical. Around the same time, European rationalism was also beginning to make inroads among English churches, with a number of leaders among the General Baptists imbibing this new skepticism toward supernatural revelation and rejecting the Trinity as an irrational and incoherent formulation. Ironically, among eighteenth-century English Baptists, the Trinity was under attack on two fronts by a peculiar coalition of biblicists who rejected tradition and rationalists who wanted to measure religion by the standards of human reason.[12] Take note of this point: if you reject the creedal heritage of the ancient church, with its two thousand years of exegesis and debate, then you are in serious danger of becoming a Baptist Unitarian. If that doesn't scare you into learning the creeds and teaching them to your children, then you probably need a refresher course on church history.[13]

My proposition is that if we jettison the creeds, then we can all too easily find ourselves jettisoning the historic faith of the Christian church, a faith that we claim is rooted in Scripture, borne out of the testimony of the apostles, and built on the foundation of Jesus Christ. The creeds are not optional décor; rather, they are a sure anchor for a biblical faith and are therefore necessary for a theologically healthy church.

How Creeds Can Invigorate Your Faith

To begin with, an obvious role for the creeds is in our public worship. A creed can be a great way of transitioning between the proclamation of the word to the liturgy of the Lord's Supper. We recite a creed after sermons to

---

12. I owe this point to Dr. Stephen R. Holmes of the University of St. Andrews.

13. I should add that the General Baptist Orthodox Creed of 1678 says that the Nicene Creed, Athanasian Creed, and Apostles' Creed should be received and believed as they contain a fitting summary of what is taught in Scripture. At the inaugural meeting of the Baptist World Alliance, one of the first things the participants did in their joint session was to recite the Apostles' Creed together.

remember that we weigh all teachings against the fabric of Scripture as it has been taught in the churches. We recite a creed before the Lord's Supper to remind us that we are united by one faith, one Lord, and one baptism, as we come to break the one loaf and share in one cup. If our worship services should be God centered, retelling the gospel of Jesus Christ and celebrating our unity with God and with each other, then the creeds are a natural tool to facilitate that kind of worship.

Second, the creeds are among the best ways of promoting unity and fellowship with other believers. Despite the many differences among Christians, the creeds constitute emblems of the biblical faith that are professed by Christians of all traditions, denominations, and backgrounds. The creeds emphasize what we have in common rather than what separates us. The creeds demarcate what is our "common faith" (Titus 1:4), what C. S. Lewis called "mere Christianity," and what Thomas Oden has called "consensual Christianity," a faith that transcends denominational divisions.[14]

Consider that reciting one of the historic creeds means that we place serious weight on holding to the one holy catholic and apostolic faith which Christians of all ages have confessed. We do not presume to think that we have to reinvent the doctrine wheel ourselves in every generation or think that no one before us has ever faced the same tough issues that we are confronting today. Publicly reciting the creeds means we stand in a single unbroken line that stretches from Jesus and the apostles all the way forward to the churches in our own day. It is a faith that is confessed weekly in the most northern parts of Europe to the southernmost regions of New Zealand. This faith is proudly owned by men and women of a multitude of races, languages, tribes, and cultures, who are united in their profession of this one creedal faith. It is a faith that has come to us through two thousand years of earnest study, intense debate, gripping prayer, violent persecution, bloodcurdling martyrdom, triumphant evangelism, and deliberate discipleship. So when we confess the Apostles' Creed in our churches, we are validating the apostolic faith and standing in solidarity with those in every place and in every age who have confessed the same faith. It means we confess *one* faith

---

14. Thomas C. Oden, *Classic Christianity* (New York: HarperOne, 2009), xx; C. S. Lewis, *Mere Christianity*, rev. ed. (New York: HarperOne, 2015).

in *one* Lord as part of *one* church. It is a church that is diverse in its many parts but still united in holding to the story of Scripture and the lordship of Jesus Christ as narrated in the creeds.

Third, pressing on, the creeds remind us who we are as Christians and that we are part of God's plan to gather his people around himself and to bring all of his children into his new creation. As N. T. Wright points out, it is certainly no accident that *symbol* was one of the words that Christians used for their creeds. They were badges to be worn by members, like a scholar's gown, which declared that "this is who we are and what we stand for." The creeds symbolically mark reciters as saying in effect, "We are renewed as *this people*, the people who live within *this* great story, the people who are identified precisely as people-of-this-story, rather than as people of one of the many other stories that clamor for attention all around."[15] Thus, when we recite the creeds, we are saying that this is what we, the church, believe about God, creation, Jesus, and the life of the age to come. This is who we are! The creed is thus a political manifesto: it declares to the powers that be—or pretend to be—that we are the people defined by this story, the story of God, the reign of Jesus, the experience of the Spirit, and the hope of the world to come.[16]

Fourth, the creeds also can and should hold an important place in our personal devotional lives. The Christians who first said *credo* or *pisteuō* ("I believe") did not do so thoughtlessly but often at risk of ostracism and even persecution. According to Thomas Oden, to say, "I believe," is "to speak from the heart, to reveal who one is by confessing one's essential belief, the faith that makes life worth living."[17] We can recite the creeds daily as a profession of faith and even use them as a model for prayer. The North African theologian Augustine prescribed that the Apostles' Creed should be recited several times a day, comparably to how the Jewish people cite the Shema from Deuteronomy 6:4–9 in the course of their daily business. The Bishop of Hippo wrote:

---

15. Wright, "Reading Paul, Thinking Scripture," 64 (italics original).

16. Luke Timothy Johnson, *The Creed: What Christians Believe and Why It Matters* (New York: Doubleday, 2003), 45.

17. Thomas C. Oden, *Classic Christianity: A Systematic Theology* (New York: HarperOne, 2009), 8.

The symbol [i.e., creed] of the holy mystery that you have all received together and that today you have recited one by one, are the words on which the faith of [the] Church is firmly built above the stable foundation that is Christ the Lord. You have received it and recited it, but in your minds and hearts you must keep it ever present, you must repeat it in your beds, recall it in the public squares and not forget it during meals: even when your body is asleep, you must watch over it with your hearts.[18]

More recently, Pope Benedict XVI has urged believers to meditate on and pray through the Apostles' Creed since it reminds believers of the pledge of faith that they made in baptism:

To rediscover the content of the faith that is professed, celebrated, lived and prayed, and to reflect on the act of faith, is a task that every believer must make his own, especially in the course of this year. Not without reason, Christians in the early centuries were required to learn the creed from memory. It served them as a daily prayer not to forget the commitment they had undertaken in baptism.[19]

In sum, we've explored how the biblical canon and the early creeds had a close and mutually influential relationship. We've also seen how the creeds are important for the church and can assist Christians in their spiritual growth. What you should take away is remembering how the creeds are shaped by Scripture and shape the reading of Scripture. The creeds give us a quick and easy way of organizing and summarizing the main blocks of biblical teaching about God, Jesus, salvation, and the age to come. That is why they are useful as aids to discipleship and can even function as a template in prayer. The creeds are like a tour guide in a cathedral where biblical teaching is laid out in various chapels within a massive monument of Christian thought. Thereafter, our reflections upon the creed should lead us deeper in solemn worship and love for God. What is more, the creeds do not

---

18. Saint Augustine, "Sermon, 215.1," in *Sermons (184–229Z) on the Liturgical Seasons*, ed. John E. Rotelle, trans. Edmund Hill; The Works of Saint Augustine 3/6 (Brooklyn: New City, 1993).

19. Pope Benedict XVI, *"Porta Fidei*: For the Indiction of the Year of Faith," 11 October 2011, Apostolic Letter, Vatican Collection.

merely summarize doctrine but also issue an invitation to explore further the work and wonder of the God who is known to us as Father, Son, and Holy Spirit. The creeds propel us to open our Bibles and to read and reflect upon them in greater depth, so that we might know God better and be equipped to walk the path he has marked out for us. It is into these depths and along these paths that we shall now boldly go!

Recommended Reading

Horton, Michael S. *We Believe: Recovering the Essentials of the Apostles' Creed*. Nashville: Thomas Nelson, 1998.

Johnson, Luke Timothy. *The Creed: What Christians Believe and Why It Matters*. New York: Doubleday, 2003.

McGrath, Alister E. *"I Believe": Exploring the Apostles' Creed*. Downers Grove, IL: InterVarsity Press, 1998.

3

I BELIEVE

I believe …

The Faith Story

The Christian life is a story of faith: of coming to faith, of keeping the faith, and of finishing in faith. No surprises then that the Creed begins with the simple statement, "I believe." This means that we are immediately dealing with a profession of faith in the Christian God and his revelation of himself to us. Of course the words *faith*, *belief*, and *trust* can mean all sorts of things to all sorts of people. Strangely enough the words *faith* and *believe* appear a lot in our culture. From Kenny Rogers's moving ballad, "She Believes in Me" to the raunchy pop lyrics of George Michael's "Faith," the words *faith* and *believe* resonate with our deepest and innermost desires. (And yes, I know that these song selections say something of my age!) Politicians will frequently appeal to people to believe in their policies and to trust in their promises. Marriage is really a faith bond between a man and a woman who have come to know, trust, and believe in each other. Precisely because life can be uncertain and painful, we look to people, institutions, and ideas to both believe in and to hope upon. We do that, risky though it is and despite the fact that it makes us vulnerable, because we genuinely think that in this person, or in this organization, or in these ideas, we will find the security for things which we cannot control ourselves.

Faith, belief, trust, hope—whatever words you like—these emerge from a deeply human experience full of dualities; experiences of life and loss, fidelity and failure, joy and grief, as well as trust and betrayal. All of life is a life of faith, whether it is faith in ourselves, our family, friends, plans, people, ideologies, institutions, or even in forces beyond ourselves. We look to something or someone to be a rock and anchor that we can cling to in a world that feels like a merry-go-round spinning out of control. The reality is that faith is an inalienable feature of human existence. We certainly have a choice in whom or what we will believe. But whether we will believe in someone or something is not a choice but a necessity; it simply is part of what it means to be human in a world that is beyond our own mastery. We all reach out in faith somewhere whether we are religious or not, because it is in our nature to stretch our hands toward another.

When the Apostles' Creed begins with the words, "I believe," it is asking people who recite it to recognize their need to know, to trust, and to belong to something beyond themselves. It is an affirmation of one's needs, needs that cannot be satisfied by anything material but are met in the faith professed by the speaker. While we have many needs like food, shelter, purpose, and companionship, perhaps our most basic need, one hardwired into our humanity, is to know God. As Augustine famously said, "You have made us for yourself, O Lord, and our hearts are restless until they find their rest in you." The strange sense of discontent and déjà vu that we experience in a God-haunted world disappears when we connect with God just as we were made to. When we say, "I believe in God," we are saying that we have reconnected with our Maker and have found satisfaction for our spiritual hunger in him.

As we begin to examine Christian doctrine through the Apostles' Creed, in this chapter we will begin by exploring the meaning of faith and examine what it really means to believe in the Christian God.

Faith as Fact: The Apostolic Testimony

The Apostles' Creed calls us to express faith in "the faith." This faith consists of the assertions made in the Creed about God, Jesus, and salvation. This "faith" is a noun, it is the sum of "faith facts" that tell us something about

God's person and work. The deposit of faith facts that are embedded in the Creed is based on the apostles' testimony to Jesus. John begins his first letter with the words: "That which was from the beginning, which we have heard, which we have seen with our eyes, which we have looked at and our hands have touched—this we proclaim concerning the Word of life. The life appeared; we have seen it and testify to it, and we proclaim to you the eternal life, which was with the Father and has appeared to us" (1 John 1:1–2). The apostolic testimony is the story of God sending the Word into the world and how it brings eternal life to all who receive it. The Creed then describes the gist of the apostolic testimony to what God had done in Jesus Christ.

At the heart of this testimony is the gospel, the royal announcement that God has brought salvation in the life, death, and resurrection of Jesus. This gospel runs across the pages of the New Testament. Jesus himself proclaimed the gospel, the "good news of the kingdom," in the course of his ministry (Matt 4:23). The apostle Paul began his letter to the Romans by describing to them "the gospel of God" (Rom 1:1). The gospel stands as the foundation of the "faith that was once for all entrusted to God's holy people" (Jude 3). The second-century church father Irenaeus got it right when he described the gospel "handed down to us in the Scriptures, to be the ground and pillar of our faith."[1] The gospel, with its news of the forgiveness of sins through faith in Jesus, provides the bedrock upon which other Christian beliefs are built up into the monument of Christian doctrine.

The Apostles' Creed calls us to believe "the faith," the faith facts which embody the apostolic testimony to Jesus and are rooted in the gospel. It is a faith which must be proclaimed to the world, imparted to disciples, and protected from distortion. This brings to mind Paul's description of evangelism as proclaiming "the message concerning faith" (Rom 10:8) and his exhortation to Timothy that deacons "must keep hold of the deep truths of the faith with a clear conscience" (1 Tim 3:9) and that Timothy himself must continue to be "nourished on the truths of the faith and of the good teaching that you have followed" (1 Tim 4:6). In other words: tell the faith, teach the faith, and defend the faith.

---

1. Irenaeus, *Against Heresies* 3.1.1.

Faith as Trust:
Believing What You Heard

While *the faith* can refer to a body of teachings to be assented to, *the act of faith* is certainly more than that. The biblical picture of faith is no stale affirmation of stationary facts. Rather, belief is something that is living, active, dynamic, personal, and even risky. Faith is primarily a way of trust and fidelity, a willingness to receive from God what he freely offers, and thereafter a disposition to act in a certain way when confronted with certain things. Faith is ultimately our trusting response to what God has done for us and promised us in the gospel, which in turn pervades every aspect of our daily lives. Faith is not an abstract virtue but is directed toward a person, Jesus Christ. Faith is our cleaving and clinging to Christ. Faith is the act where we say to Christ, "Save me, for I am yours" (Ps 119:94).

We've said a lot about faith so far. But we probably should have a definition of faith to carry with us. A good deal is said about faith in the book of Hebrews. At one point the author gives this definition of faith: "Now faith is confidence in what we hope for and assurance about what we do not see" (Heb 11:1). Faith is a firm conviction that what we *hope* for will one day *happen*. Faith is confidence about a future that looks uncertain to others. A few verses later the author says: "And without faith it is impossible to please God, because anyone who comes to him must believe that he exists and that he rewards those who earnestly seek him" (Heb 11:6). Faith is what God requires of us. To have faith means that we believe that God is there, God is with us, God is for us, and that God offers us a world beyond our own that we can scarcely imagine.

Ultimately faith is our trusting response to God's faithfulness. I like how Karl Barth put it: "Faith is trust in the divine faithfulness."[2] The notion that God is faithful is the bedrock of biblical teaching. We read in Deuteronomy that "the LORD your God is God; he is the faithful God, keeping his covenant of love to a thousand generations of those who love him and keep his

---

2. Karl Barth, *Church Dogmatics*, ed. G. W. Bromiley and T. F. Torrance (Edinburgh: T&T Clark, 1957–75), II/1:460–61 (hereafter *CD*).

commandments" (Deut 7:9). The same thought is mirrored in Paul's letter to the Corinthians: "God is faithful, who has called you into fellowship with his Son, Jesus Christ our Lord" (1 Cor 1:9). Our faith is oriented toward the God who has shown that he himself is faithful to his people. When our faith fails, our God remains faithful to us.

The first moment of believing, "the hour I first believed," is the instrument by which we experience the blessings and privileges promised in the gospel. It is by believing the apostolic testimony to Jesus, who he was and why he died and rose, that we experience the saving benefits promised us in the gospel. As Paul wrote, "By this gospel you are saved, if you hold firmly to the word I preached to you" (1 Cor 15:2). Accordingly, throughout the New Testament we read about the benefits and blessings that are given to believers. Those who believe in Jesus are justified, made right with God, by faith alone (Rom 3:27–4:25; Gal 2:15–16; Eph 2:8); faith in Jesus's name brings healing (Acts 3:16); faith provides us with full assurance (Heb 10:22); faith enables us to receive the promise of the Spirit (Gal 3:14); faith is our victory over the world (1 John 5:4); the end result of faith is "the salvation of your souls" (1 Pet 1:9). Faith is the instrument by which we access the blessings of the Father, the salvation wrought in Jesus Christ, and the graces of the Holy Spirit.

Importantly, believing is not just a one-off thing or a back-then experience that happened when we were converted to Christ; rather, the whole of our life is a constant expression of faith, an increasing effort to surrender to God, and a never-ending quest to pursue his glory. Our faith cannot be reduced to a singular moment but comprises an ongoing confidence in God and a way of life that draws its strength from the conviction that God really is for us. This faith-life has its ups and downs; it can be a struggle to daily believe that God is there and our whole lives are lived before him. In regard to this life of faith, there are some wonderful biblical images for walking in faith in a life of devotion before God. It is amazing how many times in the face of adversity that the psalmist exclaims, "I trust in you" (see Pss 13:5; 25:2; 31:6, 14; 52:8). The most paradigmatic example of faith is Abraham. Abraham responded to God's call and left his home, parents, native land, and even his ancestral gods to go and worship the Lord in Canaan, a strange and often hostile land to which the journey itself would have been peril-ous. By faith, he embraced the divine promises that he would be the father of many nations and receive an everlasting inheritance (Gen 12:1–8). He faced hardship, division, testing, opposition, war, and even infertility. In fact, everything seemed to point in the opposite direction of what God had promised him. But Abraham did not give up; instead he maintained his trust in God. So much so that the apostle Paul says about him:

> Against all hope, Abraham in hope believed and so became the father of many nations, just as it had been said to him, "So shall your offspring be." Without weakening in his faith, he faced the fact that his body was as good as dead—since he was about a hundred years old—and that Sarah's womb was also dead. Yet he did not waver through unbelief regarding the promise of God, but was strengthened in his faith and gave glory to God, being fully persuaded that God had power to do what he had promised. (Rom 4:18–21)

We find a sublime tribute to the virtue of faith in Hebrews 11. In this "Hall of Faith," we read about the struggles of Old Testament saints who kept their faith under duress. From Abel to Isaiah, these paragons of faith are paraded out to encourage the readers to persevere in the faith. These heroes were all commended by God for their faith even though "none of them received what had been promised, since God had planned something better for us so that only together with us would they be made perfect" (Heb 11:39–40).

One poignant biblical picture of faith is that of a journey, a gradual and steady march toward the new Jerusalem, the city of God (Heb 12:22–23; Rev 21:1–2). John Bunyan's *Pilgrim's Progress* captures much of the biblical and experiential reality of the faith journey, as we have to make our way beyond the slough of despond and other such treacheries. Yet the reward at the end is eternal and everlasting intimacy with our God and Savior, the Lord Jesus Christ, into whose presence we will find ourselves most welcome. Faith is what happens between the first and last steps of that journey.

Faith and Obedience: Staying Faithful

Faith and obedience and their relationship are important to understand. If we collapse faith into obedience, the result would not be faith but fealty and fear, a belief that we must obey certain rules and live a certain way in order to earn God's love. If we only have the imperative to obey apart from a sense of God's love for us, we would find ourselves on some kind of performance treadmill, constantly trying to impress God and others by our religiosity. Alternatively, if we cordon off faith and obedience too far, then faith becomes dislocated from faithfulness, and we run the risk that faith is nothing more than an abstract compilation of religious ideas that do not shape how we actually live. A faith without obedience will seek spiritual transcendence without moral transformation. That kind of faith—inactive, lazy, and without works—James says "is dead" (Jas 2:26). The fact is that real faith always expresses itself in obedient action. What we truly believe is exhibited in how we live. The Danish philosopher Søren Kierkegaard said, "As you have lived, so have you believed."[3] As Christians, we have to make sure that our walk matches our talk and that we live lives worthy of the gospel (Phil 1:27). We are not called to be fans of Jesus but to be followers of Jesus. A true follower of Jesus is one who imitates Jesus (see John 15:13; 1 Cor 11:1; 1 Pet 2:21).

Exploring faith and obedience further, it is interesting that Paul's letter to the Romans, that great letter about "justification by faith," begins and ends with reference to the obedience of faith (Rom 1:5; 16:26). Paul says that the mandate of his apostolic ministry is not to get gentiles to make decisions for Jesus, not to get them to walk down the aisle, not to get them to pray this or that prayer, or to sign this card. No, his objective is to bring gentiles to the obedience of faith. The great nineteenth-century Baptist preacher, Charles Spurgeon, once said: "We preach the obedience of faith. Faith is the fountain, the foundation, and the fosterer of obedience. Men obey not God till they believe him. We preach faith in order that men may be brought to

---

3. Niels Jørgen Cappelørn et al., eds., *Kierkegaard's Journals and Notebooks, Volume 8: Journals NB21–NB25* (Princeton: Princeton University Press, 2015), 150.

obedience."[4] Faith cannot exist without being obedient, much as the sun cannot exist without shining. The Swiss theologian Karl Barth put it well: "Faith is not obedience, but as obedience is not obedience without faith, faith is not faith without obedience. They belong together, as do thunder and lightning in a thunderstorm."[5] So while faith is not obedience, there can be no true and enduring faith without obedience. Such obedience is not driven by fear but born of love, and love always translates itself into action. As the apostle John wrote: "And this is love: that we walk in obedience to his commands" (2 John 6).

In other words, faith is not something we just do in our head, a terse list of things to assent to; it is more than that. Faith permeates and empowers our effort to obey God's commands, however imperfectly we might do it. Faith leads to conviction, and conviction cultivates action. In biblical testimony, faith expresses itself in love (Gal 5:6), faith prompts us toward good deeds (Eph 2:10; 1 Thess 1:3; 2 Thess 1:11; Jas 2:14–26), faith grows and increases (2 Cor 10:15; 2 Thess 1:3). Faith produces a harvest of spiritual fruit, propels us toward God-shaped endeavors, and drives us into loving actions. Faith in God, in other words, compels us toward obedience to God.

Faith in the Balance: Reason and Doubt

That is all well and good, but how does faith sit in relation to things like reason and doubt? Any conversation about faith has to engage the question of the reasonableness of Christianity and how to cope with doubts about the Christian story of God. A robust faith should be able to have an honest and sober discussion about these matters.

Reasonable Faith?

Faith and reason are well known to each other with theologians and thinkers of all stripes arguing whether or not they are compatible. There

---

4. Charles Spurgeon, "The Obedience of Faith," *The Spurgeon Archive*, delivered 21 August 1890, http://www.spurgeon.org/sermons/2195.htm.
5. Karl Barth, *CD*, IV/2:538.

has been a long industry in Christian thought of arguing that faith is quite reasonable. Indeed, there are some very good reasons for believing in God if you ever care to look them up![6] The existence of God explains why there is a "something" rather than a "nothing," why the universe is rationally intelligible, and why it seems wired up to produce intelligent life. The existence of God accounts for our sense of "moral oughtness," the belief that we ought to act in a certain way toward other human beings, that all human beings possess a sense of right and wrong. The existence of God makes sense of the religious experience of many peoples. God's existence is perhaps most fully revealed in the historical events of Jesus's life, death, and resurrection. That said, while faith has its reasons, reason is never the cause of faith. No one is ever argued into faith; rather, faith is what emerges from an encounter with the living God.

Reasons for God or not, there will always be those who contend that faith is nothing more than primitive, backward, superstitious, pie-in-the-sky nonsense. A common atheistic view goes something like, "Faith is authoritarian, while reason is autonomous. Faith is biased, while reason is neutral, with no axe to grind."[7] To the unbelieving world, faith and reason are like oil and water; they simply don't mix. In what was probably the ultimate insult to faith, in 1793 during the French Revolution, a Parisian courtesan was enthroned in Notre Dame Cathedral as the "goddess of reason."

The atheist jibe is that faith is always a blind faith. All faith is a desperate grasp after something that is not really there. Faith is a futile attempt to see God by closing one's eyes to the evidence of his absence. Faith is mocked as denying the blindingly obvious disproof of God's existence. But faith is not like a person blindly jumping in the dark. Faith is more like a leap into the light.[8] According to John the Evangelist, Jesus said, "I am the light of the world" (John 8:12). Because Jesus is the light, faith in Jesus brings illumination to the world around us. Faith does not obscure things; it helps us make sense of everything. Viewed through the lens of faith, science,

---

6. See William Lane Craig, *Reasonable Faith: Christian Truth and Apologetics* (Wheaton: Crossway, 1994); Tim Keller, *The Reason for God: Belief in an Age of Skepticism* (New York: Dutton, 2008).

7. Paul Helm, *Faith and Understanding* (Edinburgh: Edinburgh University Press, 1997), 3.

8. Eric Metaxas, "I am Second®," *YouTube*, 19 September 2013, https://www.youtube.com /watch?v=F_GTMgckqi4.

philosophy, logic, and ethics all become coherent in a whole new way. That is because Jesus is the one in whom "all things hold together" (Col 1:17). He is the cosmological glue of the universe. He is the reason why there is a cosmos rather than a chaos. Faith in Jesus allows me to understand more of the world than I ever knew before in unbelief. Living in light of Jesus, we see the unveiling of the mystery of the cosmos: why the world exists and for whom it exists. Furthermore, we can finally see our own place in the world and our path illumined by the rays of God's glory in Christ.

A Doubter's Guide to Faith

Faith and doubt are serious issues and must be approached with sensitivity. There can be seasons of life when God feels distant. Times when we feel like our prayers are just bouncing off the ceiling. Moments of intellectual angst over some of the odd and astounding things we read in Scripture. Days of wondering, "If God loves me and my family, then why has such misery befallen us?" There are even occasions when we momentarily crave the freedom of nonbelief to allow us to indulge in the tawdry attractions of the world that constantly assault us with their enticements.

The Bible is realistic about doubt. In the Gospel of Mark, a man begs Jesus to heal his son who suffers from convulsions, petitioning Jesus to help him if he "can." Jesus retorts that "everything is possible for one who believes" (9:23). To which the man desperately responds, "I do believe; help me overcome my unbelief" (9:24). This man believed that Jesus's miraculous healing powers were possible but no more than that; he needed help to move beyond mere possibility to absolute trust. Then there is the famous story of the disciple Thomas, who heard from the other disciples that Jesus was risen but replied, "Unless I see the nail marks in his hands and put my finger where the nails were, and put my hand into his side, I will not believe" (John 20:25). Thomas was your quintessential rationalist. Dead people don't come back to life. Maybe Jesus went to heaven, became an angel, and perhaps his spirit went to the bosom of Abraham, but daily experience tells us that dead people stay dead. How embarrassing and yet how enthralling it must have been for the risen Jesus to tell Thomas, "Stop doubting and believe" (John

20:27). Then, in the Epistle of Jude, we are told to "be merciful to those who doubt" (Jude 22). When churches argue bitterly among themselves, as was happening in the church to which Jude wrote, some people can be left confused about what they believe and wondering if they really believe. To such persons, Jude urges us to show understanding, patience, and mercy.

Many people will wonder about the intellectual credibility of their faith. After all, belief in rivers turning to blood, floating axe heads, and virgins having babies is a big pill to swallow for those of us living in the age of electricity, the internet, and iPads. Or circumstances in our lives may lead us to wonder whether God even cares. If you have not experienced moments like these, I assure you that at some point you or someone you care about probably will. Yet doubt is not always a bad thing. Doubt can be a sign of spiritual struggle, a means of growing into maturity, and a pathway into a stronger and more resilient faith. What sustains me in times of doubt is one simple thing: the complete and utter worshipability of Jesus Christ. Jesus is magnetic. I'm drawn toward him, not just to hear about him but to worship him. Once, when Jesus gave a difficult sermon about what it meant to believe in him, many of his disciples turned away and no longer followed him. Jesus asked Peter if he too wanted to leave. Peter's answer was simple: "Lord, to whom shall we go? You have the words of eternal life. We have come to believe and to know that you are the Holy One of God" (John 6:68–69). The words of Jesus are like honey in the mouth, and the story of Jesus is like music for the soul. Knowing Jesus is like being wrapped in a blanket of joy. It's not that Jesus is the only religious game in town—atheism, Buddhism, and Islam each have their own attractions—the issue is that his story is the only story worth believing. I believe in Jesus because I am moved in my heart to believe that he is who he said he is, Son of God and Son of Man. Yet I also know that believing in him makes me a better person. I have not achieved perfection or purity, but following Jesus makes me more like him: compassionate, faithful, and merciful. Compared to Jesus, everything else in the world smells like dung and tastes like expired tuna.

Doubt is real, and there is nothing to be ashamed of if one experiences it. It is comforting to remember that God's faithfulness to us is far greater and far more powerful than our doubts. God is there to help us in our doubts and to journey with us so that we might have the blessings of full confidence in him and full assurance in his promises.

Faith and Mystery: Delighting in the Unknown

The fun thing about mystery novels is that there is always some sort of strange puzzle or perilous situation that will eventually get solved by the hero, but we enjoy the surprise of discovering precisely how. Now on the one hand, Christians believe that God's mysterious purposes have been made known to them in the unveiling of Jesus Christ. In fact, the book of Revelation is about the divine disclosure of God's plan to put the world to rights. So we know how the story is going to end: a new heaven and new earth, with God's redeemed people rejoicing in it and reigning over it. But on the other hand, there are still so many uncertainties and unknowns. What does tomorrow hold for me? What has God planned for my family or my church? What is my part in God's designs? What foes will emerge, what trials will we face, what failures will we experience, and how will God bring us through it? Every day that we wake and walk upon this world is another page in the great mystery of God's plan and purposes. Every day is another step into the journey toward the new Jerusalem. Every day is another improvised performance by the church, the company of the gospel, in the divine drama. Every day is another day of delighting in the mystery of the unknown.

Faith means following Jesus into the mystery of God. Faith is filled with a curiosity that longs to be satisfied, and faith compels us to imagine something we can scarcely comprehend. Faith emerges from that sneaking suspicion that everything is not as it always appears to be. Faith arises from that gnawing doubt that reality goes deeper than it looks. Faith is knowing that I see and sense something beyond myself that draws me closer and that won't let me go. Faith is born out of a mysterious curiosity that is singularly dissatisfied with answers that leave no room for the transcendent. Faith, like Neo in the *Matrix*, takes the red pill. Faith, like Alice in Wonderland, follows the rabbit down the hole. Faith is what happens when something stirs in the quietness of our own soul, so that suspicion gives way to conviction, and mystery turns into marvel.

Let me finish by saying that the Apostles' Creed calls us to a rich and vibrant faith in the God whom it describes. We've seen that Christian faith is based on the apostolic testimony and rooted in the gospel. Faith is our act of trust in God's very own faithfulness. A genuine faith will always express itself in faithfulness and obedience to God. What is more, our creedal faith is credible and can withstand rationalist attacks and can even survive the dark nights of doubt and despair. Our faith launches us, ready or not, into the mystery of God's person and plan, as we wait for the day when God fully and finally dwells with his people. This faith, as expressed in the Apostles' Creed, is no list of stale facts. It tells a story about God, about Jesus, about us, and about the world to come. The challenge for us is to make sure that it is this story, this faith, and not something else, that shapes us and molds us into the God-lovers, the Christ-followers, and the Spirit-possessors that God chose us to be. Hopefully, by reading the Apostles' Creed, reciting it, and learning it, we will be among those "who keep God's commands and hold fast their testimony about Jesus" (Rev 12:17).

Recommended Reading

Byron, John, and John Lohr, eds. *I (Still) Believe: Leading Bible Scholars Share Their Stories of Faith and Scholarship*. Grand Rapids: Zondervan, 2015.

Keller, Timothy J. *The Reason for God: Belief in an Age of Skepticism*. New York: Dutton, 2008.

McGrath, Alister E. *Doubting: Growing Through the Uncertainties of Faith*. Downers Grove, IL: InterVarsity Press, 2006.

Moran, Gabriel. *Believing in a Revealing God: The Basis of the Christian Life*. Collegeville, MN: Liturgical Press, 2009.

Taylor, S. S. "Faith, Faithfulness." Pages 487–93 in *New Dictionary of Biblical Theology*. Edited by T. D. Alexander and Brian S. Rosner. Downers Grove, IL: InterVarsity Press, 2000.

4

BELIEVING *in the* FATHER

I believe in God, the Father almighty,
creator of heaven and earth.

The One True God

The first line in the Apostles' Creed means that our faith is directed toward the one and only God. The God of creation, the God of the covenant, and the God of Jesus Christ. The God who is the great "I AM" (Exod 3:14), the "LORD Almighty" (Ps 24:10), the God of Abraham, Isaac, and Jacob (Gen 50:24; Exod 2:24; Deut 1:8). This is the God who Scripture says made the world, called the patriarchs, rescued Israel from slavery in Egypt, entered into covenant with them, gave them the law, and promised to rescue the world through Israel. This God is so magnificent that the biblical authors literally pile up image upon image, milk every metaphor they can find, and use every superlative at their disposal to describe God's majesty and might. God is like an eagle (Deut 32:11), a refuge (Ps 9:9), a refiner (Mal 3:3), a rock (Ps 18:2), a fortress (Ps 144:2), and a tower (Ps 61:3). The list of descriptions goes on and on.

The Triune God

It is important to stress that while Christians profess belief in *one God*, it is the *triune God* in whom we believe. There is one God who exists as three distinct and yet equal persons consisting of Father, Son, and Holy Spirit. The monotheism of Christians is different from the monotheism of Jews and Muslims precisely on this matter of the Trinitarian nature of God's being. The Trinity can be a hard doctrine to get your head around. For a start, how can anyone say that 1+1+1 = 1? Then there is the problem of balancing God's unity and diversity. If you overemphasize God's oneness, then you can end up saying something like the Father, Son, and Spirit are simply three costumes worn by a single divine being (i.e., the heresy called *modalism*). If you overemphasize God's threeness, then you end up with three gods (i.e., the heresy of *tritheism*) or else a senior "God" and two lesser "gods" (i.e., the heresy called *monarchianism*). None of these are sufficient to describe God as he has revealed himself in the gospel of Jesus Christ.

The doctrine of the Trinity is neither a philosophical mind game nor an exercise in bending the meaning of words. The doctrine attempts to describe the identity of God as he is known in the act of salvation and in the experience of the early church. First, we have to remember that the gospel itself is implicitly Trinitarian. The gospel points to a God who exists as Father, Son, and Holy Spirit. The salvation that the gospel promises portrays the Father as choosing, Christ as redeeming, and the Spirit as renewing—all in a unified work by distinct persons in a single godhead. As Kevin Vanhoozer puts it, "The very logic of the gospel—the declaration that God enables believers to relate to God the Father in Jesus Christ through the Spirit—implies the divinity of the Son and Spirit as well."[1] Second, while no biblical text gives an explicit Trinitarian formula corresponding precisely to what we find in the Nicene and Athanasian Creeds, still we do find the ingredients for their formulations in the Bible and biblical pressures that push us to construct Trinitarian categories in order to make sense of what we are reading. In that sense, the Trinity becomes a type of interpretive key, generated by the biblical texts, that helps us make sense of the biblical texts themselves.

Let me give a couple of examples of the biblical roots of the Trinity. To begin with, there is the Trinitarian statement at the end of Matthew's Gospel where the risen Jesus commands believers to baptize in the name

---

1. Kevin J. Vanhoozer, "The Triune God of the Gospel," in *The Cambridge Companion to Evangelical Theology*, ed. T. Larsen and D. J. Treier (Cambridge: Cambridge University Press, 2007), 17.

of "the Father and of the Son and of the Holy Spirit" (Matt 28:19). Here baptism is an act where one is immersed into the reality of the one God known in the three persons of Father, Son, and Holy Spirit. To read it in a non-Trinitarian manner would create theological absurdities. Catholic biblical scholar John Meier comments: "Certainly, one could hardly imagine a more forceful proclamation of Christ's divinity—and incidentally, of the Spirit's distinct personality—than this listing together, on a level of equality, of Father, Son, and Spirit. One does not baptize in the name of a divine person, a holy creature, and an impersonal force."[2]

Then there are texts like Paul's benediction at the end of 2 Corinthians, where the apostle blesses his readers with the words, "May the grace of the Lord Jesus Christ, and the love of God, and the fellowship of the Holy Spirit be with you all" (2 Cor 13:14). If you read this benediction in a modalist sense, it seems needlessly repetitive for God to bless believers three times under three different names for no apparent reason. Then again, if you read the benediction in a monarchian sense, it seems rather impoverished as God's blessing is mediated through two lesser gods rather than coming directly from him. But if you read Matthew 28:19 and 2 Corinthians 13:14 with a Trinitarian set of lenses, then these two passages take on a new degree of coherence and profundity. The risen Jesus sends us out to continue the mission of the triune God. The apostle blesses a congregation with actions that spring from the very heart of the triune God.

The early church maintained the oneness of God while also affirming that God exists as three distinct persons, who perform three distinct yet cooperative roles within the acts of creation, revelation, and redemption. As Hippolytus wrote:

> The Father decrees, the Word executes [the decree], and the Son is mani-
> fested [by the Spirit], through whom we come to believe in the Father. The
> dispensation of harmony leads straight back to one God, for God is one. It
> is the Father who commands, the Son who obeys and the Holy Spirit who
> gives understanding. The Father is above all, the Son is through all, and

---

2. John P. Meier, *Matthew*, NTM 3 (Wilmington, DE: Liturgical Press, 1980), 371–72.

the Holy Spirit is in all. We cannot think of God in any other way than as Father, Son, and Holy Spirit.[3]

Trinitarian theology is best performed by a process of negation and elimination. It is generally easier and less problematic to say what the Trinity is not—not one God with three faces, not three Gods, not a hierarchy consisting of one big God with a supreme angel and a divine power—than to say what the Trinity actually is. Otherwise you can end up messing with the threeness and oneness of God in some way. Even so, the affirmative consensus of Christians over the centuries, borne of scriptural study, forged in prayer, confessed in baptism, and experienced in worship, is that God is Father, Son, and Holy Spirit existing in one substance, one power, and one eternity.

A Father for Us All

The first person of the Trinity is God the Father. The Father is the person of the Godhead whom we regard as the creator of the universe, the revealer of the divine nature, and the sender of the Son. The fatherly imagery underscores the person within the Godhead whose identity is associated with the deity's supreme power and divine paternal care. God as Father speaks to the transcendence, sovereignty, and love within the Godhead.

The concept of God as Father is amply attested in Israel's Scriptures.[4] The Israelites rarely addressed God as "Father," probably to avoid connotations of divine sexual liaisons associated with polytheistic myths in the ancient Near East. However, we find that in the Old Testament God is the "Father" of Israel in the sense of calling and creating the nation to be the children of his covenant (see Exod 4:22; Deut 32:6, 18; Jer 31:9; Hos 11:1). Elsewhere God is called "a father to the fatherless, a defender of widows" (Ps 68:5), which underscores his compassion and caring nature. The imagery of God's fatherhood is apt because Israel owes its existence to God and possesses the

---

3. Hippolytus, *Against Noetus* 14, as cited in Gerald L. Bray, ed., *We Believe in One God*, vol. 1 of *Ancient Christian Doctrine*, ed. Thomas C. Oden (Downers Grove, IL: IVP Academic, 2009), 77.

4. See Christopher J. H. Wright, *Knowing God the Father through the Old Testament* (Oxford: Monarch, 2007), esp. 77–98.

status of sons, royal heirs of the heavenly Lord. God's fatherhood and Israel's sonship are also grounds for rebuke, as God disciplines the nation for their disobedience much like a father who disciplines a wayward son (see Isa 1:2–4; 30:1, 9; Mal 1:6). At the same time, Israel's redemption is indelibly connected to God's fatherhood of the nation, since the prophets attest that God will not abandon his children to hardship forever. As such, Isaiah beseeches God to be merciful to the remnant returning from exile because "you are our Father, though Abraham does not know us or Israel acknowledge us; you, LORD, are our Father, our Redeemer from of old is your name" (Isa 63:16). Later he adds, "You, LORD, are our Father. We are the clay, you are the potter; we are all the work of your hand" (Isa 64:8). In the context of Isaiah, God does not abandon Israel to exile, even though they are rebellious sons and daughters. Rather, God is bound by his fatherly love to redeem them and restore them to places of honor in his family.

The notion of God as father was peripheral in Judaism and yet was central in Jesus's life and teaching. We learn about God's fatherhood primarily as we see it in relationship to Jesus's own sonship. Jesus enjoyed a unique Father-Son relationship with Israel's God. John calls Jesus "the one and only Son, who is himself God and is in closest relationship with the Father" (John 1:18). There are copious instances in the Gospels where Jesus talks about God as "my Father" in such a way as to make clear that he truly knows the Father, often referring to what the Father has revealed to him and what the Father will do for him and others. Such is the Father-Son relationship that in the garden of Gethsemane, we see Jesus praying to the Father in a mixture of despair and grief about his coming fate, yet still committing himself to what the Father has willed for him. What is more, Jesus teaches about God's fatherly love with such beautiful and riveting images, like the story of the father running to meet his rebellious son who has finally returned home (Luke 15:11–32). And there is the promise that whoever follows Jesus's teaching will be loved by "my Father" (John 14:23). The risen Jesus tells Mary that he is going to ascend to "my Father and your Father, to my God and your God" because the risen Lord brings us into fellowship within the triune God (John 20:17). Think about that for a moment. If we know Christ as our Savior, then we have his Father as our Father, and the Spirit as our

Comforter. I think John put it best when he wrote in his epistle: "See what great love the Father has lavished on us, that we should be called children of God" (1 John 3:1). Lavish indeed that former rebels are now adopted children of the glorious Father!

God as Father is crucial to the notion of prayer in the New Testament. Jesus himself prayed to God as Father. It is quite prominent in Jesus's high priestly prayer for the disciples (John 17), but also in Jesus's agonizing over his own fate in Gethsemane (Matt 26:39, 42). Jesus taught his disciples to pray to God as "our Father" in the Lord's Prayer (Matt 6:9). Paul writes that because believers have been adopted into God's family and share in the Holy Spirit that they can now cry out to God with the intimate words, "*Abba*, Father," in their heartfelt pleas before the divine throne (Gal 4:6; Rom 8:15). Christian prayer moves us to seek out the blessings and comfort of our heavenly Father.

There is also something particularly Christian about praying to God as Father. In other religions, calling God one's own father would be problematic if not impossible. Crying out to God as Father would be irreverent for Jews, blasphemy to Muslims, weird for Buddhists, and mean something entirely different for Hindus. Such a claim to enjoy God's fatherhood is crucial, however, for the Christian idea of God and for the distinctive nature of Christian worship. God is not a distant deity, not an impersonal power, not a divine monad without personality or purpose. God is the one who made Christ our brother and the Holy Spirit our comforter, and adopted us as sons and daughters of his royal and everlasting kingdom. God gives us gifts like a father spoiling his children.

But Isn't This Just Too Patriarchal?

There is a potential downside to this language of God as Father. First, many of us will have had bad experiences with our own fathers. Fathers who were absent, distant, or abusive cause deep emotional pain and lasting psychological wounds in men and women who were hurt because of the failures of their earthly fathers. The emphasis on fatherhood can also sound very patriarchal and appear to be another example of maleness being associated with power and authority. Mary Daly complained that "if God is male, then the male is God."[5] Is "God the Father" simply a projection of patriarchal power into God's own character, so that maleness is associated with God's authority, and femaleness with submission? Where does all of this leave women then? The fact is that Christian theology, with its "God the Father" representation of the deity, potentially becomes a means of providing religious currency to patriarchal systems that are often demeaning, disempowering, and abusive of women. As such, many feminist theologians argue that we should abandon this representation of God as Father or at least expand it to include the notion of God as Mother to balance the disparities.

The biblical statements about God as Father represent real challenges to how we situate fatherhood in relation to language, culture, and theology. This is a genuine stumbling block for many, and we've got to get a firm grasp on what God's fatherhood does and does not mean for our faith.

First, we have to remember that all theological language is analogical. That is to say, our finite language can never fully capture the infinite nature of God. All language about God, scriptural and theological, is at best an approximation of what God is like and is not a final and concrete description of his being. All conversations about God—whether in English, Greek, Arabic, French, or whatever—will only approximate what God is truly like. Even the language of divine fatherhood is only an apt approximation and is not an exhaustive explanation of God's being.

Second, it is worth pointing out that, even with the prevalence of fatherly language for God, there is also a sizeable number of places where God is described in maternal imagery. In Isaiah, God is portrayed as a mother in birth for Israel (Isa 42:14; similarly Deut 32:18). Isaiah says that God is like a nursing mother who will not abandon her children in the way that other mothers have (Isa 49:14–17). God comforts Israel like a mother comforting a frightened child (Isa 66:13). Thus, in the biblical description, there is more to God than fatherhood, and we should trace out the maternal imagery for a fuller picture of God's character.

---

5. Mary Daly, *Beyond God the Father: Toward a Philosophy of Women's Liberation* (Boston: Beacon, 1973), 19.

Third, like it or not, we have to accept that God is revealed in Scripture as the Father of Israel, of Jesus, and of Christians. Fatherhood is part of God's revelation of himself, even while it does not exhaust everything to be said about God's nature. While a more generalized image of the first member of the Godhead as something like the "prime mover" or "ground of all being" might be more gender inclusive and carry less potential for cultural offense, we cannot just abandon this image of God as Father without serious injury to our doctrine of God. That is because the word "father" is part of Jesus's own language for God, not functioning as a dispensable category but intrinsic to the identity of God as the sender of Jesus. When we believe in Jesus, we are grafted into the Father-Son relationship within the triune Godhead so that Jesus's Father becomes our Father. God's fatherhood is part of the particularity of God's self-disclosure. He reveals himself as Father: the Father to Israel, the Father of Jesus, and even the Father of believers.

Fourth, it should go without saying that fatherhood can be associated with notions of love, closeness, and protection across cultures and languages as well. Fatherhood is not all patriarchy and power. When I hear people complain about the fatherhood of God in the Bible as patriarchally oppressive, I ask them two questions: "Do you like your dad?" and "Do you take comfort in knowing that your dad loves you?" Yes, I for one know that there are certainly some bad fathers out there, but generally speaking, most reply with "Yes, I like my dad and I'm glad he loves me!" Here's the thing: fathers do love their children and they constitute an important source of joy and strength in a child's life. If there is *anything* good about human fathers, then there is *something* infinitely good about God's fatherhood. For those of us who had bad fathers, no fathers, or lost our fathers, God the Father is the only father we might have now. David Meece sings wonderfully about this theme in his song, "My Father's Chair." In this tearjerker, a child laments the emptiness of his father's absence yet takes comfort in the fact that he has a heavenly Father with a royal throne beyond the veil of this world and so he sings, "Someday I'll share my Father's chair." The song echoes a vital truth: God is the Father of the fatherless.

Several years ago I was on holiday with my family in a charming little English town called Bude. On one Sunday evening, when everyone else was too tired for a late church service, my father-in-law and I decided that we'd go and find a service to attend. We stumbled across a charming Methodist church, which held its worship services in a small room off a back street. In the small congregation we sang a chorus that I hadn't had the pleasure of singing before, "Father God I Wonder," by Ian Smale. It's a wonderful song of praise about God's fatherhood and our privileges as his children (though the melody always reminds me of the Rolling Stones song "Paint It Black"). To paraphrase the chorus: "How did I exist without knowing that God is my Father?" How much happier we are, knowing that our heavenly Father did not spare his own Son but gave him up so he could adopt sinners like us into his family. Some of us for various reasons, often sad reasons, might find it hard to relate to God as Father. However, when properly understood, the news that God is our Father is good news indeed.

God Almighty

The immediate adjective that the Apostles' Creed uses to describe God the Father is "almighty." Here we are presented with what theologians call God's omnipotence, his infinite power and ability to achieve his purposes. To say that God is "almighty" is to say that he possesses all might. His power is not limited by anything beyond his own character and being. God always works to bring about what he intends to do, and not a single molecule in the universe can thwart him or frustrate his purposes.

The notion of God as mighty and powerful is rooted in biblical testimony. In the Old Testament, Israel's redeemer was the King of glory, enthroned in heaven, "The LORD Almighty" is his name (1 Sam 4:4; Ps 24:10; Isa 51:15). God's might is what the Israelites trusted to make things right amidst constant rise and fall of ancient Near Eastern empires around them (Ps 59:5–9). What is more, a testimony to the sky-high Christology of the New Testament is that God the Father and Jesus the Lamb are both identified by John of Patmos as the *pantokratōr*, the "Almighty," who transcends time, brings justice to the earth, and dwells forever with his people in the new Jerusalem (Rev 1:8; 4:8; 11:17; 15:3; 16:7, 14; 19:6, 15; 21:22). The

God of the Bible is not wimpy or withdrawn but is master and commander of everything in heaven and on earth.

Let me stress that discussions about God's might, ability, and power should not be considered in the abstract. It is not like we are discussing how much charge is contained in an AA battery or how much horsepower there is in a new Mercedes engine. We are talking rather about God as the one who wills to win the world over with his love. This divine power stretches from creation through the cross to the new creation. God's power is the reason why we trust in him to do all things for us, in us, and even through us. God's limitless power is why we can place limitless faith in him, knowing that God is able to do immeasurably more than all we ask of him.

Such is God's immense power that he made this world by mere decree. God's word uttered in the beginning brought into being the whole universe from literally nothing. God's creative action speaks to his singular supremacy over every single molecule and subatomic particle in cosmic existence. In what can only be described as a cosmic irony, God's infinite power is ultimately displayed in the crucifixion of Jesus. It is in the weakness, shame, humiliation, and powerlessness of Jesus Christ on the cross that we see the power of God at work to save humanity from the evil of the age. Mark's account of the crucifixion scene stresses this totally strange power-in-weakness when he narrates the mocking words of the chief priests uttered against Jesus: "'He saved others,' they said, 'but he can't save himself!'" (Mark 15:31). What the chief priests literally say is that Jesus is not *able* or *powerful* enough (Gk. *dynatai*) to save himself. There is a double irony here. First, readers of the Gospels already know that Jesus is powerful enough to save himself; he could easily come down from that cross and command twelve legions of angels to get him some instantaneous payback on his tormentors. Jesus has power over the demonic realm and even bosses the weather around the way we might bark orders at a puppy. The second irony is that it is precisely in this state of powerlessness that God's power to redeem is at work. Jesus's death brings the redemption that the prophets had long ago proclaimed. In the crucifixion of Jesus, in the apex of agony, in the summit of suffering, in the depths of degradation, we see God's power unleashed on an unsuspecting world. Do you want to know what God's power looks like? Well, it looks nothing like the coercive power of emperors or tyrants. God's power doesn't rely on guns or gold, much less the threat of violence to bring victory. God's power comes to us in the cross, in the height of humiliation and in the zenith of disempowerment; there, in of all places, God's power rescues and redeems, purifies and purchases a people for himself. No wonder that Paul tells the Romans that he is "not ashamed of the gospel" because, he adds, it is the "power of God that brings salvation to everyone who believes" (Rom 1:16). The gospel, as the power of God, might just as well be called the *omnipotence of God* to create and redeem a people for himself.[6]

Sceptics have always liked to lampoon the idea of an almighty God by posing several paradoxes. Could God make a rock so heavy that he cannot lift it? The question is a catch-22 because if God cannot make such a rock or cannot lift such a rock, then he is by definition not all-powerful. C. S. Lewis, however, noted that these are not really serious objections to divine omnipotence but just silly games with words. God's omnipotence means that God has power to do all that is intrinsically possible, not the intrinsically impossible. God cannot make a triangle with four sides or any propositional absurdity. Not because God's power meets a limit but because nonsense remains nonsense even if we preface it with the question, "Can God . . . ?"[7] Word games aside, God can do all that is proper and fitting for an omnipotent being. The only limit to his power is the contours of his character and the consistency of his nature.

The notion that God is almighty is a great source of comfort for believers. For no matter how terrible or tragic our circumstances, we can rest assured knowing that our God is *able* to do immeasurably more than what we ask and *able* to bring about the best for those who love him.

---

6. Karl Barth, *A Shorter Commentary on Romans* (Farnham, Surrey, UK: Ashgate, 2007; repr., London: SCM, 1959), 10–11.

7. C. S. Lewis, *The Problem of Pain* (New York: HarperOne, 2001), 48.

Creator and Creation

I heard a funny joke a while ago about a group of scientists who challenged God to a contest over who could design and build a better human being. God happily accepted the challenge and met the scientists at the designated laboratory where the contest would take place. God took a clump of clay and began to build Adam 3.0, when he suddenly noticed that the scientists were doing the exact same thing. So God promptly walked over to the scientists' table, took their clay away from them, and said, "Ahem, excuse me chaps, but this is my clay; I made it for myself. You go and make a man out of your own clay!" The contest was over. Human beings are made and designed to be clever. We can map DNA sequences, uncover cosmic mysteries of the universe like dark matter, theorize quantum mechanics, and even create artificial intelligence. However, when it comes to making something out of nothing, we are not in God's league. Even when people try to play God, they always seem to come up well short.

God is the creator; he and no other. Probably the best biblical summary of God as creator is given in Nehemiah: "You alone are the LORD. You made the heavens, even the highest heavens, and all their starry host, the earth and all that is on it, the seas and all that is in them. You give life to everything, and the multitudes of heaven worship you" (Neh 9:6). The point of this and other biblical texts is to say that God relates to creation as its author and architect. God and God alone made all that exists, immaterial or material, matter or antimatter. There is nothing in the heavens or on the earth that does not owe its existence to God. God is the cosmic artist who fashioned the universe and made it not only good but fitting for the purpose of displaying his glory.

What is arguably implicit within the creation narrative of Genesis 1–2 is that God made the world *ex nihilo*, that is, "from nothing." We find tacit hints of this in the New Testament. Paul suggests that resurrection is modeled on creation because God is the one who "gives life to the dead and calls into being things that were not" (Rom 4:17). The author of Hebrews sets forth an article of faith on creation with these words: "By faith we understand that the universe was formed at God's command, so that what is seen was not made out of what was visible" (Heb 11:3). The doctrine of creation from nothing means that prior to creation God was the only reality. It tells us that before space, time, and matter existed, God was himself the infinite boundary of all being, a self-existing and self-sufficient person, apart from whom there was literally no one or nothing other. And God brought forth the universe from nothing, since there was no reality other than himself. God did not work over preexisting matter or simply mold primeval chaos into a pristine cosmos. He made the universe by sheer fiat. He spoke, and a universe was born, space-time began, galaxies began to coagulate, and eventually planets began to form.

People interpret Genesis 1 in all sorts of ways: a literal creation with seven twenty-four-hour days; a progressive creation where the days correspond to long periods of time; a gap theory with a punctuated intermission of billions of years between v. 1 and v. 2; or a symbolic reading which is compatible with some form of theistic evolution. The question of whether we should take the story literally did not begin in the aftermath of Charles Darwin's *The Origin of Species* but goes all the way back at least to Augustine. Augustine wrote voluminous amounts on the creation story with a focus on its literary properties (i.e., what the author was trying to say) and its symbolic value (i.e., what it taught about the future). The problem is that many of these debates about the "literalness" of Genesis might just be missing the point. The language is highly poetic, strikingly vivid, and constructed in a discernible literary structure with an obvious parallelism in the description of the various "days." The biblical creation story is fundamentally concerned with the identity of the creator and how creation is to relate to him. The primary intention then is more about constructing a theistic *worldview* and not concerned with the nitty-gritty *workings* of how God made the universe. The Israelites, burrowed in the polytheistic civilizations of the ancient Near East with various gods associated with the cycles of nature, were a unique people with their claim that there was one God. So one does not worship the heavenly bodies but the divine being who made them. In sum, Genesis 1–3 provides a dramatic account of God's actions as creator to make the heavens and the earth, *Homo sapiens*, and their habitat, to set humanity as priest-kings in God's glorious temple centered in Eden.

If we attempt to press the biblical creation story into the grid of a wood-enly literalistic reading, we end up betraying its historical context, literary purposes, and theological claims. Genesis 1 is written up in the genre of an ancient Near Eastern creation story in order to contest and challenge competing accounts of the world's origins as narrated in other ancient Near Eastern creation stories from Babylon and Mesopotamia. Genesis 1–3 functions within the Pentateuch as the background to Israel's covenant life so that his people might know that the LORD is no mere tribal God but the one and only God, maker of heaven and earth, who calls Israel to be his people. Genesis 1–3 introduces us to crucial theological insights about God's nature and God's purpose, not least his goodness, his absolute sovereignty, his providence, the mysterious entrance of evil, humanity's fall into disobedience, and God's promise to put the world to rights through the skull-crushing victory of Eve's offspring.

The biblical references to God as creator—not just in Genesis 1, but I'm thinking here broadly of the Psalms, Job, and the Prophets—inform us about how God relates to creation and his creatures. God is not the creation—so no pantheism; God does not inhabit creation like an impersonal force—so no panentheism; God did not make the world and then permanently go off to lunch—so no deism; nor did an evil demigod create the world—so no Gnosticism. When we confess that God is creator of heaven and earth, we are saying that God is distinct from creation, God is sovereign over creation, God loves his creation, God is concerned with creation, and God remains active in creation.

God's authorship of creation is the most basic and shared confession of all monotheistic faiths. However, the distinctly Christian view of creation is that it was brought into being as an act of the triune God. Creation is a cooperative effort by all members of the Godhead. How so? The biblical witness is clear that God is the creator (see Gen 1:1; Isa 45:18; Mark 13:19; Eph 3:9). However, specific roles are assigned to the specific members of the Godhead within the act of creating itself. God the Father is the one "from whom all things came" (1 Cor 8:6; see Mal 2:10; Rom 11:36; Heb 2:10). Jesus Christ is the one "through whom all things came" (1 Cor 8:6) and "in him all things were created" (Col 1:16). The Spirit of God was active in creation as the one who "hovered" over the primordial waters to bring life into existence (Gen 1:2) and is generally associated with the impartation of life into living creatures (Job 33:4; John 6:63; Rom 8:10). In the analogy of Irenaeus, we might say that the Son and Spirit were the hands that the Father used in the creation of the world.[8] We can aver that whereas the Father is the ground of creation, the Son is the principle of creation, and the Spirit is the divine power active in creation.[9] Hans Urs von Balthasar said that the Father has chosen to be "Almighty," not by solely creating but by eternally begetting the Son and breathing the Spirit who freely create with the Father as much as for the Father.[10]

God was not pressed or pushed to create. God made the universe out of his satisfaction with his own glory and to share his glory with others. In the Psalms we see how God's glory is the manifestation of his "love and faithfulness" (Ps 115:1). God glorifies himself when he sends his love and shows his faithfulness to others. God is love (1 John 4:16), and there is divine love within the Trinity as the Father loves the Son (John 3:35; 5:20) and the Holy Spirit is the bond of love between them just as he is in the church (Rom 5:5; 15:30; Col 1:8). God is compelled by the nature of his own being to share the internal love between the triune persons externally with creatures made for the purpose of enjoying his love and responding in faithfulness to him. God's overarching purpose, then, is to glorify himself by the effusion of his holy love upon creatures that are little miniatures of himself. God creates with the sole intent of creating a bride for the Son and to unite himself with his creation. The world is the bridal chamber for the ultimate union of God with humanity to be consummated in the new creation. There, redeemed humanity will experience the full measure of the love and faithfulness of the Godhead and even be made partakers of the divine nature, that is, made to share in the eternal life of God and the bond of love within the persons of the Godhead (2 Pet 1:4).

---

8. Irenaeus, *Against Heresies* 2.30.9; 4.20.1.

9. Stanley J. Grenz, *Theology for the Community of God* (Nashville: Broadman & Holman, 1994), 101–6.

10. Hans Urs von Balthasar, *Theodrama: The Last Act* (San Francisco: Ignatius Press, 1998), 66.

The Story Thus Far

The first words of the Apostles' Creed compel us to speak out about the faith that has sprung up from within us. In the Creed, we profess that we believe in the triune God. The God in whom Christians believe is the all-powerful creator of the universe, revealing himself as Father, Son, and Holy Spirit. Christian faith is an expression of our trust, assent, and hope in God, and God is first of all to us a loving father. Our God is almighty, he reigns over all, and he is limitless in the expanse of his sovereignty. Our heavenly Father is the creator, the author and architect of the universe, which is why we owe him our worship and our thanksgiving.

Recommended Reading

Bird, Michael F. "Part Two: The God of the Gospel: The Triune God in Being and Action." Pages 87–231 in *Evangelical Theology: A Biblical and Systematic Introduction*. Grand Rapids: Zondervan, 2013.

Bray, Gerald. *The Doctrine of God*. Downers Grove, IL: InterVarsity Press, 1993.

Holmes, Stephen R. *The Quest for the Trinity*. Downers Grove, IL: InterVarsity Press, 2012.

Sanders, Fred. *The Deep Things of God: How the Trinity Changes Everything*. Wheaton: Crossway, 2010.

Thompson, M. M. *The Promise of the Father: Jesus and God in the New Testament*. Louisville: Westminster John Knox, 2000.

Walton, John H. *The Lost World of Genesis One: Ancient Cosmology and the Origins Debate*. Downers Grove, IL: InterVarsity Press, 2009.

5

BELIEVING *in the* SON— DIVINE *and* HUMAN

I believe in Jesus Christ, his only Son, our Lord.

Jesus and the Meaning of "God"

As someone who has lived in the UK and Australia and traveled all over the USA, I would hazard a guess that about 60–80 percent of people in Western cultures claim to believe in God, but only 5–20 percent—depending on what city you live in—attend a church with any regularity. Many sociologists blame this disparity on the distrust that even God-fearing people have in institutionalized religion or attribute disinterest in attending a parish to the reputation of churches for harboring hypocrisy. But there is a better explanation for this phenomenon of churchless religion. Just ask the non-churchgoing folks about the God they believe in. In my experience, if you ask most people what they mean by "God," they usually think of something like a benign old man who lives in heaven. Or they have in mind a cosmic version of Morgan Freeman, a wise old figure, full of fatherly wisdom, who sends good people to heaven and condemns bad people to hell, yet is mostly disinterested in the affairs of everyday people and is quite happy to live and let live. To be perfectly honest, I would not get out of bed early on Sunday morning and try to drag snooty teenagers, capricious middle schoolers, and cranky toddlers to church to hear about a God like that. If that was the kind of God that I believed in, why bother going to church to learn about him or to experience him, when I could just as well get the same buzz by watching a rerun of *Miracle on 34th Street* in the comfort of my own home. If you have an impoverished view of God, then you'll have a low view of church to match it.

Tom Wright tells a story about talking to college students while he was a chaplain:

For seven years I was College Chaplain at Worcester College, Oxford. Each year I used to see the first year undergraduates individually for a few minutes, to welcome them to the college and make a first acquaintance. Most were happy to meet me; but many commented, often with slight embarrassment, "You won't be seeing much of me; you see, I don't believe in god." I developed a stock response: "Oh, that's interesting; which god is it you don't believe in?" This used to surprise them; they mostly regarded the word "God" as a univocal, always meaning the same thing. So they would stumble out a few phrases about the god they said they did not believe in: a being who lived up in the sky, looking down disapprovingly at the world, occasionally "intervening" to do miracles, sending bad people to hell while allowing good people to share his heaven. Again, I had a stock response for this very common statement of "spy-in-the-sky" theology: "Well, I'm not surprised you don't believe in that god. I don't believe in that god either." At this point the undergraduate would look startled. Then, perhaps, a faint look of recognition; it was sometimes rumored that half the college chaplains at Oxford were atheists. "No," I would say; "I believe in the god I see revealed in Jesus of Nazareth."[1]

Wright's anecdote is extremely apt. The God of Christians is radically different from the culturally prevalent images of a supreme divine being found in TV programs and posted on the covers of holiday greeting cards. The God we believe in is not some charmingly senile old man swaying back and forth on his rocking chair in heaven. Rather, the God we believe in is the God who is revealed as the man Jesus of Nazareth. In fact, I would go

---

1. N. T. Wright, "Jesus and the Identity of God," *Ex Auditu* 14 (1998): 44.

so far as to say that for us, Jesus defines what we mean by "God." When we speak of this God, we see him as a helpless child being nursed in his mother's arms in a guest room in Bethlehem, a young boy growing in strength and wisdom in rural Galilee, an angry prophet denouncing the injustices of the day in the hustle and bustle of Jerusalem, and a tortured morass of human flesh cruelly crucified under the dark clouds at Golgotha. The story of Jesus is the story of God becoming one of us and sharing in our humanity so that he might redeem humanity. When Christians talk about Jesus, it can never be in the abstract or in the sanitized descriptions of civil religion. No, never; for the God we know can only be described in light of the life, death, and resurrection of Jesus. As Martin Luther said, "No other God have I but thee, born in a manger, died on a tree."

What we'll explore here and in the next chapter are various facets of Jesus's identity, including his human and divine natures as well as the contours of his messianic mission.

When the Time Had Fully Come

Jesus is our window into the mystery of God. That is not to say that no one knew about God before the coming of Jesus. God has revealed himself in nature, in Israel's history, and in the Scriptures. However, all of this was preparatory for the definitive and climactic revelation of God in the person and work of Jesus. The Old Testament, Irenaeus said, was really God's apprenticeship, preparing for the coming of Jesus the Word.[2] In a similar vein, the author of Hebrews begins his sermonic epistle with the words, "In the past God spoke to our ancestors through the prophets at many times and in various ways, but in these last days he has spoken to us by his Son, whom he appointed heir of all things, and through whom also he made the universe" (Heb 1:1–2). There is something final and definitive about God's revelation of himself in Jesus. Jesus is very much the climax to the biblical story since he came to make good on the promises given to the patriarchs,

---

2. Irenaeus, *Against Heresies* 4.12.4.

to show God's faithfulness to his covenant with Israel, to usher in the kingdom, and to draw the nations into God's love and peace. That is why we find Paul talking about how God's plan has culminated in Jesus. "When the set time had fully come," Paul tells the Galatians, "God sent his Son, born of a woman, born under the law, to redeem those under the law, that we might receive adoption to sonship" (Gal 4:4–5). God sent Jesus to redeem Israel so that a redeemed Israel might be the channel for the redemption of the world. Luke records much the same in Paul's speech in the synagogue of Pisidian Antioch: "We tell you the good news: What God promised our ancestors he has fulfilled for us, their children, by raising up Jesus" (Acts 13:32–33). Jesus is God's "yes" to Israel, and his resurrection is the specific sign that all the promises are granted and given without delay (2 Cor 1:20). His appearance is the manifestation of the "kindness and love of God our Savior" (Titus 3:4), and "he has appeared once for all at the culmination of the ages to do away with sin by the sacrifice of himself" (Heb 9:26).

Jesus is God's definitive revelation of himself, and that revelation is God's offer of salvation to all who believe in him. Anybody who has been to Sunday school can probably cite John 3:16 by heart, and I suggest that this verse is not just a good evangelistic message but the heart of biblical theology. God's plan has always been to show his love to the world in his beloved Son, and that love triumphs over all adversity. God's victory in the death and resurrection of Jesus is the proof that God's love wins.

I hope it's clear as well that the sending of Jesus was not Plan B, not an emergency measure to be activated when Adam tripped up or when things with Israel seemed to go awry. God had always intended to unite himself with creation through his Son. That is why Paul says in his panoply of poetic praise in Ephesians that God's intention was "to bring unity to all things in heaven and on earth under Christ" (Eph 1:10). God from all eternity intended to put all things in subjection to his Son so that the Son will reign over God's new world with God's redeemed people. Creation will be regained, renewed, restored, and renovated—the new will be as the old, only better—and once more God will put a human in charge of it, and this human's name is Jesus!

Jesus the God-Man

The two main features of a biblical and orthodox Christology are that Jesus is *fully* human and *fully* divine. In Jesus there is a union of deity and humanity in one person. The eternal Word of God becomes flesh according to John the Evangelist (John 1:14). The term used to describe this is *incarnation*, which is shorthand for the *enfleshing* of God the eternal Son in human form. In the incarnation, Jesus's divine nature is married to a human nature. Note, Jesus is not a divine being who *pretends* to be human (Docetism) nor is Jesus a human who *becomes* divine (adoptionism). He is fully human and fully divine at the same time.

The New Testament speaks to the full humanity of Jesus. He has a human birth, childhood, adulthood, and death. He has a fully orbed existence at the emotional level with grief, sorrow, joy, frustration, love, and anger, as well as a complete physical existence with tiredness, hunger, and thirst. Jesus comes as bone to our bone and flesh to our flesh. Jesus bleeds and breathes like us since he is truly one with us. He speaks with a human voice, he prays with human needs, he laughs as one among friends, he cries human tears, and he walks in human sandals. In the story of Jesus we see divine majesty clothed in human frailty.[3]

The incarnation was the instrument by which God was able to reconcile us with himself and even to unite us to himself. The Son who knew no sin became sin to make sinners righteous. He took on mortality in order to make humans immortal. Although he was rich, for our sakes he became poor and he tasted human death so that we would taste divine glory. The author of Hebrews captures this wonderfully when he writes, "Since the children have flesh and blood, he too shared in their humanity so that by his death he might break the power of him who holds the power of death—that is, the devil. . . . For this reason he had to be made like them, fully human in every way, in order that he might become a merciful and faithful high priest in service to God, and that he might make atonement for the sins of the people" (Heb 2:14–17). Jesus became a priestly mediator to stand

---

3. Thomas Torrance, *Incarnation: The Person and Work of Christ* (Downers Grove, IL: InterVarsity Press, 2008), 185.

between God and humanity precisely through his incarnation. To redeem these children where they are, the Son had to become what they are. By sharing in their human existence, he was able to defeat the devil, destroy death, and provide atonement for sins.

Thus, the humanity of Jesus is a redemptive necessity, for only a fully divine and fully human person can be our mediator. Athanasius put it bluntly when he said that "what is not assumed cannot be redeemed." If Jesus is only partly human, then he can only partly save us. If Jesus does not have a soul, then he cannot save our souls. If Jesus does not have a real, physical human body, then he cannot redeem our bodies. Yet if he is fully human, then he can fully save us.

The New Testament also affirms the full deity of Jesus. The man Jesus of Nazareth is the incarnation of God the eternal Son. He is not an angel from God, not an emanation of God, nor a demigod but fully and equally God with God the Father. The Jesus of Holy Scripture is God in the flesh with a fully orbed humanity. This is why Matthew calls him "Immanuel," meaning "God with us" (Matt 1:23; Isa 7:14). In the Gospel of John, Jesus is the "I am" who existed even before the time of Abraham and is identifiable with the Lord who revealed himself to Moses in the burning bush (John 8:58; Exod 3:14). The apostle Paul consistently uses the monotheistic language of the Old Testament used to describe Israel's God to describe Jesus as one who is part of the identity of the God of Israel (Phil 2:5–11/Isa 45:23; 1 Cor 8:6/Deut 6:4). Paul and Peter both refer to Jesus as "God our Savior," indicating that Jesus is the God who saves his people (Titus 2:13; 2 Pet 1:1).

In the mind of the later church fathers, Jesus relates to the divinity of the Father as "light from light," so that Jesus is fully and equally divine with the Father.[4] Jesus is not a lesser divine light; rather, Jesus shines with the same divine light of the Father. To use a more philosophical way of putting it, Jesus shares the same essence as God the Father. He is comprised of the same "stuff" or "being" as it were (Greek *ousia* and Latin *substantia*). While this language might seem foreign to the world of the New Testament, it is really just using the standard philosophical language of the day to restate in

---

4. The thought is perhaps grounded in biblical texts such as Pss 4:6; 104:2; Isa 9:2.

technical terms that Jesus is, as Paul and John both profess, equal with God in every way (see John 5:18; Phil 2:6).

The nature of Jesus's sonship, while it entails his submission to the Father's will, does not in any way imply his inferiority to the Father. The primary meaning of sonship language is to convey Jesus's unique relationship with Israel's God. While "Son of God" was a title referring to the Messiah (Mark 1:1; John 20:31; Rom 1:4; 2 Cor 1:19), even so, Jesus's sonship cannot be reduced to the mantle of earthly kingship. Rather, Jesus's sonship signifies his close relationship with Israel's God, as emphasized by references to Jesus as the "beloved" son at his baptism, at the transfiguration, and in the parable of the wicked tenants (Mark 1:11; 9:7; 12:6). The Gospel of John in particular emphasizes the Father's unique love for his one-of-a-kind Son in several places (John 3:35; 5:20). Jesus was evidently conscious of that relationship as early as his boyhood (Luke 2:49). In his prophetic career, Jesus frequently prayed to God as "Father" (Matt 11:25; Luke 23:46; John 17:1) and instructed his disciples to also address God as "Father" (Matt 6:9; Luke 11:13). Such intimate language was integrated by the early church in their own prayer life (Rom 8:15; Gal 4:6). Jesus accordingly urged his followers to see his own Father as their Father. Furthermore, the Pauline and Johannine statements about the "sending" of the Son into the world further underscore the fact that God the Father sends the preexistent Son to carry out his mission (John 3:16–17; 5:23; 10:36; Rom 8:3; Gal 4:4–5).

Importantly, Jesus's sonship does not have a historical beginning, because he is the eternal Son. Jesus does not become the Son at his birth, baptism, or at the resurrection. Whereas a Roman general could be appointed as a "son of god" through adoption by the "divine" emperor and be made his heir, Jesus was the Son of God by virtue of his divine nature. Jesus's identity and relationship with the Father precedes his earthly life. The Father always had a Son and the Son always had a Father. The eternal nature of that relationship was largely inferred from the economy of redemption. As Wolfhart Pannenberg put it, "If God has revealed himself in Jesus, then Jesus's communion with God, his Sonship, belongs to eternity."[5] In which case, Jesus's

---

5. Wolfhart Pannenberg, *Jesus—God and Man* (Philadelphia: Westminster, 1968), 154.

divine sonship is not simply a *function* of his earthly life, but is proper to his very *person* from all eternity. Epiphanius commented on Matthew 16:16, saying, "If Christ is the Son of God, by all means he is God. If he is not God, he is the not Son of God. But since he himself is the Son, and as the Son takes up all things from the Father, let us hold this one inseparably in our heart because there is no one who escapes his hand."[6] Or, to paraphrase the American comedian Stephen Colbert, "If the Son of a Duck is a Duck, then the Son of God is God!"

Theologians of a Lesser Son

Others in the ancient church, however, did not hold to this conception of the Son as sharing the same *being* as the Father. In the early fourth century, an Alexandrian preacher named Arius argued for a more hierarchical order within the Godhead, with the Father alone as fully divine and Jesus as a being who was lesser than the Father, though still greater than the angels. So on Arius's view, Jesus was a created being, the greatest created being by all accounts, but still a creature nonetheless. It was an attractive option for many, as it solved the problem of the apparent plurality within the Godhead by demoting Jesus to a lesser status than fully divine. It also enabled adherents to speak of the exclusive divinity of the Father and retain the unity and oneness of God. Arius's views garnered widespread support among ecclesiastical and political elites of the day and took some fifty years to fully flush out of the church. Thankfully, however, many church leaders like Athanasius opposed Arianism and for good reason. The Arian view ran into two basic problems.

First, if Jesus was a heavenly creature, then he could not be a savior. Athanasius's rebuttal against Arianism was devastating, as he argued that no creature can redeem another creature. If Jesus is creature, then on Arius's own terms Jesus cannot save humanity since he himself is part of the created

---

6. Epiphanius, *Interpretation of the Gospels* 28, as cited in Manlio Simonetti, *Ancient Christian Commentary on Scripture: Matthew 14–28*, ed. T. C. Oden (Downers Grove, IL: InterVarsity Press, 2002), 45.

order. The problem was that Arius was effectively sawing off the branch the church had been sitting on. "What Arius had done," writes Gerald Bray, "was to offer a solution to the problem of Christ's divinity that destroyed the very essence of our salvation. If Christ was the being whom Arius claimed he was, then he was not God. And if he was not God, he was as far away from him as we are and therefore totally unable to do anything for us."[7]

Second, while Arius agreed that Jesus should be worshipped, it was an inconsistent position to hold if Jesus was a created being. If God alone is to be worshipped (Matt 4:10; Luke 4:8), and if there are prohibitions against worshipping angels (Rev 22:8–9), then how can one worship Jesus if Jesus is merely a supreme angelic being? The worship of an angel or even a super angel would be idolatrous and blasphemous because no one but God is worthy of the church's worship. Viewed this way, if Arianism was true, then it made the church's gospel a theological fallacy and rendered the church's worship absolutely blasphemous.

The incarnation of God as a human being is the load-bearing symbol of the Christian faith. Christians believe that "God was reconciling the world to himself in Christ" (2 Cor 5:19), only because Jesus is the one in whom "the fullness of the Deity lives in bodily form" (Col 2:9). So when rock star Joan Osborne sings in her mocking and melancholic ballad, "What if God was one of us?" we can answer, "Yes, he was, hallelujah to heaven!" And when Osborne asks, "If God had a name, what would it be?" we can scarcely contain our joy from crying out, "Jesus!" Stirring as Joan Osborne's song is, she can't hold a candle to Charles Wesley who put it much better when he wrote those moving words: "Veiled in flesh the Godhead see, Hail th'incarnate deity, pleased as man with men to dwell, Jesus our Emmanuel."

Two Natures

Now if Jesus is fully divine and fully human, then the next problem is how do Jesus's divine and human natures relate to each other? Over the course

---

7. Gerald Bray, "The Deity of Christ in Church History," in *The Deity of Christ*, ed. C. W. Morgan and R. A. Peterson, Theology in Community (Wheaton: Crossway, 2011), 170.

of church history there has been a propensity to overemphasize either his humanity or his deity. For instance, some thought that the divine Logos indwelled the man Jesus, with the Logos effectively just replacing Jesus's soul (i.e., Apollinarianism). Imagine a lump of clay with a marble inside of it, with the clay representing Jesus's body and the marble representing his soul. Then imagine that we took out the marble and replaced it with a ping-pong ball, with the ping-pong ball representing Jesus's divinity or the person of the Logos. Others held to the two natures blended together in one person to produce an entirely new nature (i.e., Monophysitism). The best way to illustrate this view is along the lines of two ingredients dropped into a blender, like Worcestershire sauce and ketchup being mixed together to produce a Kilpatrick sauce. Still others contended that the two natures remained side by side but entirely compartmentalized from each other, almost making Jesus into two persons (i.e., Nestorianism). The best analogy would be something like a jar filled with water and oil that do not fully mix together but remain separate.

However, the view that won the day was that Jesus had two natures—divine and human—which were united but unmixed in his one person. This view is called *hypostatic union* and was formally ratified by the church at the Council of Chalcedon (AD 451). The basic thrust of the Council was to affirm that Christ possesses everything true of a person and he possesses everything that is true of both the human and divine natures.[8]

The Mediator Is the Message

All of this talk about Jesus's divine and human natures might seem a bit confusing. We've got some ancient words like *ousia*, various heresies like modalism and adoptionism, plus technical terms like *hypostatic union*. Yet we shouldn't disregard this as obscurant theological gobbledygook, because the history of the discussion is the history of trying to explain something

---

8. Oliver D. Crisp, "Desiderata for Models of the Hypostatic Union," in *Christology Ancient and Modern: Explorations in Constructive Dogmatics*, ed. O. D. Crisp and F. Sanders (Grand Rapids: Zondervan, 2013), 31–34.

important about God and Jesus. When Paul wrote that "there is one God and one mediator between God and mankind, the man Christ Jesus" (1 Tim 2:5), we need to describe precisely *how* Jesus mediates between the divine and human realms in his own person. The most cogent answer, arrived at after scriptural study, and the final verdict of the church's best theological minds is that Jesus is fully divine and fully human, expressed in the Latin formula: *vere Deus, vere homo* ("truly God, truly human"). That is not to say that we or others can fully comprehend the entirety of the incarnation; it remains an ineffable and yet glorious mystery. But what we can claim to know is that God is to us what he is in Jesus Christ: God from God, Son of God and Son of Man, Lord and Savior. And that is why it makes sense to believe that "the Word was with God, and the Word was God" and that "the Word became flesh and made his dwelling among us" (John 1:1, 14). It is why it makes sense to say that "God was reconciling the world to himself in Christ" (2 Cor 5:19), and why it makes sense to worship him. Jesus unites the divine nature with human flesh so that humanity might for all time be united with God and enjoy him forever.

Recommended Reading

Bloesch, Donald. *Jesus Christ: Savior and Lord*. Downers Grove, IL: InterVarsity Press, 1997.

McGowan, A. T. B. *The Person and Work of Christ: Understanding Jesus*. Milton Keynes: Paternoster, 2012.

Rae, Murray, and Stephen Holmes, eds. *The Person of Christ*. New York: T&T Clark, 2006.

Torrance, Thomas F. *Incarnation: The Person and Life of Christ*. Downers Grove, IL: InterVarsity Press, 2008.

6

BELIEVING *in the* SON— MESSIAH *and* LORD

I believe in Jesus Christ, his only Son, our Lord.

Jesus the Messiah

There is sadly a major deficiency in the Apostles' Creed since the Creed moves from Jesus's birth (ca. 4 BC) to his death under the prefecture of Pontius Pilate (AD 30) with no reference at all to his life, teaching, and earthly mission. In the exact place where one might expect to find some mention of Jesus's ministry, all we get instead in our English version of the Creed is a comma.[1] It would have been great if we had a short summary of Jesus's career at this point in the Creed much like what we find in the apostolic sermons recorded in Acts (Acts 3:13–15; 10:36–43; 13:22–38). Such an omission is unfortunate and attributable to the fact that the life of Jesus was not a major point of contention in the second-century church, whereas more ferocious debates were waged over Jesus's identity and his relationship to God the Father. The Apostles' Creed, therefore, focuses on Jesus's identity in the context of a wider narrative about God and salvation, rather than summarizing Jesus's teaching and the achievement of his death and resurrection. Nonetheless, this gap in the Creed needs to be appropriately filled out for a robust and thick description of Jesus's work.

---

1. See N. T. Wright, *How God Became King: Getting to the Heart of the Gospels* (London: SPCK, 2012), 259–62.

To help us fill in this gap, we should remember that "Jesus Christ" is not a name, as if his parents were Mrs. Mary Christ and Mr. Joseph Christ, but comprises an honorific title with the effective meaning "Jesus is the Christ." So when the Apostles' Creed refers to "Jesus Christ," we should think of it as a reference to Jesus in his messianic office as *the Christ*, as the long-awaited deliverer of Israel. The designation "Christ" is from the Greek word *Christos*, which itself is a translation of the Hebrew word *mashiah*, meaning "anointed one" (and from which comes the word *Messiah*). So for us, the mention of Jesus as "Christ" or "Messiah" should automatically evoke the wider gospel narrative pertaining to Jesus's messianic ministry in Galilee and Judea.

The Messiah was a future end-time king who is intimated in the Old Testament. Several Old Testament passages provided ample material for Jewish authors in the intertestamental period to imagine what a coming messianic deliverer might look like, what he might do, and when he might come (Gen 49:10; Num 24:17; Dan 7:13–14; Zech 4:14). Many looked forward to a day when a messianic leader would save Israel from evil, regather the scattered tribes of Israel, renew the covenant, establish justice, build a new temple, and save God's people from pagan oppressors. Some Jews looked for an earthly military leader to do this, others for a heavenly agent accompanied by an angelic army or a son of David and son of Aaron to jointly lead God's people into a new Israelite empire.[2]

While not all Jews were anxiously awaiting a messiah, nonetheless Jesus came onto the scene at a time when Palestine was on a sociopolitical knife edge, where rebellion was a constant possibility, banditry was rife, sectarian tensions were widespread, and various prophetic figures drew large crowds and were often violently scattered by Roman forces. It was in this environment that Jesus proclaimed the kingdom of God, called twelve disciples to be the vanguard of a restored Israel, referred to himself as the "Son of Man" with clear echoes of Daniel 7, entered Jerusalem like the shepherd king of Zechariah, promised to rebuild the temple just as the Messiah was supposed to do, was charged with being a messianic pretender at his trial, died a vicarious death like a king suffering on behalf of his subjects, and

---

2. See Michael F. Bird, *Are You the One Who Is to Come? The Historical Jesus and the Messianic Question* (Grand Rapids: Baker, 2009), 31–62.

was mocked by his tormentors as "King of the Jews" in the *titulus* above the cross. What I'm getting at is that Jesus—in word and deed, in symbol and story—proclaimed himself to be Israel's Messiah, often tacitly or implicitly, but clearly enough for those with eyes to see it.

If so, the incarnation was not a random visitation of God at some point in time, in some obscure place, to whatever people who were around at the time. Far from it! The incarnation was the climax of Israel's story about the long-awaited visitation of God in the coming of his messianic king. It's about the moment when God would lead Israel into a new exodus, embark upon the renewal of the covenant, redeem creation, and even rescue gentiles, and all of this through a new son of David.

Messiah, Cross, and Kingdom

How do we bring together the messianic office of Jesus with his crucifixion and the advent of the kingdom? What is the link between them and why do they belong together? Many Christians have a resolute focus on the cross, and with good reason, for on the cross we see God's deliverance of sinful people by Jesus's atoning death and his triumph over evil. That does not mean, however, that Jesus's life is just a warm-up act to Calvary or merely a catalogue of anecdotes for Sunday school lessons. We should not inadvertently forget that Jesus's death is part of God's kingdom project to establish his reign on earth as it is in heaven, that it is part of the story of God's rescue of creation. Jesus's life, teaching, and death all belong under this singular heading of "the kingdom of God."

Jesus's messianic career is not simply the hors d'oeuvres to the atonement! Emil Brunner writes:

> The view that because our one aim is to proclaim "Christ Crucified" the story of His life does not actually belong to the Gospel, is equally mistaken. The Early Church, rightly, held the opposite opinion, when she called the four books which tell the story of the life of Jesus, "the Four Gospels." As the life of Jesus can only be rightly understood from the

point of view of the cross—the object of the Fourth Gospel is to show this—so, conversely, the Cross of Jesus can only be understood in light of His life, as its culmination.[3]

We must remember that Jesus's message of the kingdom of God is indelibly connected to his death because Jesus is crucified as king; in fact, it is Jesus's death that establishes the kingdom's saving power for all time. Jesus's final week in Jerusalem brought several running themes of his ministry—kingship, victory, and salvation—to their gripping conclusion. Joel Green writes:

> Everything—his interpretation of Israel's Scriptures, his practices of prayer and worship, his astounding choice of travel companions, his crossing of the boundaries of clean and unclean, his engagement with children, his miracles of healing and exorcism—leads to the cross. Calling twelve disciples as representative of a restored Israel, weaving the hopes of a new exodus and the eschatological era into his ministries of word and deed, speaking of fulfillment of God's promises to Israel, his prophetic action in the temple in anticipation of a temple not made by human hands. . . . This led him to a form of execution emblematic of a way of life that rejected the value of public opinion in the determination of status before God and inspired interpretations of his death that accorded privilege to the redemptive power of righteous suffering. The way was opened for Jesus's followers to accord positive value to his shameful death, and thus to learn to associate in a meaningful way what would otherwise have been only a clash of contradictory images: Jesus's heinous suffering and his messianic status. . . . Thus, Jesus was able to gather together Israel's history and hopes and from them a view of himself as the one through whose suffering Israel, and through Israel the nations, would experience redemption.[4]

---

3. Emil Brunner, *The Christian Doctrine of Creation and Redemption* (London: Camelot, 1952), 283.
4. Joel B. Green, "Kaleidoscopic View," in *The Nature of the Atonement*, ed. J. Beilby and P. R. Eddy (Downers Grove, IL: InterVarsity Press, 2006), 163–65.

What links Jesus's ministry and death together is his messianic vocation to inaugurate the kingdom of God. In Jesus's work, God was finally becoming king of Israel, bringing a new exodus, establishing a new covenant, teaching the way of covenantal righteousness, calling Israel to its appointed vocation, defining law by love not by debate about legal minutia, reminding people of God's special concern for the poor, and calling the religious leaders to account. That mission was fulfilled, not cut short, by his death where Jesus gave his life as a ransom for many (Mark 10:45), proving that he was the suffering servant of Isaiah (Mark 14:24), the smitten shepherd of Zechariah (Mark 14:27), and the persecuted righteous one of the Psalms (Mark 15:24).

Here's the gist: kingship and cross go together. The upshot is that we should not think of Jesus as a crucified savior and only later as the reigning Lord. Instead, we see Jesus as king, not despite the cross but precisely because of it and even upon it! As Irenaeus wrote, "He whom the Jews had seen as a man, and had fastened to the cross, should be preached as the Christ, the Son of God, their eternal King."[5] God's reign is connected to the redemptive act manifested in the death of Jesus the Messiah. The wood of the cross is not only a new tree of life, but it is the throne from which the victorious Prince of Life reigns eternally. Jeremy Treat sums up well the relationship between the cross and kingdom:

> While many Christians either champion the kingdom or cling to the cross, Scripture presents a mutually enriching relationship between the two that draws significantly from the story of Israel and culminates in the crucifixion of Christ the King. In short, the kingdom and the cross are held together by the Christ—Israel's Messiah—who brings God's reign on earth through his atoning death on the cross. The kingdom is the ultimate goal of the cross, and the cross is the means by which the kingdom comes. The cross is not the failure of Jesus' messianic ministry, nor simply the prelude to his royal glory, but the apex of his kingdom mission, the throne from which he rules and establishes his kingdom.

---

5. Irenaeus, *Against Heresies* 3.12.6.

The shocking paradox of God's reign through Christ crucified certainly appears foolish to fallen human logic, but perceived through faith, it is the very power and wisdom of God (1 Cor 1:18–2:5). May we ever follow Calvin's exhortation to imitate even the penitent thief on the cross, who "adores Christ as a King while on the gallows, celebrates His kingdom in the midst of shocking and worse than revolting abasement, and declares him, when dying, to be the author of life."[6]

The Lord Jesus

In addition to the designation of "Christ" or "Messiah," Jesus is also called "Lord." The title "Lord" (*Kyrios*) conveys that Jesus carries the weight of divine authority. *Kyrios* is not a technical title for a deity but simply denotes a person who has authority over someone or something. In the ancient world slaves would refer to their masters as *Kyrios* (Greek) or *Dominus* (Latin). In the Gospels, when Jesus is addressed as "Lord," it usually means no more than "Sir" or "Master."[7] However, there are other occasions where the designation of Jesus as "Lord" is intended to convey Jesus's divine identity. The resurrection and exaltation of Jesus drove the early church to refer to Jesus as "Lord" in ways identical to how the Old Testament refers to God as YHWH. We need to remember that the Hebrew name for God, the Tetragrammaton YHWH, and the more general title *Adonai*, were usually translated in the Septuagint, the Greek version of the Old Testament, with *Kyrios* ("Lord"). So when Paul says that Jesus is the "one Lord" through whom all things come (1 Cor 8:6) and "every tongue [will] acknowledge that Jesus Christ is Lord" (Phil 2:11) he was using YHWH-language to describe Jesus as the "Lord." The purpose of this blend of scriptural allusion and devotion to Jesus is to underscore the unequaled status given to Jesus by God the Father.

---

6. Jeremy R. Treat, "Exaltation in and through Humiliation: Rethinking the States of Christ," in *Christology Ancient and Modern: Exploration in Constructive Dogmatics*, ed. O. D. Crisp and F. Sanders (Grand Rapids: Zondervan, 2013), 113–14.

7. The exception perhaps is Matthew 7:22 where Jesus describes himself as the eschatological "Lord" of the end of history.

In several other instances the lordship of Jesus constitutes the overarching canopy for the New Testament witness to Jesus. For a case in point, Psalm 110 with its "the LORD says to my lord: 'Sit at my right hand until I make your enemies a footstool for your feet'" was *the* favorite text of Christian preachers in the early church. Flip through any New Testament concordance and you'll find citations, allusions, and echoes of Psalm 110 literally and literarily everywhere. A christological reading of Psalm 110 gave strong impetus to the view that Jesus was the singular highest authority in heaven and earth, indeed, in the whole cosmos. In addition, Paul tells us that when the Judean leaders and Roman authorities killed Jesus, they did not put a mere man to death, rather, "They crucified the Lord of glory" (1 Cor 2:8). The Roman and Judean authorities, political powers and religious leaders alike, conspired to destroy Jesus, but Jesus was exalted by the Father to share his divine radiance, his glory. By calling Jesus the "Lord of glory," Paul brazenly applies an attribute associated with God—the "God of glory" (Acts 7:2; Rom 3:23; 5:2; 1 Cor 10:31; 11:7; 2 Cor 1:20; Rev 21:23)—to Jesus. Furthermore, the place where Jesus's glory will be supremely manifested is of course his second coming, an event that will demonstrate Jesus's lordship par excellence. His return at the end of history will be the revelation of Jesus as the Lord who is arrayed in heavenly splendor and invested with divine power. For this reason, Aramaic speakers in the early church regarded the return of the Lord, *marana tha* in Aramaic, as the coming of Jesus to judge the world (1 Cor 16:22; Rev 22:20; Didache 10.6)—Maranatha! Come, Lord! The final and climactic manifestation of Jesus as Lord will take place at his second coming when he will rescue believers from the coming wrath (1 Thess 1:10), gather them to himself (2 Thess 2:1), and overthrow lawless authorities (2 Thess 2:8). It is the moment where Jesus will be by might what he is by right: the *pantokratōr*, the divine master and commander over everything and everyone! So, to sum up, whether it was expositing Scriptures like Psalm 110, contemplating the glory of God in Christ, or waiting for Jesus's return—for the early Christians all of it was saturated with the imagery of Jesus as Lord.

The lordship of Jesus Christ was not merely a doctrinal formula but something that pervaded the witness, work, and worship of the early church.

Have a brief glance through the book of Acts and you'll notice as clear as day that baptism, thanksgiving, prayers, hymns, praise, and celebratory meals all take place in the context of devotion to Jesus Christ as the Lord. In the early church, the word and example of the Lord Jesus carried preeminent authority (1 Cor 7:10; 11:1; 1 Thess 4:15; 1 Pet 2:21). The preaching of the gospel was the proclamation of Jesus as Lord (Acts 2:36; 5:14; 8:16; 9:5; 10:36; 28:31; 2 Cor 4:5; 2 Thess 1:8). Knowing God meant knowing the lordship of Jesus Christ (Eph 1:17; 2 Thess 1:8). In fact, the most basic definition of a Christian is one who confesses Jesus as Lord, because it is by such a confession that one is saved (Rom 10:9–10) and such a confession can only be made with the help of the Holy Spirit (1 Cor 12:3). On top of that, on a more chilling note I have to say, Paul declares that if anyone does not love the Lord, then he or she is cursed (1 Cor 16:22). Evidently, loving the Lord Jesus is an expression of new covenant loyalty.[8]

We should also add that there is a sharp and subversive claim made with the profession that Jesus is Lord. In the Roman world of the first century, Caesar was venerated as "Lord" over the realms he ruled, not just politically but religiously too. Worship of the emperor all over the empire, usually localized in form and varied in intensity, ensured the devotion of his subjects. In ancient media like coins, pottery, and poetry one can find celebration of the emperor as both a god and a mediator before the gods. In inscriptions one reads things like "Emperor [Augustus] Caesar, god and lord" and "Nero, the lord of the whole world." In this context, picture what it would be like to confess that Jesus is Lord. Visualize yourself standing on a street in downtown Rome, announcing that a Jewish man from a far province, who was put to death by a Roman governor, had been installed as King of kings and Lord of lords! To some it might sound disgusting, while to others it would mark you as a political dissident. N. T. Wright rightly observes, "To come to Rome with the gospel of Jesus, to announce someone else's accession to the world's throne, therefore, was to put on a red coat and walk into a field with a potentially angry bull."[9]

---

8. D. E. Garland, *1 Corinthians*, BECNT (Grand Rapids: Baker, 2003), 774.
9. N. T. Wright, "Romans," in *The New Interpreter's Bible*, ed. L. E. Keck, 12 vols. (Nashville: Abingdon, 2002), 10:423.

Imagine that you are in an extravagant hotel in Berlin during the 1930s for a dinner party attended by a mix of lawyers, doctors, businessmen, and military officers. While the evening is mostly polite and cordial with small talk on everything from the stock market to the latest operas, a military officer suddenly taps his glass and proposes a toast to the *Führer*, Adolf Hitler. Then, as everyone stands and raises their glasses, you, being the committed Christian you are, interrupt and propose an alternative toast. Everyone is startled and looks at you as you proudly utter in your best German, "Jesus der Jude aus Nazaret ist der wahre Führer" ("Jesus the Jew from Nazareth is the true Führer").[10] You probably wouldn't have long before the Gestapo came and took you away to a very nasty place for making such a subversive claim. Lest I appear to overstate the political dimensions of Jesus's lordship, keep in mind that Nero did not have Christians thrown to the lions because they said, "Jesus is Lord of my heart." The Romans were not interested in the internal dispositions of people's lives. Confession of Jesus as Lord was always a scandalous and subversive claim. Profession of a "lord" is not merely religious language for adoration on some spiritual plane; it is also a matter of social and political allegiance. When it came to who was running the show, the Christians knew that there were only two options, either the son of Augustus or the son of David. By singing and preaching about Jesus as Lord, they were opting for the latter, a claim regarded by political authorities as seditious. As N. T. Wright suggests, "For Paul, Jesus is Lord and Caesar is not."[11]

For us today though, "The term 'Lord' has become one of the most lifeless words in the Christian vocabulary."[12] When the title "Lord" lost its reverence, it also lost its relevance and was reduced to something like "a spiritually meaningful religious leader." That is such a travesty because adoration of Jesus as Lord is neither an empty confession nor a vague religious platitude. More likely, as Kennedy himself adds, "To enter into its meaning and to give it practical effect would be to re-create, in great measure, the

---

10. Michael F. Bird, *A Bird's-Eye View of Paul: The Man, His Mission and His Message* (Nottingham: Inter-Varsity Press, 2008), 83–84.

11. N. T. Wright, *Paul in Fresh Perspective* (Minneapolis: Fortress, 2009), 69.

12. H. A. A. Kennedy, *St. Paul's Epistle to the Philippians*, 439, as cited in C. F. H. Henry, *God, Revelation, and Authority* (Wheaton: Crossway, 1999), 2:239.

atmosphere of the Apostolic Age."[13] I concur with Kennedy. To confess that Jesus is "Lord" is to announce that he is Lord of all. At the name of Jesus, every knee shall bow—every Christian, every Jew, every Muslim, every Hindu, and every atheist—and they will confess that Jesus Christ is Lord. I don't know whether you've thought about it, but this is deeply offensive and disturbing stuff to postmodern sensibilities. Confession of Jesus as Lord implies that all religions are not equal. Jesus is not a leader who has his authority curtailed by politicians or sociologists telling him which areas of life he's allowed to give people advice on. Jesus is the boss of everyone's religion, politics, economics, ethics, and everything. Jesus is not interested in trying to capture a big chunk of the religious market; to the contrary, he's in the business of completely monopolizing it with the glory, justice, and power of heaven. And he has every right to do so; after all, as the firstborn of all creation, the cosmos is his work and inheritance. Consequently, Abraham Kuyper was right to declare that "there is not a square inch in the whole domain of human existence which Christ who is Sovereign over all, does not cry: 'Mine!'"[14] If that is the case, then true discipleship is about dutifully and faithfully living out the lordship of Jesus Christ. Discipleship means ordering our lives according to his story, symbols, teaching, and authority. Evangelism is not about asking people to try Jesus the way they might try a new decaf mochachino latte from Starbucks. It is more like *declaring* the victory of the Lord Jesus over sin and death, *warning* of the judgment to be made by the Lord Jesus over all rebellion, and *inviting* people to find joy and satisfaction in the life and love that come from the Lord Jesus Christ.

What we should take away is that in the unfolding story of the New Testament, the preincarnate Son who divested himself of divine glory in his incarnation is now fully invested by the Father with divine authority over every realm. What the Lord God of Israel does in creation and redemption is now, in some way, exercised through the lordship of Jesus Christ. When Jesus is named "Lord," it is usually in the context of affirming that he carries the mantle of the Father's full authority and that he is the Father's

---

13. Kennedy, *Philippians*, 439.

14. Cited in James D. Bratt, *Abraham Kuyper: A Centennial Reader* (Grand Rapids: Zondervan, 1998), 461.

agent for rescuing Israel and putting the world to rights. Confession of Jesus as Lord was not a matter of mere assent or intellectual affirmation. It was a life-and-death issue. It meant standing up to the Caesars of the world who usurped for themselves the praise and power that rightly belonged to God. As Christians today, our highest vocation is to live our lives under the canopy of Jesus's lordship and to make it clear to all that "this Jesus," whom men and women reject, is Lord of all. What is more, the Lord Jesus will bring justice to our sin-cursed earth and then flood the world with the *shalom* of heaven.

In light of this, we should reflect on the words of Paul who said, "Grace to all who love our Lord Jesus Christ with an undying love" (Eph 6:24). To love the Lord is to love Jesus's lordship. We do that knowing that Jesus is neither a tyrant nor a despot. While Jesus is Lord of all, he is also Lord for all. The goodness, kindness, love, and compassion of Jesus as our Savior is also reflected in Jesus as our Lord. If we were to make a Christian psalm book, the most common refrain should be, "The Lord Jesus is good and his love endures forever" (Pss 100:5; 106:1; 107:1; 118:1, 29; 136:1)!

This Jesus

I have to confess that high school was a particularly glum time for me. What is more, the last day of high school was a fitting monument to my misery. At my high school graduation ceremony we had to endure a number of speeches, which were so boring that they could warrant charges of crimes against humanity.

First, we had a local businessman give us a pep talk about success, telling us how to be winners and how to access the formula for achievement. It was not just that it was painfully boring, but it was really ironic that his own business went bankrupt about a month later. I subsequently learned that he delivered his talk to us while insolvency accountants were going through his books to see if his business was in any way salvageable!

Second, we had a lecture from a local doctor on personal hygiene. Let me say that I have never quite seen or heard such a graphic and full account of the dangers of testicular cancer. The climax of his discussion was showing us a poster with three male monkeys sitting in trees, holding their genitals, with a caption underneath that read, "Monkeys check theirs, do you check yours?" Every time someone mentions the words "proctologist" or "vasectomy," I always think of those poor monkeys.

Third, just when I thought it could not get any worse, we then had our religious guest deliver a third talk. I was not from a religious home, I had no religious friends, and I regarded religion with little more than disdain. The speaker was the school chaplain, a local Baptist pastor, and I have to confess that for some reason something he said stuck with me and lodged itself in my mind like a splinter I couldn't get out. He said, "The most important decision you will ever make is whether you chose to accept or reject Jesus Christ as Savior." At the time I just shook it off as religious mumbo jumbo, but his challenge remained with me, those words haunted me, and years later I would recall those words and could see that they were preparing the way for my own coming to Christ.

The reason why accepting or rejecting Christ is such an important decision is because Jesus is the most important person to have ever lived in all of history. The most confronting issue about Christian faith is not any single idea—as if "Christianity" can be reduced to an "idea"; rather the most challenging aspect of Christian faith is a person: Jesus. Jesus of Nazareth is a towering figure of world history and he lives, not in the pages of history books but in the experience of his love and in the testimony to him as carried by his followers. He refuses to be merely one teacher in a buffet of religious gurus. Jesus claims a unique role as "the way" to God and a superlative authority as "Lord." We can disbelieve him, but no one can ignore him. Jesus comes to us with a question, "Who do you say I am?" (Matt 16:15), an invitation, "Take my yoke upon you and learn from me, for I am gentle and humble in heart, and you will find rest for your souls" (Matt 11:29), and a command, "Come, follow me!" (Matt 4:19). Hopefully our study of this aspect of the Apostles' Creed has equipped us to answer the question, accept his offer, and follow the command!

The Story Thus Far

To sum up, the Apostles' Creed calls us to believe in Jesus Christ, God's Son, and our Lord. The central substance of that claim is that (1) Jesus is the Messiah who brings Israel's story to fulfillment, (2) Jesus is the Son of God with a messianic mission and a unique filial relationship to Israel's God, and (3) Jesus as Lord is installed as the highest authority in heaven and on earth. Obviously much more could be said about Jesus; more is obviously implied and demanded, not least about his divine and human natures. What suffices for now is to note that whatever we say about God's glory, love, will, and word, we must say in reference to Jesus, for Jesus defines for us what God's glory, love, will, and word mean!

Recommended Reading

Bird, Michael F. "The Story of Jesus and the Identity of God." Pages 460–87 in *Evangelical Theology: A Biblical and Systematic Introduction*. Grand Rapids: Zondervan, 2013.

Matera, Frank. *New Testament Christology*. Louisville: Westminster John Knox, 1999.

Strauss, Mark L. *Four Portraits, One Jesus: An Introduction to Jesus and the Gospels*. Grand Rapids: Zondervan, 2007.

Wright, N. T. *The Challenge of Jesus: Rediscovering Who Jesus Was and Is*. London: SPCK, 1999.

7

BELIEVING *in the* VIRGIN BIRTH

*He was conceived by the power of the Holy Spirit
and born of the Virgin Mary.*

Messiah in the Manger

Back in the early 1980s in Britain there was a late-night comedy show called *Not the Nine O'Clock News*, featuring actors like Rowan Atkinson of Mr. Bean fame. In one particular episode, there was a comical parody of a Church of England worship service. During the service, the congregation recited the Apostles' Creed from "the new revised version of the new revised version of the Book of Common Prayer," which said about Jesus's birth, "[W]ho was conceived by the Holy Ghost, born of the Virgin Mary. No, don't laugh, it could happen. After all, they can do it in a test tube these days." Quite clearly, the notion that Jesus was born to a young Galilean girl who was still a virgin has proven to be one of the most objectionable and mocked beliefs of the Christian faith. And yet, there it is right in front of us, right there in the Apostles' Creed, to be confessed by Christians as part of our holy faith.

It is no wonder then that belief in Jesus's virgin birth was a touchstone of orthodoxy at the height of the fundamentalist vs. liberal controversy in the early twentieth century. In the midst of all the controversy, some theologians could pretend to be orthodox and bluff their way through Christ's deity, the atonement, and the resurrection. Speaking in opaque terms, using wishy-washy images, and making vague pronouncements that nobody really understood, you could sound conservative to conservatives and liberal to liberals. However, the one subject that you could never bluff your way through was the virgin birth. Either you believed that Mary miraculously became pregnant before sexual intercourse or you did not. Either you held that Jesus was conceived by a supernatural event or you claimed that he was conceived from the natural processes of human procreation.

What we'll do in this chapter is look at the complex historical issues related to affirming the virgin birth, and then (and much more interesting to my mind) discuss the real meaning and significance of Jesus's birth.

Sceptics at the Manger

When it comes to the virgin birth, or more properly we should say, the "virgin conception," there is a whole swath of critical issues that one could examine. Such issues include the parallels between the virgin conception and ancient stories about the birth of other religious and political heroes, the question of the sources behind the nativity accounts in the Gospels, discussions about the Old Testament citations in the nativity stories, doubts about Luke's census under Quirinius, the differences between the versions of Matthew and Luke, questions about whether there are any implicit references to a virgin conception in Paul (Gal 4:4) and Mark (Mark 6:3), and so forth. To be brief, those of a more critical mind try to arouse suspicion about the historical character of the virgin conception by pointing to things like how the Roman emperor Augustus was supposedly conceived through his mother being impregnated by the god Apollo.[1] Based on these comparisons, Dom Crossan and Jonathan Reed argue: "If you take Jesus' conception story literally, take Augustus' literally. If you take Jesus' conception story metaphorically, take Augustus' metaphorically."[2] Others assert that according to the earliest tradition, Jesus was regarded as coming from the "seed of David,"

---

1. Suetonius, *Augustus* 94.4.
2. John Dominic Crossan and Jonathan L. Reed, *Excavating Jesus: Beneath the Stones, Behind the Texts* (San Francisco: HarperOne, 2001), 88.

meaning physical descent from David's line, with Joseph therefore being Jesus's real biological father (Acts 13:23; Rom 1:3; 2 Tim 2:8). For others, they emphasize that the virgin conception is a late development found only in Matthew and Luke with no explicit mention made in Mark, Paul, and John. Some critics find great succor in the fact that the doctrine of the virgin conception was far from unanimous in the second-century church. The Ebionites said Jesus was born through a normal human conception. Marcion said Jesus was so heavenly that he wasn't physically born at all but just appeared on the scene. Valentinus said that Jesus passed through Mary's body like water through a pipe without taking on any of her yucky humanity. And Justin Martyr said that Jesus was born of the virgin Mary. So for many critics, the virgin conception can be glibly dismissed as mythical, a doctrinal latecomer, and disputed even by those professing a Christian faith.

Speaking Up for the Son of Mary

The challenge we face in discussing the virgin conception is that we could so easily get bogged down canvassing the critical issues about its history and the formation of the doctrine that we forget to look at what the affirmation of the virgin conception even means for Christian belief and what relevance it has for the church's witness today. While I am quite aware of the danger of getting stuck in an intractable quagmire of debate, even so, the critical issues of the virgin conception's historicity and theological importance cannot be ignored. So, without doing full justice to the topic, I'll offer a few short comments now.[3]

First, the critical perspective should not be prematurely dismissed since some correct observations are made and some valid protests are lodged. There are some things here that will make you scratch your head, and no

---

3. For fuller helpful treatments on the historical and theological matters, see C. E. B. Cranfield, "Some Reflections on the Subject of the Virgin Birth," *SJT* 41 (1988): 177–89; Thomas F. Torrance, "The Doctrine of the Virgin Birth," *Scottish Bulletin of Evangelical Theology* 12 (1994): 8–25; Michael F. Bird, "Birth of Jesus," in *Encyclopedia of the Historical Jesus*, ed. Craig A. Evans (New York: Routledge, 2008), 71–74; Oliver D. Crisp, *God Incarnate: Explorations in Christology* (New York: T&T Clark, 2009), 77–102; Andrew T. Lincoln, *Born of a Virgin?: Reconceiving Jesus in the Bible, Tradition, and Theology* (Grand Rapids: Eerdmans, 2013).

one should be yelled down for asking honest questions raised by reading the biblical texts. We are not here to peddle our assumptions but to engage in a close and detailed reading of the texts that will hopefully vindicate them.

Second, the relative absence of the virgin conception from most of the New Testament suggests that the doctrine has only relative importance for mapping the identity of Jesus. Note, I did not say that the virgin conception is unimportant or irrelevant but only that it has *relative* importance within the wider topic of the person and work of Jesus Christ. While a view of Jesus that denies the virgin conception might be problematic, a story of Jesus without it is not necessarily deficient. To say otherwise would be to render Mark, John, Paul, and the writer to the Hebrews as christologically challenged for not mentioning Jesus's birth. For such reasons, I'm inclined to understand the nativity stories as a clarification to Jesus's divine sonship rather than the necessary grounds for it. As a doctrine, the virgin conception is not essential to Christian testimony, but neither is it completely dispensable since it features prominently in a fully orbed doctrine of Jesus's person. Or, in the words of J. G. Machen, "even if the belief in the virgin birth is not necessary to every Christian, it is certainly necessary to Christianity."[4]

Third, I am not prepared to accept that the story of the virgin conception was a late creation intended as a christological parody of stories about ancient persons who were supposedly born of strange and supernatural circumstances. I remain convinced that, historically, there was rumored to be something suspicious or at least out of order about Jesus's birth; hence the accusation that Jesus was illegitimate, or in Aramaic slang, a *mamzer*.[5] An accusation of illegitimacy of course does not prove the virgin conception but is certainly consistent with it. What is more, the nativity stories exhibit a distinctive Palestinian flavor and reflect the piety of Jewish Christians. They are based on traditional materials, especially the hymns like Mary's *Magnificat*, so that they cannot be dismissed as adaptations of pagan myths by a gentile-dominated church late in the first century.[6]

---

4. J. G. Machen, *The Virgin Birth of Christ* (New York: Harper, 1930), 396.

5. See John 8:19, 41 and discussion by Scot McKnight, "Calling Jesus *Mamzer*," *Journal for the Study of the Historical Jesus* 1 (2003): 73–103.

6. See Michael F. Bird and James G. Crossley, *How Did Christianity Begin? A Believer and Non-Believer Examine the Evidence* (London: SPCK, 2008), 18–21.

Fourth, whether one likes it or not, the virgin conception is part of the faith received in the global church—affirmed in the biblical canon, annunciated in ancient creeds, and rehearsed in the Reformed confessions—and we should not think that we are at personal liberty to highlight the text with our cursor and then hit the delete button. Karl Barth knew full well the cupboard of critical objections to the virgin conception and he accepted that one could conceivably hold to a high view of Jesus without it. He stated, "There is certainly nothing to prevent anyone, without affirming the doctrine of the Virgin birth, from recognising the mystery of the person of Jesus Christ or from believing in a perfectly Christian way. It is within God's counsel and will to make this possible, just as it cannot be at all impossible for Him to bring anyone to the knowledge of Himself even beyond the sphere of the Church visible to us."[7] However, Barth also recognized that this was not necessarily a wise course, as the church had historically embraced the "miracle of Christmas" as part of the story of the incarnation. For Barth, the virgin conception is a sure sign that Jesus is truly God and truly man, a sign that cannot nonchalantly be pushed aside to avoid offending rationalistic sensibilities. Thus Barth adds, "But this does not imply that the Church is at liberty to convert the doctrine of the Virgin birth into an option for specifically strong or for specially weak souls. The Church knew well what it was doing when it posted this doctrine on guard, as it were, at the door of the mystery of Christmas. It can never be in favour of anyone thinking he can hurry past this guard. It will remind him that he is walking along a private road at his own cost and risk. It will warn him against doing so. It will proclaim as a church ordinance that to affirm the doctrine of the Virgin birth is a part of real Christian faith."[8] The virgin conception is not up for negotiation, as it is a part of the biblical teaching and a consistent feature of the church's testimony to Jesus. We are free to raise questions, test interpretations, and offer fresh ones, but we are not free to roll our eyes and move on to other matters if we are to believe in Jesus as Christians.

---

7. Barth, *CD*, I/2:181.
8. Barth, *CD*, I/2:181.

Why the Virgin Birth?

Rather than get bogged down in the (de)merits of demythologizing the nativity story or engaging in apologetic arguments for the virgin conception's historicity, we will do better if we focus our time asking what the story of Jesus's birth is about and what function it has within the constellation of Christian teaching. In short, what does the virgin conception teach us about God, Jesus, and humanity?

It Is Not about Sinlessness

To begin with, let's be clear as to what the virgin conception is not about. The virgin conception is definitely not necessary for Jesus to be sinless. If one is operating with the assumption that human characteristics are transmitted seminally, that is, exclusively through the male line, then the absence of a father would be necessary for Jesus to be born without a human propensity for corruption and without its associated guilt (i.e., original sin). However, there is nothing in the nativity accounts that suggests that Jesus's sinlessness is at stake. In addition, we know that children receive DNA from both of their parents, mother and father, and Jesus evidently possessed human DNA at least from his mother. So a virgin conception cannot be a necessary requirement for apprehending a mode of humanity partitioned away from human fallenness since biology teaches us otherwise. On this point, Mark Strauss is quite right:

> Some have argued it was necessary to protect Jesus's sinless nature, but the narratives themselves do not indicate this purpose. The Messiah could have entered human life free from sin with or without a virginal conception. Nor is Scripture explicit on the details of the conception. Did God create the sperm for Mary's egg? Did he create a fertilized embryo? The latter question raises questions about how Jesus could have been fully human if he had no physical connection to Mary or Joseph. The former raises the question of how Jesus could have avoided Mary's sinful nature. The Roman Catholic answer is the immaculate conception, whereby

Mary herself was born free from sin. But this doctrine has no basis in Scripture. In the final analysis, the details remain a mystery. What is certain from the text is that the conception of Jesus was a supernatural act of God, confirming that God himself was about to accomplish the salvation which no human being could achieve.[9]

A Son Is Born to Us!

When it comes to the *meaning* of the virgin conception, there are several salient points that are umbilically connected to it.

First, the virgin conception makes clear that Israel was the vehicle by which God's deliverance was brought into the world. God's Son comes into the world as an Israelite man. Jesus could not have been Roman, Syrian, Parthian, or American; he had to be an Israelite. God's plan has always been to reach the world through Israel, thus it had to be as a son of Israel that the Son of God was born. The Old Testament, in typology (Isa 11:1–5) and in prophecy (Mic 5:1–5), looks forward to a coming son of David who shall lead God's people out of exile and into a new day of deliverance. Furthermore, a redeemed Israel would lead to the redemption of the world, so part of the Messiah's job description was to heal the nations and to rule over them on God's behalf (Isa 2:2–4; Amos 9:11–12; Mic 4:1–5; Zech 8:23). In which case, the virgin conception is not only the fulfillment of biblical prophecy but also the validation of the biblical claim that God's deliverance comes through the people, promises, story, and covenants of Israel. The infancy story explains God's mission to bring the sons of Adam into a relationship with himself through the sons of Israel. That plan is executed, in fact, through one very special son of Israel, the messianic seed of Abraham, a royal son of David, a new son of Adam, the son of Mary, who is in fact the beloved and begotten Son of God.

Second, the virgin conception underscores the dominant role of the Holy Spirit in Jesus's ministry. Notice how the Apostles' Creed states that "he was

---

9. Mark Strauss, *Four Portraits, One Jesus: An Introduction to Jesus and the Gospels* (Grand Rapids: Zondervan, 2007), 415.

conceived by the power of the Holy Spirit." The Spirit is an underrated and yet highly prominent partner in Jesus's life and ministry. Jesus was not only born from the Spirit's work (Matt 1:18, 20; Luke 1:35) but the Spirit animated Jesus's entire ministry (Luke 4:1, 14; 10:21). Remember that Jesus did not do any mighty deeds or preaching until such time as he was baptized and received the Holy Spirit (Matt 3:16). Thereafter, the Spirit was the leading partner in the relationship. For instance, we are told that the Spirit "led" or "drove" him into the wilderness for his time of temptation (Mark 1:12; Matt 4:1; Luke 4:1). Elsewhere Luke reports that Jesus did his work "in the power of the Spirit" (Luke 4:14). Jesus's work by the "Spirit of God" was also the proof that "the kingdom of God" had at last arrived (Matt 12:28//Luke 11:20). The virgin conception is, then, the first reminder of the role of the Spirit in Jesus's life, ushering in the kingdom and bringing about redemption.

Third, the virgin conception provides a clarification to Jesus's identity as the preexistent and eternal Son of God made flesh. Matthew and Luke both connect the virgin conception to their wider narrative aims to disclose Jesus's identity as God's Son. The upshot is that Jesus was not simply a holy man whom God honored with divine status. Jesus was not a cosmic ghost disguised as a man dispensing philosophically savvy self-help advice to be true to ourselves. Rather, the virgin conception is the first expression of the belief that Jesus is both a human son of Adam and the divine Son of God. It shows us that Israel's long-awaited "son of David" is also "Immanuel, God with us." The virgin conception is the first clue we have to the incarnation, a union of humanity and divinity in the person of Jesus, even if the precise mechanism for that union is left unexplained. Or, as Barth put it, the virgin conception is the event that describes how "in Jesus Christ God comes forth out of the profound hiddenness of His divinity in order to act as God among us and upon us."[10]

Fourth, the virgin conception means that God's new world was at last becoming a reality. The virgin conception signifies that the coming kingdom and the renewal of creation had already entered human existence through the heavenly power that entered Mary's womb. N. T. Wright comments:

---

10. Barth, *CD*, I/2:182.

Actually, the strange story of Jesus's being conceived without a human father is so peculiar, particularly within Judaism, and so obviously open to sneering accusations on the one hand and the charge that the Christians were simply aping the pagans on the other, that it would be very unlikely for someone to invent it so early in the Christian movement as Matthew and Luke. But there's more to it than just that. The virginal conception speaks powerfully of new creation, something fresh happening within the old world, beyond the reach and dreams of the possibilities we currently know. And if we believe that the God we're talking about is the creator of the world, who longs to rescue the world from its corruption and decay, then an act of real new creation, anticipating in fact the great moment of Easter itself, might just be what we should expect, however tremblingly, if and when this God decides to act to bring this new creation about.[11]

On this line of thought, the birth of Jesus is the first sign of a new world being born, a new age dawning upon our own. A world pregnant with anticipation and hope finds itself in the final throes of labor pains as it receives the gift of new spiritual life from heaven in the person of the Christ child.

Fifth, the birth of Jesus teaches us about the victory of God and the vanquishing of Satan. Let me show you a biblical nativity story that I'm sure you seldom see. Imagine a woman in the throes of childbirth, screaming in pain, with her legs spread apart. Imagine also that standing over the woman is a seven-headed dragon, who is crouched, poised, salivating, and ready to devour the child as soon as it is expelled from the birth canal. It reads like a nativity scene directed by Quentin Tarrantino, doesn't it! But cast your eyes over Revelation 12:

A great sign appeared in heaven: a woman clothed with the sun, with the moon under her feet and a crown of twelve stars on her head. She was pregnant and cried out in pain as she was about to give birth. Then another sign appeared in heaven: an enormous red dragon with seven

---

11. N. T. Wright, "Power to Become Children: Isaiah 52.7–10 and John 1.1–18," sermon preached at Cathedral Church of Christ, 25 December 2007, http://www.ntwrightpage.com/sermons /Christmas07.htm.

heads and ten horns and seven crowns on its heads. Its tail swept a third of the stars out of the sky and flung them to the earth. The dragon stood in front of the woman who was about to give birth, so that it might devour her child the moment he was born. She gave birth to a son, a male child, who "will rule all the nations with an iron scepter." And her child was snatched up to God and to his throne. The woman fled into the wilderness to a place prepared for her by God, where she might be taken care of for 1,260 days. Then war broke out in heaven. Michael and his angels fought against the dragon, and the dragon and his angels fought back. But he was not strong enough, and they lost their place in heaven. The great dragon was hurled down—that ancient serpent called the devil, or Satan, who leads the whole world astray. He was hurled to the earth, and his angels with him. Then I heard a loud voice in heaven say: "Now have come the salvation and the power and the kingdom of our God, and the authority of his Messiah. For the accuser of our brothers and sisters, who accuses them before our God day and night, has been hurled down. They triumphed over him by the blood of the Lamb and by the word of their testimony; they did not love their lives so much as to shrink from death. (Rev 12:1–11)

The scene depicts the cosmic battle between the forces of evil and the hosts of heaven as the context for the birth of Jesus. The woman in question is not Mary; rather, she is the messianic community through whom Jesus is born. The child is obviously the Messiah, hence the citation of Psalm 2:9 and his rule over the nations with an iron scepter. The messianic child is removed by God from the malevolent grasp of the red dragon. The removal is allusive of Jesus's ascension and exaltation. What is important here is that Jesus's birth and the blood that he sheds constitute the victory of God over Satan. God's plan to repossess the world from the dominion of darkness is launched in the birth of a child who is destined to defeat the dragon that rages against the people of God. The birth of Jesus marks the beginning of the end of evil, sin, pain, and death.

Final Verdict on the Virgin Birth

To wrap things up, the virgin conception is not a Christianized version of pagan mythology nor an odd tale of God's onetime enterprise at running a Galilean fertility clinic for teenage girls. The virgin conception tells us about Israel's hopes coming true, about God's Son made flesh, about the Spirit's power in Jesus's life, about a new world dawning, and about God's victory over Satan through the offspring of Eve. In short, the Christian faith is a Christmas faith, celebrating the fact that God became one of us through the Holy Spirit overshadowing Mary's body. It is a glorious story about God's Spirit, Mary's womb, God's Word made flesh, and angels singing, "Peace on earth."

The Story Thus Far

We believe that the God who made the world sent his Son into the world. The name of his Son is Jesus of Nazareth, the son of Mary. This Jesus shares fully in the Father's divinity and completely in our humanity—a divinity same in substance to the Father coupled with a humanity that is identical to our own. He is appointed as Israel's Messiah and the Lord of the whole world. He comes to the world, not on a fiery chariot accompanied with apocalyptic portents nor cloud surfing with an entourage of angels. Rather, he comes to us in humility through the vessel of a young Jewish girl. He comes as flesh to our flesh, as bone to our bone, to be God with us and God for us. When we profess that we believe in Jesus Christ, this is the one upon whom we set our hopes.

Recommended Reading

Bird, Michael F. "The Birth of Jesus" and "The Ministry of Jesus." Pages 365–82 in *Evangelical Theology: A Biblical and Systematic Introduction*. Grand Rapids: Zondervan, 2013.

Cranfield, C. E. B. "Some Reflections on the Virgin Birth." *Scottish Journal of Theology* 41 (1988): 177–98.

Lincoln, Andrew T. *Born of a Virgin: Reconceiving Jesus in the Bible, Tradition, and Theology*. Grand Rapids: Eerdmans, 2013.

Machen, J. G. *The Virgin Birth of Christ*. New York: Harper, 1930.

8

BELIEVING *in the* CROSS— THE OFFENCE *of the* CROSS

He suffered under Pontius Pilate,
was crucified, died, and was buried.

"And They Crucified Him"

The single uncontested fact about Jesus of Nazareth was that he was crucified in Jerusalem sometime around AD 30. He was executed at the behest of the Jerusalem high priest and on the order of Pontius Pilate. That Jesus "was crucified, died, and was buried" is probably the only line of the Apostles' Creed that even atheists could confess with a clear conscience. The problem is that we can all too glibly mouth the words "was crucified" without reflecting on them and without experiencing the horror that the words held for ancient audiences. The reality is that we have grown accustomed to the cross as a thing of religious art, fashionable jewelry, and theological symbolism. It might as well be the McDonald's sign or the Apple logo. A cross on a building or on the front of a book indicates a religious brand rather than the most terrifying torture we can imagine. However, the cross remains one of the most distinctive symbols of what lies at the heart of Christianity; it tells us what God is like, how much God loves us, and what it means to follow

Jesus. The cross is something disciples must explore time and time again as they strive to make its meaning and power wash over them afresh.

The Foolishness of the Cross

Our culture is still Christian enough not to be affronted and shaken by the crucifixion of Jesus. By virtue of our exposure to it, we are desensitized to the point that the shock and revulsion of the word *crucifixion* is lost on us. So remember this and remember it well, nobody who ever saw a crucifixion ever thought about turning it into a piece of artwork or modeling jewelry after it. Crucifixion meant degradation, death, shame, and cruelty. Crucifixion was the Roman way of saying, "If you dare to mess with us, there is no limit and no restraint on the violence that we will do to you." If you had ever seen a crucifixion, and they were common in places like Judea, the experience would have been truly terrifying. It would leave you with irrepressible memories of naked half-dead men dying a protracted death for days on end, covered in blood and flies, their flesh gnawed at by rats, theirs members ripped at by wild dogs, their faces pecked at by crows, the victims continually mocked and jeered by the torturers who enjoyed their craft, perhaps even with relatives nearby weeping uncontrollably yet entirely helpless to do anything for them.[1] This is why the Roman philosopher and jurist Cicero called crucifixion "the most cruel and terrifying penalty."[2] The Jewish historian Josephus, who had the horrible misfortune of seeing several of his friends crucified, labeled crucifixion "the most pitiable of deaths."[3] Maurice Goguel said that crucifixion

> represented the acme of the torturer's art: atrocious physical sufferings, length of torment, ignominy, the effect of the crowd gathering to witness the long agony of the crucified. Nothing could be more horrible than the sight of this living body, breathing, seeing, hearing, still able to feel, and yet reduced to the state of a corpse by forced immobility and absolute

---

1. N. T. Wright, *The Day the Revolution Began: Reconsidering the Meaning of Jesus' Crucifixion* (San Francisco: HarperOne, 2016), 54.
2. Cicero, *In Verrem* 2.5.165 (Greenwood, LCL).
3. Josephus, *Jewish War* 7.202–3 (Thackeray, LCL).

helplessness. We cannot ever say the crucified person writhed in agony, for it was impossible for him to move. Stripped of his clothing, unable even to brush away the flies that fell upon his wounded flesh already lacerated by the preliminary scourging, exposed to the insults and curses of the people who can always find some sickening pleasure in the sight of the tortures of others, a feeling which is increased and not diminished by the sight of pain—the cross represented miserable humanity reduced to the last degree of impotence, suffering, and degradation. The penalty of crucifixion combined all that the most ardent tormentor could desire: torture, the pillory, degradation, and certain death, distilled slowly drop by drop.[4]

To put it bluntly, crucifixion was the attempt to manufacture a temporary hell for its intended victim. Death by crucifixion denied the humanity of its victim and even destroyed something of the humanity of those who had become capable of inflicting it on another human being. Facing up to the sadistic horror of crucifixion might actually be an important task because, as Martin Hengel noted, "Reflection on the harsh reality of crucifixion in antiquity may help us to overcome the acute loss of reality which is to be found so often in present theology and preaching."[5] Balthasar was right: "If theology is to be Christian, then it can only be a theology which understands in dynamic fashion the unsurpassable scandal of the Cross."[6]

For outsiders, whether Jewish, Roman, or Greek, the Christian veneration of a crucified man was indeed scandalous if not outright madness. When Paul said that the cross was a stumbling block to Jews and foolishness to Greeks, he was not engaging in hyperbole (1 Cor 1:18–23). We can find manifold instances where the cross courted mockery and scandal by those who heard its message.

---

4. Maurice Goguel, *The Life of Jesus*, 535–36, as cited by Herman C. Waetjen, *A Reordering of Power: A Socio-Political Reading of Mark's Gospel* (Minneapolis: Fortress, 1989), 232.

5. Martin Hengel, *Crucifixion in the Ancient World and the Folly of the Message of the Cross* (London: SCM, 1977), 90.

6. Hans Urs von Balthasar, *Mysterium Paschale*, trans. A. Nichols (Edinburgh: T&T Clark, 1990), 56.

A Stumbling Block to Jews

To begin with, many Jews associated crucifixion with the pronouncement of Deuteronomy 21:22–23 about the accursedness of anyone hung upon a tree.[7] Justin Martyr's Jewish dialogue partner, Trypho, believed that "to be crucified and to die thus shamefully and dishonorably via the death which has been cursed in the law" makes it simply impossible to suppose that Jesus was the Messiah. For Trypho the "so-called Messiah" of Christians became "dishonorable and disreputable" by being hung upon a cross and falling under "the last curse in the law of God."[8] Trypho, like other Jews we can suppose, simply could not conceive how someone suffering the worst of covenant curses could be the one in whom God demonstrated his covenant faithfulness. In their mind a Messiah was meant to serve, save, and even sum up Israel in himself. God would reveal his saving righteousness in the reign of the Messiah who redeemed Israel from her enemies. Israel would rise up with their messianic leader to rule over the surrounding nations.

And therein lies the problem. As N. T. Wright points out, "The cross is offensive to Jews because a crucified Messiah implies a crucified Israel. Israel rejects the proffered Messiah precisely because she understands this. . . . If the Messiah dies under the law's curse, that means that Israel stands under the same curse: that is part of the meaning of Galatians 3:10–14. Calvary means that Israel also must die between two thieves, must share in the fate of the ungodly."[9] Paul argued in places like Romans 8:1–4, 2 Corinthians 5:19–21, and Galatians 3:10–14 that Israel was in fact under the curses of the covenant, and the Messiah took that curse into himself so that Israel would be set free from it and the blessings of the patriarchs could at last reach the gentiles. Paul's messianic reading of the curse of the law is decidedly apologetic and meant to show that it was God who was the one behind the crucifixion of the Messiah.

---

7. See 11Q19 (Temple Scroll) 64.6–13; Philo, *On the Special Laws* 3.151; Josephus, *Jewish Antiquities* 4.202, 264–65; Gal 3:13.

8. Justin Martyr, *Dialogue with Trypho* 32.1; 94.5 (*ANF*).

9. N. T. Wright, *Pauline Perspectives: Essays on Paul 1978–2013* (London: SPCK, 2013), 8.

Foolishness to Greeks

Greek and Roman perspectives about Christian faith in a crucified man did not fare much better. Hengel wrote, "The heart of the Christian message, which Paul described as the 'word of the cross,' ran counter not only to Roman political thinking, but to the whole ethos of religion in ancient times and in particular to the ideas of God held by educated people."[10] Crucifixion, after all, was the punishment of slaves, bandits, and enemies of the state. It was particularly offensive to Romans that the Christians honored as a god a person whom Roman authorities had executed as a common criminal. No wonder that Roman political leaders regarded the Christian faith as a pernicious superstition that had blown in from the east.[11] Marcus Cornelius Fronto, an orator and rhetorician, condemned Christians in a lost speech that is now preserved only in fragments within Minucius Felix's *Octavius.* Fronto said that "the religion of the Christians is insane, in that they worship a crucified man, and even the instrument of his punishment itself."[12] Similarly, Augustine records how the famous anti-Christian philosopher Porphyry of the third century discussed the shame associated with the Christian worship of a crucified god. Porphyry wrote about the story of a man who went to the temple of Apollo to ask the god what he might do to dissuade his wife from being a Christian. In Porphyry's account, Apollo answered the man as follows: "Let her continue as she pleases, persisting in her vain delusions, and lamenting in song a god who died in delusions, who was condemned by judges whose verdict was just, and executed in the prime of life by the worst of deaths, a death bound with iron."[13] The earliest piece of anti-Christian graffiti is the famous *Alexamenos* inscription, dated to around AD 200, found on Palatine Hill in Rome, on what probably was a school to train imperial slaves. The inscription presents a man with a donkey's head hanging on a cross, while another man faces toward the cross in a pose of worship. The words "Alexamenos worships his god" are etched underneath. The allegation is clear: Christians worship a crucified ass! It is

---

10. Hengel, *Crucifixion*, 5.
11. Pliny the Younger, *Epistulae* 10.96.4–8; Tacitus, *Annales* 15.44.3; Suetonius, *Nero* 16.3.
12. Minucius Felix, *Octavius* 9 (Rendall, LCL).
13. Augustine, *The City of God* 19.23 (LCL).

easy to plot the recurring themes: superstition, silliness, and insanity. No wonder that Justin Martyr could opine that "they say our madness consists in the fact that we put a crucified man in second place after the unchangeable and eternal God, the Creator of the world."[14]

Folly to Postmodern Minds

Sadly, things never change and the cross is still foolishness to secular Jews and postmodern Greeks. The idea that God inflicts a judicial penalty on Jesus for the sins of others as the grounds for salvation has prompted a flurry of derisive criticism. Many theologians of past and present have struggled to come to terms with the cross as a sacrifice for humanity's sins and the ordained means by which divine wrath is turned away.

Objections to an atonement theology of this species have been raised on the ground that such an act would contradict the divine command to love others without thought of retribution. Substitutionary atonement perpetuates the myth of redemptive violence where divinely sponsored violence is said to overcome human violence. Vociferous protests have been lodged that it is fundamentally unjust for God to punish an innocent man for the crimes of the guilty. The notion of a punitive and substitutionary death has been castigated as the lingering residue of a medieval theology which had a macabre fascination with sin and suffering. Furthermore, according to a radical feminist critique of the atonement, "Christianity is an abusive theology that glorifies suffering. . . . Is it any wonder that there is so much abuse in modern society when the predominant image of theology is of 'divine child abuse'—God the Father demanding and carrying out the suffering and death of his own son? If Christianity is to be liberating for the oppressed it must be itself liberated from this theology."[15]

If that were not bad enough, we might consider the sheer irrationality and pointlessness of the cross in contemporary thinking. For instance, the novel *Life of Pi* by Canadian author Yann Martel is about a young Indian

---

14. Justin, *First Apology* 13.4 (*ANF*).

15. Joanne Carlson Brown and Rebecca Parker, "For God So Loved the World?," in *Christianity, Patriarchy, and Abuse: A Feminist Critique*, ed. J. C. Brown and C. R. Bohn (New York: Pilgrim, 1989), 26.

boy whose parents own a zoo. The curious child one day stumbles into a Catholic church, where a priest explains to him the story of Jesus's death and the atonement. Piscine then later recounts what it was like to hear this Christian story of crucifixion and redemption:

> And what a story. The first thing that drew me in was disbelief. What? Humanity sins but it is God's Son who pays the price? I tried to imagine Father saying to me, "Piscine, a lion slipped into the llama pen today and killed two llamas. Yesterday another killed a black buck. Last week two of them ate a camel. The week before it was painted storks and grey herons. And who's to say for sure who snacked on our golden agouti? The situation has become intolerable. Something must be done. I have decided that the only way the lions can atone for their sins is if I feed you to them."
>
> "Yes, Father, that would be the right and logical thing to do. Give me a moment to wash up."
>
> "Hallelujah, my son."
>
> "Hallelujah, Father."[16]

For critics of Christianity, whether they are Jewish or Greek, ancient or postmodern, the cross is the epitome of religion gone crazy. For many the story of the cross is shameful, affronting, absurd, nonsensical, and plain unjust. Polycarp wrote to the Philippians that they should do their best to bear the "testimony of the cross," yet he knew that if they did that there would instantly rise up "enemies of the cross" for whom they must pray.[17] How little times have changed! So be warned! Whenever the cross is raised, there will quickly gather a gaggle of mockers to hurl insults at it. And yet, none of the sneers, taunts, or profanities hurled at the cross and at those who raise it up can change the fact that the cross is a beacon of light in a world that is cold, brutal, and dark. For upon the cross we encounter the depth of God's mercy for those who were once children of disobedience and his love for those once enslaved to the present evil age. The cross is hope, joy, peace, and love, and nothing uttered by Caiaphas or written in the *New York Times* can ever change that.

---

16. Yann Martel, *Life of Pi* (New York: Harcourt, 2001), 58–59.
17. Polycarp, *To the Philippians* 7.1; 12.3.

Embracing the Shame of the Cross

What I personally find so striking is that despite the foolishness, horror, and the shame associated with crucifixion, the cross quickly became the most cherished symbol of the Christian faith. Mark's portrayal of Jesus shows that the cross defines the very meaning of kingdom, where *kingdom* is redefined as power in weakness, strength in suffering, and victory in sacrifice (Mark 8:31–9:1; 10:35–45; 15:1–32). Luke depicts the cross, not as the end result of a series of unfortunate events, but part of the divine plan, often using the Greek word *dei* ("it is necessary") to locate Jesus's death as part of God's foreordained purposes (Luke 9:22; 17:25; 22:37; 24:7, 44). According to John, Jesus's death is a revelation of divine glory (John 12:23; 13:31–32) and motivated by divine love (John 3:16; 15:13). The apostle Paul preached a message of "Christ crucified" because it is the very "power of God" (1 Cor 1:17–18, 23). Paul even regarded his own identity as indelibly and somewhat mysteriously connected to the death of Jesus to the point that he could say that "I have been crucified with Christ" and "the world has been crucified to me" (Gal 2:20; 6:14). The author of Hebrews offers a stirring exhortation to his readers to remember Jesus, who "for the joy set before him ... endured the cross, scorning its shame" (Heb 12:2). That word "joy" is hard to miss and it would strike Romans, Greeks, and Jews as virtually incomprehensible to associate crucifixion with any kind of joy. John of Patmos peppers references to Jesus's crucifixion across the pages of his Apocalypse. Jesus is for John the "Lamb who was slain from the creation of the world," locating his death as part of God's prepromised plan to rescue his people from the mire of an evil world (Rev 13:8). The New Testament authors are then overwhelming witnesses to the crucicentric faith of the early church and the centrality of the cross in their proclamation.

Let me add an important point that the cross was not simply an item of theological interest. The cross visibly and audibly imposed itself in the worship, stories, symbols, and ethics of the first Christians. In worship, the cross appears in early Christian hymns and poems like the famous Christ-hymn of Philippians 2:5–11, which at its climatic midpoint celebrates how Jesus was "obedient to death—even death on a cross" (v. 8). And we can hardly forget the heavenly hymn in Revelation 5 where multitudes around the throne sing, "Worthy is the Lamb, who was slain, to receive power and wealth and wisdom and strength and honor and glory and praise" (v. 12). In the later church, the hymns of Romanos the Melodist (ca. AD 490–556) are filled with beautiful and rhythmic descriptions of the cross and its achievement. In his "Victory of the Cross" he wrote, "In your opinion the cross is an instrument of folly, but all creation sees it as the throne of glory. On it Jesus is nailed, like a king waiting to be hailed."[18]

When it comes to stories, a browse over the Gospels shows that when the church talked about God's promises, God's kingdom, and God's Messiah, they all led to the same place: Golgotha and the empty tomb. The story of the cross appears through the exhortations of 1 Peter, Hebrews, and the letters of Ignatius of Antioch. The symbolism of the cross is powerfully evoked in the sacraments of baptism and the Lord's Supper. Descending into the waters of baptism symbolizes dying with Christ and entering into solidarity with his death (Rom 6:1–8). In the Lord's Supper, the wine reminds us of Jesus's blood shed for us, and the bread reminds us of Jesus's body broken for us, pointing to the sacrificial nature of Jesus's death and its role in brokering a new covenant (Matt 26:28; Mark 14:24; Luke 22:20; 1 Cor 11:25; Heb 10:29).

The presence of staurograms in early manuscripts is a further indication of the veneration of Jesus's death in Christian writing materials. A staurogram is formed by superimposing the Greek letters *rho* and *tau* together to make a distinctive symbol to stand in place of the words "cross" (*stauros*) and "crucify" (*stauroō*) and it functions as both a *nomen sacrum* or "sacred name" and visual representation of the cross. Staurograms appear in some of the earliest New Testament papyri in the late second century.[19] Tertullian referred to the late second-century practice of making the sign of the cross: "At every forward step and movement, at every going in and out, when we put on our clothes and shoes, when we bathe, when we sit at the table, when we light the lamps, when on the couch, on a seat, and in all the ordinary actions of life, we trace the sign of the cross on our foreheads."[20]

---

18. R. J. Schork, *Sacred Song from the Byzantine Pulpit: Romanos the Melodist* (Gainesville: University Press of Florida, 1995), 130.

19. See further Larry W. Hurtado, *The Earliest Christian Artifacts: Manuscripts and Christian Origins* (Grand Rapids: Eerdmans, 2006), 135–54.

20. Tertullian, *The Crown* 3 (*ANF*).

The point I'm driving at is this: despite the mockery and shame associated with crucifixion and despite the utter folly of a crucified Messiah to all and sundry, the early church narrated the story of the cross as the climax of God's plan, and they embraced the symbol of the cross as the instrument through which God's kingdom was achieved. If we are to live out the story of the cross, then one of the first things we have to do is get inside the passion story and grasp, not superficially but on a deep level, the full sweep of the story of the cross.

Pontius Pilate and the Passion of Jesus

The Apostles' Creed mentions that Jesus was crucified "under Pontius Pilate." Pilate was a Roman aristocrat who was appointed by the Roman Emperor Tiberius as the prefect of Judea from AD 26–36. In regards to his character, to put it mildly, Pilate was a thug in toga. The first-century Jewish authors Philo and Josephus have nothing but scathing contempt for him. Philo described Pilate as "naturally inflexible, a blend of self-will and relentlessness" known for "the briberies, the insults, the robberies, the outrages, and wanton injuries, the executions without trial constantly repeated, the ceaseless and supremely grievous cruelty."[21] They refer to his needlessly provocative action in having Roman troops enter Jerusalem with imperial standards bearing the emperor's images despite the clear offense that these images had for the Jewish residents. When a crowd came to Caesarea to petition Pilate to withdraw the standards, he initially refused their request; yet after their persistence, he had the delegation surrounded by troops and threatened with execution if they did not cease their protest. It was only the delegation's willingness to die that forced him to back down and withdraw the standards from Jerusalem.[22] In another incident, Pilate seized funds from the temple treasury to fund the construction of an aqueduct. The seizure of sacred funds incensed many, and when some began to agitate,

---

21. Philo, *On the Embassy to Gaius* 301–2 (Colson, LCL).
22. Josephus, *Jewish Antiquities* 18.55–59; *Jewish War* 2.169–74; Philo, *On the Embassy to Gaius* 299–305.

Pilate had his soldiers infiltrate the crowd in disguise and on his secret order attack them with clubs.[23] Jesus warned about the necessity of repentance before judgment, using the story of Pilate massacring Galilean pilgrims in or around the temple as the prime example.[24] Finally, Pilate ordered the killing of Samaritans on a pilgrimage at Mount Gerizim. The Samaritans lodged a protest with Vitellius, the governor of Syria, who removed Pilate and had him sent back to Rome, and that is the last we hear about him in our ancient sources.[25]

Compared to Josephus and Philo, the Evangelists offer a fairly sympathetic characterization of Pilate. They portray him as inquisitive about Jesus and yet puzzled about what to do with him. In the Evangelists' accounts, Pilate regards Jesus as an innocent though perhaps deranged prophet, who had driven the high priests into a frenzied call for his execution. The Evangelists accent Pilate's finding Jesus innocent of any charge (Luke 23:22; John 19:4) and his willingness to release Jesus (Luke 23:16, 20, 22; Acts 3:13). Even Pilate's wife had a dream about "that innocent man" and urged her husband to have no part in the trial condemning him (Matt 27:19). Pilate, however, true to his character, appeased the crowd by releasing the murderer Barabbas and "had Jesus flogged, and handed him over to be crucified" (Mark 15:15; cf. John 19:16). According to Matthew, Pilate tried to absolve himself of any responsibility in Jesus's death by symbolically washing his hands and saying, "'I am innocent of this man's blood,' he said. 'It is your responsibility!'" (Matt 27:24). Nevertheless, the Christian tradition has never allowed Pilate to shirk responsibility for his part in the death of Jesus. Luke describes John and Peter recounting in prayer how "Herod and Pontius Pilate met together with the gentiles and the people of Israel in this city to conspire against your holy servant Jesus, whom you anointed" (Acts 4:27). In Paul's sermon in the synagogue at Pisidian Antioch, he mentioned how the Judean leaders "found no proper ground for a death sentence, [so] they asked Pilate to have him executed" (Acts 13:28). In Paul's first letter to Timothy, he prefaces his charge to Timothy with the words, "In the sight of

---

23. Josephus, *Jewish Antiquities* 18.60–62; *Jewish War* 2.175–77.
24. Luke 13:1–5.
25. Josephus, *Jewish Antiquities* 18.85–89.

God, who gives life to everything, and of Christ Jesus, who while testifying before Pontius Pilate made the good confession" (1 Tim 6:13).

Thus, in Christian memory, Pilate was the weak and vicious Roman official who, however reluctantly, did the bidding of the Jerusalem leadership to have Jesus of Nazareth executed. Pilate is then the very epitome of Psalm 2:2 where kings and rulers foolishly "band together against the Lord and against his anointed." Pilate's place in history is owed exclusively to the fact of his involvement in Jesus's death, and Christians have accordingly reviled him for it. An archetypical portrayal of Pilate comes from the musical *Jesus Christ Superstar*, which presents Pilate singing about a distressing dream he had concerning a Galilean man, who was wrongfully killed, and afterward he can see thousands of millions crying for this man. The song then ends with the somber line, "Then I heard them mentioning my name and leaving me the blame." Such is Pilate's memory, a mixture of notoriety with tragedy, for he met the Son of God and handed him over to be crucified to placate the priestly class and their bloodthirsty rent-a-crowd.

Consider this: Pontius Pilate, a second-tier Roman aristocrat sent to a backwater Roman province, is the only other person besides Jesus and Mary named in the ancient creeds of the Christian churches. No apostles, biblical figures like Moses or Abraham, or any of the Roman emperors are named. The inclusion is deliberate and important. It points to the historical circumstances pertaining to Jesus's death in Jerusalem on the Passover of ca. AD 30. We cannot dehistoricize the mission of Jesus and the passion narrative. We cannot talk as if Jesus was a heavenly figure who just decided to float down from heaven at some random point in history, borrowed a human body, taught earthly stories with heavenly meanings, promised everlasting life to anyone who would assent to his claims, and then irritated the Judean leaders for the sole purpose of getting them to crucify him so he could pay a sin-debt that humanity owed an angry and vengeful God in heaven. That, I submit, is a type of evangelical Gnosticism that narrates a gospel detached from the story of Scripture and the historical setting of Jesus's ministry.

We need to situate Jesus's death in the context of his career and locate his career in the coordinates of prophetic hopes for Israel's future. Jesus was born into the world of Roman Palestine and the messy sociopolitical circumstances of the day. Israel had suffered under the domination of one pagan kingdom after another: Assyria, Babylon, Persia, Greece, the Ptolemies, the Seleucids, and eventually Rome. At this time many, such as Simeon, were looking for the "consolation of Israel" (Luke 2:25). The travelers to Emmaus were waiting for someone to "redeem Israel" (Luke 24:21), while others were longing for God to "restore the kingdom to Israel" (Acts 1:6) and to usher in the "times of refreshing" (Acts 3:19). This involved a whole constellation of hopes from Israel's Scriptures that were diversely interpreted by various Jewish groups. The chief elements of those hopes included a reconstitution of the twelve tribes of Israel, the final end to the lingering effects of exile, a new exodus, abundant agricultural prosperity, a renewed covenant, the building of a new temple, the return of the Lord to Zion, the advent of one or more messianic figures, the defeat of pagan kingdoms, and the pilgrimage of gentiles to Zion to worship Israel's God. These hopes were often also combined with the expectation of a time of tribulation, the resurrection of the dead, and a final judgment. Jesus saw his death as part of this narrative. His death was the instrument for Israel's forgiveness, the defeat of Satan, the renewal of the covenant, and the inclusion of the gentiles in God's saving purposes. Jesus saw himself as the suffering servant of Isaiah, the mistreated righteous one of the Psalms, and the smitten shepherd of Zechariah, who would enter into the tribulation of wrath and by his death win redemption for Israel so that a transformed Israel would transform the world.

This is the script that Jesus followed in his ministry. Jesus busted up a dispute among his disciples about greatness by setting forth his own vocation which he described in these words: "For even the Son of Man did not come to be served, but to serve, and to give his life as a ransom for many" (Mark 10:45). The background to this saying is probably Jesus's reflection on the fourth Servant Song of Isaiah (52:13–53:12). In this saying, Jesus is the representative of Israel, who dies as a ransom for the iniquities of the nation and returns to life to usher in Israel's restoration from exile ahead of the new creation. The Last Supper tradition, as Luke and Paul narrate it, includes Jesus's memorable words that "This [bread] is my body given for you" and "This cup is the new covenant in my blood, which is poured out for you" (Luke 22:19–20; 1 Cor 11:24–25). The annual Jewish festival of Passover, which celebrated Israel's redemption from Egypt, is taken up by Jesus and turned into a memorial meal celebrating the new exodus that would be achieved by his approaching death. Jesus says, in word and symbol, that his death would be the central and climactic moment toward which Israel's story had been heading. A new sacrifice would be offered, a new covenant made, sins would be forgiven, and Israel's restoration to covenant standing would be effected. You should get the idea by now. God's intention to renew Israel, to forgive their sins, and to broker a new covenant all hinges on the work of the Messiah to take the curse of their disobedience upon himself and to bear it upon that cross.

By confessing that Jesus "suffered under Pontius Pilate," we are proclaiming that what looks to outsiders like just another case of Roman brutality turns out to be in fact the means by which God restores Israel's covenant and reconciles the nations to himself. Jesus was not crucified because he was in the wrong place (Jerusalem), at the wrong time (Passover), doing the wrong thing (causing a commotion), which upset the wrong people (the high priest), during the watch of the wrong governor (Pontius Pilate). Rather, "Jesus resolutely set out for Jerusalem" (Luke 9:51) to embrace his "baptism" and to drink the "cup" of divine wrath (Mark 10:38–39; Luke 12:50), to die as a "ransom for many" (Mark 10:45//Matt 20:28), to "lay down" his life for his friends (John 15:13), and to shed his blood for the new covenant (Luke 22:20; 1 Cor 11:25). By refusing to save himself, he is able to save others (Mark 15:31–32). By submitting himself to the powerlessness of the cross, he shows us the kingdom of God coming in power (Mark 9:1). Pilate may have thought he was running the show in delivering Jesus over to be crucified. However, on closer inspection, we see that Pilate's wickedness and weakness were conscripted by God as the means whereby his saving promises came to fruition. It was really *God* who delivered Jesus over to death for our sins and raised him to life for our justification (Rom 4:25) and *God* who "did not spare his own Son, but gave him up for us all" (Rom 8:32). The jealously of the priestly leadership and the injustice of a Roman governor were the evil that God used for good to forgive the sins of many through the death of his Son. In fulfillment of the scriptural promises, Jesus's death brought about the end of exile—not only Israel's exile from the divine presence but even more importantly the exile of Adam and Eve from the garden of Eden. Jesus's crucifixion brought about the end of enmity and the end of estrangement between God and humanity. It was here that God was starting to make all things new (Isa 42:9; 48:6; Rev 21:5).

Recommended Reading

Bird, Michael F. "The Death of Jesus." Pages 385–434 in *Evangelical Theology: A Biblical and Systematic Introduction*. Grand Rapids: Zondervan, 2013.

Chapman, David. *Ancient Jewish and Christian Perceptions of Crucifixion*. Grand Rapids: Baker, 2010.

Longenecker, Bruce W. *The Cross before Constantine: The Early Life of a Christian Symbol*. Minneapolis: Fortress, 2015.

Wright, N. T. *The Crown and the Fire: Meditations on the Cross and Life in the Spirit*. Grand Rapids: Eerdmans, 1995.

9

BELIEVING *in the* CROSS—
THE VICTORY
of the CROSS

He suffered under Pontius Pilate,
was crucified, died, and was buried.

Living the Story of the Cross

The reason why the cross was etched onto the walls of catacombs, drawn on the margins of manuscripts, and sung about in ancient hymns was because it was paramount for the church's faith. For the early church, the cross was the paradigmatic symbol of what it believed, why it behaved as it did, and what it stood for. The church was not a religious club interested in the minutia of Hebrew exegesis and maintaining purity from the unclean masses. It was not a Judean liberation movement preaching a mixture of apocalyptic revival and armed revolution with the Torah in one hand and a sword in the other. It was not an association of Roman gentry who liked to pass the time discussing philosophy, politics, and religion in between drinking games and sex with concubines. Nor was the church interested in ingratiating itself into the benefaction of imperial elites by casting itself as dependents of the Roman gods and their emperor. Instead the early Christians were focused on telling the story that the God of Israel had launched the long-awaited rescue of his people through the cross of the Messiah. While quite cognizant of the shame and scandal of the crucifixion in the surrounding culture, the church's project, if we can speak coherently of one, was to proclaim the good news of the cross of Jesus and to live out the pattern of the cross in their own lives. This brings us to the next aspects of the cross that the Apostles' Creed requires we reflect on, namely, atonement and discipleship.

The Atonement

We are told in the New Testament that Jesus died "for us" and "for our sins." But what does the "for" actually mean? What does Jesus's death do for us and how does his death change our standing before God? These questions all center on the subject of the atonement where we will investigate the achievement and inner workings of Jesus's saving death.

To get our bearings, the word "atonement" derives from the Old English word "onement," meaning to unite or to attain a state of "at-one-ness."[1] Thus, in the Christian story, God deals with the problem of human sin through the cross and restores humanity to a relationship with himself by the cross of Jesus. The cross then brings those who were far off from God into a state of oneness with God by faith in Jesus as their Savior. However, in browsing over the subject of atonement we are led toward an immediate and intractable problem. Whereas the early church reached a consensus on the nature of Jesus's person as fully divine and fully human, it never attempted to reach a similar consensus on the atonement, either its mechanics or its effects. Instead, the church was quite happy to merely confess that Jesus's death was *pro nobis* ("for us") but without explicating precisely how. Generally speaking, the theologians of the church have been content to deploy the many biblical images for the atonement as seemed fitting to the theological occasion but without zeroing in on a theological epicenter to the atonement.

We can neatly sum up what the cross achieved by tracing out the biblical testimony to the saving effects of Jesus's death. In Holy Scripture we learn that Jesus's death:

---

1. Graham Cole, *God the Peacemaker: How Atonement Brings Shalom*, New Studies in Biblical Theology 25 (Downers Grove, IL: InterVarsity Press, 2009), 20, 24.

- Provides a ransom for sins (Matt 20:28; Mark 10:45).
- Protects from the tribulation and future judgment (Matt 23:37–39).
- Ushers in the new covenant (Mark 14:22–25 and parallels).
- Restores Israel and draws the nations into the family of Abraham (Mark 9:12; Luke 1:68; 2:38; 23:27–31; John 11:51–52; Acts 3:18–21; 13:25–29; Gal 3:13; Rev 5:9–10).
- Rescues us from the kingdom of darkness and the present evil age (Gal 1:4; Col 1:14).
- Reconciles us from enmity (Rom 5:10–11; 2 Cor 5:18–20; Eph 2:16; Col 1:20, 22).
- Redeems us from slavery (Rom 3:24; 8:23; 1 Cor 1:30; 7:23; Gal 3:13; 4:5; Eph 1:7, 14; Col 1:14; Titus 2:14; Heb 9:12; 1 Pet 1:18; Rev 5:9).
- Justifies us from condemnation (Rom 3:24; 5:9; Gal 2:21).
- Provides forgiveness of sins (Matt 26:28; Luke 1:77; 24:47; Acts 2:38; 5:31; 10:43; 13:38; 26:18; Eph 1:7; Col 1:14; 3:13; Heb 9:22; 1 John 1:9; Rev 1:5).
- Brings peace to our hostility with God (Isa 53:5; Acts 10:36; Rom 5:1; Eph 2:14–17; Col 1:20).
- Heals our wounds and brokenness (Exod 15:26; Isa 53:5; Mal 4:2; 1 Pet 2:24).
- Cleanses our moral impurities (1 Cor 6:11; Titus 2:14; Heb 1:3; 9:14–22; 10:2, 22; 2 Pet 1:9; 1 John 1:7, 9; Rev 7:14).
- Provides an example to be followed (Phil 2:5–11; Heb 12:1–3; 1 Pet 2:21).

It is very difficult to reduce the effect of the cross to just one of these images. This rich array of biblical images in its entirety possesses an abundant testimony to our peace with God, our sins cancelled, divine anger set aside, all enmity ended, and all hostilities ceased. They tell us in triumphant chorus that nothing now can separate us from the love of God in Jesus the Messiah. Because of the cross we have communion with God the Father, union with God the Son, and life in the Holy Spirit.

That said, if someone sitting next to you on a bus asked, "Why did Jesus have to die?" it would be impractical to go through a dense compilation of biblical teaching on the matter. Indeed, one could spend a bus ride from Anchorage to Buenos Aires, combing through the relevant verses and consulting commentaries to try and do justice to the topic. If only for the sake of practicality, we need a succinct yet accurate working definition of what Jesus's death achieved in order to be concise and clear on the subject. But what could we say? Which image should we reach for? How do we describe the historical, cosmic, and theocentric event of the cross if all we have time for us is a short tweet or a two-minute conversation?

Well, the Apostles' Creed is a good pointer in this regard. Toward the end of the creed it mentions as an article of faith the belief in the "forgiveness of sins." The theme of forgiveness is as wonderful a picture as any of how Jesus's death removes our sins and enables us to enter into a relationship with God as our Father. The promise of forgiveness is an aptly abbreviated summary of the message of the gospel. Forgiveness is one of the blessings explicitly named in the new covenant (Jer 31:34), it is the one image that Jesus used to interpret the purpose of his death at the Last Supper (Matt 26:28), it is part of the missionary command given by the risen Jesus to the disciples (Luke 24:47; John 20:23), and it appears frequently in apostolic preaching (Acts 2:38; 5:31; 8:22; 10:43; 13:38; 26:18) and teaching (Rom 4:7; Eph 1:7; Col 1:14; 1 John 1:9; 2:12). In fact, Robert Yarbrough notes that "the story of Jesus's life from infancy to ascension, is dominated by the account of his mission to provide forgiveness."[2] As such, talking about "forgiveness" should easily be our go-to image for unpacking the significance of Jesus's death, the atonement, and the offer of salvation.

So far we've got "atonement" as the restoration of our relationship to God through the cross, and the "forgiveness of sins" as the favorite club in our golf bag to describe what the cross achieved, but something is still missing. How does the atonement work? How does Jesus's death actually provide the mechanism for believers to be forgiven, healed, cleansed, and justified? What happens at the cross to make us holy, righteous, and blameless before God? Imagine that the atonement is a car. Some theologians like to look

---

2. Robert Yarbrough, "Forgiveness and Reconciliation," in *New Dictionary of Biblical Theology*, ed. T. D. Alexander and B. S. Rosner (Downers Grove, IL: InterVarsity Press, 2000), 501.

under the hood to check out what kind of engine is driving the whole thing. When we examine this topic, we are pursuing what is traditionally known as the theory of the atonement. Here the objective is to provide a biblically sound and internally coherent account of how the cross brings about the various things like redemption, rescue, reconciliation, and more. Over the course of church history a number of theories have been set forward to describe the inner workings of the atonement. See them in the table below:

Recapitulation	Jesus's death replays the story of Adam except that, unlike Adam, Jesus is successful over sin and obedient to death on the cross.
Ransom	Jesus paid the price for the release of humanity from Satan.
Victory	Jesus's death is a triumph over evil and the devil.
Moral Influence	Jesus's death changes our inward disposition and enables us to love others.
Exemplar	Jesus's death provides an example of love for believers to emulate.
Satisfaction	Jesus's death satisfies the debt of God's honor that our sins affronted.
Governmental	Jesus's death shows God's displeasure with sin and Jesus's death pays the debt caused by our transgression of God's justice.
Penal Substitution	Jesus died as our representative and substitute and takes away the penalty meant for us.

I do not have time and space to offer a lengthy summary, appreciation, and critique of all of these theories of the atonement. Suffice to say for now that each of them is saying something that is either true or at least partially true. Jesus's death is a *recapitulation* in the sense that he sums up in himself the stories of Adam and Israel. By rehearsing human existence, he is able to redeem us from the mire of human depravity. In other words, he became what we are so that we might become what he is. Jesus's death is a *ransom* by paying the price for our sins and releasing us from the power of sin and from the grip of evil. Jesus's death is a *victory* over the world, flesh, and Satan. On the cross of Jesus, God defeated the powers of this age and transferred us from the domain of darkness to the kingdom of the Son of his love. Jesus's death is a *moral influence* insofar as it demonstrates a divine love that compels us to love others. The cross teaches us that those who have been forgiven much will in turn love much. Jesus's death is an *example* of self-sacrifice in that believers are to imitate the self-giving nature of the cross in their mutual relationships with each other and even in marriage. Jesus's death is a *satisfaction* that makes reparation for our offenses against God. On the cross, God's justice and love are satisfied, and God is able to be just and the justifier of those who have faith in Jesus. Jesus's death can be thought to be *governmental* in the sense that it expresses God's displeasure with sin, and God chooses to pass over the sins that have been committed by people. Jesus's death is a *penal and substitutionary* sacrifice because our sin is condemned in his flesh, he bears our sin upon the cross, and he suffers the curses of our transgressions.

The question that keeps theologians awake at night is which theory is the fairest of them all or which theory is one to rule them all? Many forthrightly argue for the prominence of penal substitution, while others urge the paramount nature of victory, and others again stress the significance of ransom as the determinative model of the atonement. In many ways this is an unnecessary question, since all of the theories are required for a broad and comprehensive account of the atonement. There is a kaleidoscope of atonement images in Scripture, and it would be most unwise to choose merely one to the neglect of others. Scot McKnight contends that theories of atonement are like the strings on a violin. He comments:

> The magic of a violin is the capacity for the violinist to make each string work in harmony with the others to create the appropriate sound. If a violinist somehow managed to play only one string on the violin, the sound could never be complete. Some theories of atonement ask violinists

either to pluck all but one string or to play gospel music as though only one string really mattered. I want to contend that we need each of these strings, and that we need to ask for a violinist with a bow that can stroke the strings so well that the potency of each string creates a harmonious composition that puts our hearts at rest.[3]

I want to affirm McKnight's basic point that we should embrace the testimony to the atonement in the entire witness of Scripture and not arbitrarily accent a few prized passages. That said, I still think some strings on our violin might get more use than others, or some theories of the atonement might have a greater capacity to be the integrative piece that connects them all altogether. To switch metaphors, the theories of the atonement might be like the spokes on a wheel, and while there are several spokes on each wheel, one theory might be better described as the hub to which all the other spokes are connected.

My exegetical and theological intuition is to gravitate toward the victory theory as the integrative model for the atonement since it effectively combines the motifs of recapitulation, representation, ransom, sacrifice, and triumph. The victory model places Jesus's death *for us* in its proper coordinates as an apocalyptic event that reveals God's rescue plan against the evil powers (Gal 1:4). Paul writes how the triumph of the cross over the dark powers is achieved by the cancellation of the written code that stood against believers (Col 2:13–15). This meshes nicely with the theological contours of Romans 8 and 1 Corinthians 15, which move seamlessly from sacrifice-in-place-of-others (Rom 8:1–3; 1 Cor 15:3–5) to victory-over-evil (Rom 8:35–39; 1 Cor 15:54–57). Athanasius commented on Hebrews 2:14 that Jesus "took to himself a body such as could die, that he might offer it as his own in the stead of all, and as suffering through his union with it, on behalf of all, 'Bring to naught him that had the power of death, that is the devil; and might deliver them who through fear of death were all their lifetime subject to bondage.'"[4] According to John, "The reason the Son of God appeared was to destroy the devil's work" (1 John 3:8), and this occurs

---

3. Scot McKnight, *A Community Called Atonement* (Nashville: Abingdon, 2007), 114.
4. Athanasius, *On the Incarnation* 20.5–6 (*NPNF²*).

through his death as a propitiatory sacrifice for the whole world (1 John 2:2). In Revelation, in every age the church rehearses their victory over Satan by triumphing over him by the blood of the Lamb (12:11).

On Golgotha, Jesus lets the powers do their worst to him, he takes the full brunt of sin, he drinks the dregs of judgment, and he allows death to hold him in its clutches. But in the midst of a powerless death emerges the divine power to forgive, redeem, and renew. The verdict of condemnation is cancelled, the debt of sin is paid, the justice of God is satisfied, and the power of evil is broken. The fatal wound of Jesus deals a fatal blow to death. The powers of this present darkness shiver as the looming tsunami of the kingdom of God draws ever nearer. The despots of the world live in denial as much as they live on borrowed time. Satan's force is spent, and his worst is no match for the best of the Son of God. This is a robust atonement theology, for whichever corner we turn, we are always led to the victory of God. I love how John Murray put it: "Redemption from sin cannot be adequately conceived or formulated except as it comprehends the victory which Christ secured once for all over him who is the god of this world, the prince of the power of the air. . . . It is impossible to speak in terms of redemption from the power of sin except as there comes within the range of this redemptive accomplishment the destruction of the powers of darkness."[5]

Imagine a family on a long road trip with Dad driving, Mom in the passenger seat, and a teenage boy and little girl in the backseat. Then all of a sudden a bee flies in through the window. The little girl is violently allergic to bee stings and she naturally panics as the bee buzzes around her. The big brother does his best to try to swat the bee but only serves to drive it closer to his sister. The mother is screaming for her husband to pull over and let the bee out. Yet just when the bee is about to land on the little girl, the Dad reaches back and luckily snatches the bee in his grasp and squeezes it tight. He keeps one hand on the wheel of the car, shifts his eyes back to the road, lets out a little grimace of pain, and then opens his hands. The crushed bee falls to the floor. The girl relaxes, and the trip continues. The bee's potentially fatal sting for the little girl is absorbed in her father's hand, and the bee

---

5. John Murray, *Redemption: Accomplished and Applied* (Grand Rapids: Eerdmans, 1955), 50.

itself is destroyed and unable to alarm anyone again. In the same way, Jesus takes the sting of sin, which is death, into his own body; he destroys evil's power to enslave so that death and evil cannot reign indefinitely over God's people. That is the cross, the story of victory through sacrifice.

Cruciformity

The cross is not merely a tenet of faith that we are required to assent to; it is a manifesto we are to follow. Christians are not called merely to believe in the cross but more properly to live it out. We are to live lives that are patterned after and shaped by the cross. Michael Gorman has a great word for this. He calls it "cruciformity." Gorman defines it like this: "Cruciformity is an ongoing pattern of living in Christ and of dying with him that produces a Christ-like (cruciform) person," and "cruciformity misunderstood as the human imitation of Christ is indeed an impossibility. However, cruciformity is the initial and ongoing work of Christ himself—by his Spirit sent by God—who dwells within each believer and believing community, shaping them to carry on the story."[6] In practice this means that the cross must shape our spirituality, our vision, our values, our attitudes, our behavior, our goals, our ministry, what we fear, what we flee from, and what we try to be as individual Christians and as churches.[7] There is so much we could say here, yet suffice for now we'll abbreviate it under the headings of *identity*, *imitation*, and *resistance*.

Identity: "I Have Been Crucified with Christ"

To begin with, cruciformity means that our sense of identity is determined by our relationship to the cross of Christ. The English church historian David Bebbington noted that in the nineteenth-century interdenominational newspaper, *The British Weekly*, the most frequently preached

---

6. Michael Gorman, *Cruciformity: Paul's Narrative Spirituality of the Cross* (Grand Rapids: Eerdmans, 2001), 48–49, 400.

7. Michael F. Bird, *A Bird's-Eye View of Paul: The Man, His Mission and His Message* (Nottingham: Inter-Varsity, 2008), 162–66.

text for sermons was Galatians 2:20.[8] You don't have to like cricket and crumpets to know that those Victorian-era Brits were probably onto something. The passage reads, "I have been crucified with Christ and I no longer live, but Christ lives in me. The life I now live in the body, I live by faith in the Son of God, who loved me and gave himself for me" (Gal 2:20). Paul is saying here that he has no independent existence and no separate identity apart from the crucified and risen Jesus. The entire scope of his bodily existence is singularly determined by the fact that the body of the Son of God was crucified for him, and the Son of God now lives in him. Think about that. If we take Paul's self-description as our own, it means that the only life in me is Christ living through me. It means that I am who I am only as I am in Christ Jesus. The significance of Paul's self-description in Galatians 2:20 is that when I know who I am in Christ, then I know my place in this world and the purpose of my life.

Even more so today, we are constantly being defined by peers, employers, agencies, and social conventions. People will try to define us by our occupation, our gender, our race, our nationality, our language, our politics, our marital status, even our sexuality. While any of that might be true of us, and much of it can legitimately remain meaningful for us, yet none of it ultimately defines who we are. Paul says that "there is neither Jew nor Gentile, neither slave nor free, nor is there male and female, for you are all one in Christ Jesus" (Gal 3:28). Being part of the Messiah means the negation of anything that either elevates us over others or belittles us before others. If the cross counts, then labels don't matter. You are defined by your faith in the crucified and risen Son of God. You are saved and signed by the cross. In case you haven't heard, in liturgical churches there is a particular role called a crucifer. (Not to be mistaken for *crucifiers*—those who crucify other people; the additional "i" makes a big, big difference!) A *crucifer* is a person who is appointed to carry the cross, a crucifix mounted on top of a processional staff, into the church at the beginning of a worship service. He or she is literally a "crossbearer." So if you want to know who you are, then know this: if you believe in Jesus, if you have any affection for him, if

---

8. David Bebbington, "The Gospel in the Nineteenth Century," *Vox Evangelical* 13 (1983): 24.

you cling to his cross for dear life, then you are a crucifer, a crossbearer. By baptism you are dipped and dyed into the cross, by the Lord's Supper you are fed and blessed by the cross, by the Holy Spirit you are united with the Son of God, who was crucified, buried, risen, and ascended for you.

Imitation: "You Should Follow in His Steps"

Cruciformity also means that we are called to imitate the way of the cross. One of the most confronting words of Jesus has to be his command to the disciples about following him to Jerusalem: "Whoever wants to be my disciple must deny themselves and take up their cross daily and follow me" (Luke 9:23). If one is trying to start a populist movement in Galilee or even endeavoring to launch a modern megachurch in Georgia, this does not strike me as a motto that is going to attract a large flock of followers. And yet Jesus lays it on the line. It's all or nothing. No halfway house, no try-before-you-buy, no cooling-off period. Jesus demands that his disciples be willing to take up their cross daily and follow him. He chose the horrific image of crucifixion to make it clear what following him would cost. The image of carrying the cross is thus metaphorical for self-renunciation and self-giving for the sake of others. To follow Jesus's way is to imitate Jesus's self-giving love in journeying to the cross.

The fact is that people are mimetic creatures; we naturally copy and imitate others. That's how we pick up accents and how we acquire bad habits. In New Testament ethics, imitation features very prominently, as believers are called to imitate the example of godly leaders and especially to imitate the example of Jesus. When it comes to marriage, Paul exhorted husbands with the words, "Husbands, love your wives, just as Christ loved the church and gave himself up for her" (Eph 5:25). A chauvinistic patriarchy and other power games find no place in marriages where the husband loves his wife as Christ loved the church. The majestic Christ-hymn in Philippians is perhaps the summit of Paul's Christology, setting forth as it does the story of Jesus's obedience to death upon the cross and his exaltation by God the Father. Yet there is no getting away from the fact that the hymn is cited primarily for ethical instruction. Paul enjoins the Philippians, "In your relationships with one another, have the same mindset as Christ Jesus" (Phil 2:5). We are not just to sing Philippians 2:5–11 but to imitate it within our churches in order to cultivate humility! The apostle Peter urged his readers to walk the path of the cross in their own lives: "To this you were called, because Christ suffered for you, leaving you an example, that you should follow in his steps" (1 Pet 2:21). For Peter, to step out in faith is to walk the path of Jesus as he approached the cross. When it comes to perseverance, the author of Hebrews says, "Consider him who endured such opposition from sinners, so that you will not grow weary and lose heart" (Heb 12:3). This is more than a polite reminder; it's a call to rehearse the perseverance that Jesus himself faced when under trial. According to the Gospel of John, Jesus gave his disciples a new command: "Love one another. As I have loved you, so you must love one another. By this everyone will know that you are my disciples, *if* you love one another" (John 13:34–35; emphasis added). Now, I have read over this verse many times. Yes, I have to love others; I already knew that. Nothing new to see here. However, the truly shocking nature of the command did not register until I read Francis Schaeffer's exposition of this text. Schaeffer pointed to the conditional nature of the command, the "if" upon which our discipleship is based. Schaeffer says that Jesus "gives the world the right to judge whether you and I are born-again Christians on the basis of our observable love toward all Christians."[9] The authenticity of our Christian faith will be determined by the world on the basis of whether we have a self-giving and self-sacrificing love like Jesus. The cross is the criterion for genuine discipleship. In other words, cruciformity is what separates the fans from the followers.

Resistance: "The World Has Been Crucified to Me, and I to the World"

Finally, disciples who cling to the cross will consistently find themselves engaged in resistance against the world around them. Paul can say that "the world has been crucified to me, and I to the world" (Gal 6:14). Paul

---

9. Francis A. Schaeffer, *The Mark of the Christian* (Downers Grove, IL: InterVarsity Press, 1970), 22.

is engaging here in an explicit renunciation of the values of the world and stakes his claim in favor of Christ's cross and his kingdom. Worked out in practice, discipleship of this order will mean dying daily to what the world has to offer, saying no to sin and yes to holiness, grasping Christ and letting go of worldly trinkets, and seeking the kingdom and not worldly praises. Of course, this is easier said than done. We are constantly bombarded in every form of media to be conformed to the spirit of the age in everything from politics to ethics and from fashion to religion. We are tugged and pulled in every direction, to the left and to the right, enticed by hawkers with promises of pleasure or power at every turn, with shadowy figures trying to stoke fires of doubt underneath us. One obstacle after another is placed in our way to try to wear us down and force us out of the race. The world whispers in our ears, "Why stand up for Jesus when it is so much easier to kneel before me? Why suffer the shame of the cross when you can have the pleasure and power I offer you?" The hardest thing about temptation is that it is often very tempting. But in this context of adversity, faithfulness to the cross is rebellion against the world. When we affirm that our identity and pattern of life come from the cross and not from the world, we are confessing that we cannot be bought or broken. We will take up our cross, finish the race, turn the other cheek, love our enemies, walk the extra mile, refuse to repay evil for evil, and bless when we are cursed.[10] The single greatest act of defiance we can show against those who would destroy us is to continue in Christlikeness. That is true of disciples for one reason: we have been crucified with Christ, and the world is crucified to us.

The Crux

On reflection, there are good reasons why the cross matters and why it was included in the Apostles' Creed. The cross tells the story of God's love embracing a world characterized by a mixture of brokenness and rebellion. The cross proves God's love for Israel and that his purposes for creation

---

10..N. T. Wright, *Simply Jesus* (London: SPCK, 2011), 171, 176.

cannot be thwarted. The cross speaks about grace, forgiveness, cleansing, redemption, life, a renewed covenant, a new heaven and a new earth, and the triumph over evil. The cross prompts believers to a countercultural way of life built on imitating the self-giving love of the Son of God. In which case, the cross proves to be the nonnegotiable element of the Christian faith. To preach Jesus is to preach his cross, to follow Jesus is to carry one's own cross, to worship Jesus is to raise up the cross. The cross cannot be reduced to a footnote under the heading of "incarnation." The cross cannot be relegated to an appendix on divine love because it is the supreme mode of divine love. The cross cannot be torn away from the Christian story without tearing the very fabric from which the story is woven. Or, as John Stott put it, "There is then, it is safe to say, no Christianity without the cross. If the cross is not central to our religion, ours is not the religion of Jesus."[11]

The Story Thus Far

We believe that the triune God determined in eternity past to unite himself to creation through the Son. And so it was that the Son became the man Jesus of Nazareth, the son of Mary, Immanuel, "God with us." His messianic task meant that he came to Israel to announce and enact the kingdom, to usher in the new exodus, and to renew the covenant—a renewal that will even encompass the nations and bring them into the inheritance of Israel. He was rejected, mocked, and killed, and yet in the cruelty of crucifixion his mission was fulfilled. Jesus took the curse of Israel's transgression upon himself, and the weight of the sins of the world fell upon him. He died "under Pontius Pilate" as an atonement for sins so that Jews and gentiles could know the peace of God and life everlasting.

---

11. John Stott, *The Cross of Christ* (Downers Grove, IL: InterVarsity Press, 1986), 68.

Recommended Reading

Bird, Michael F. "The Death of Jesus." Pages 385–434 in *Evangelical Theology: A Biblical and Systematic Introduction*. Grand Rapids: Zondervan, 2013.

Cole, Graham. *God the Peacemaker: How Atonement Brings Shalom*. New Studies in Biblical Theology 25. Downers Grove, IL: InterVarsity Press, 2009.

Gorman, Michael J. *Cruciformity: Paul's Narrative Spirituality of the Cross*. Grand Rapids: Eerdmans, 2001.

McKnight, Scot. *A Community Called Atonement*. Nashville: Abingdon, 2007.

BELIEVING *That* JESUS LIVES

He descended to the dead.
On the third day he rose again.

Holy Saturday

During the season of Easter, many Christians tend to get very excited about Good Friday and Easter Sunday. But Holy Saturday seems to be a down day in between church services. Good Friday has all the wonderful preaching of the atonement, and Resurrection Sunday bubbles over with the promise of eternal life and beatific visions of a new heaven and new earth. Sadly, many would find it hard to imagine anything other than a kind of halftime show that could fill the gap in between these two momentous events. However, there is definitely something in between the cross and the empty tomb that is very important: the descent of Jesus to the underworld. Christ's descent to the place of the dead has traditionally been celebrated on Holy Saturday. Now, I think it is probably fair to say that there is no line in the creed more misunderstood and more neglected than this one. It is the poor cousin of the christological doctrines and yet is important for a fully orbed understanding of the work of Jesus Christ. So it is definitely worth inclusion in the Apostles' Creed and merits a detailed examination, since most Christians either have only the vaguest grasp of the subject or else they are entirely ignorant of it.

So where was Jesus between Good Friday and Easter morning? Where did Jesus's spirit go? To begin with, Jesus was not in heaven during this time. When Mary Magdalene met the risen Jesus, he told her, "Do not hold on to me, for I have not yet ascended to the Father. Go instead to my brothers and tell them, 'I am ascending to my Father and your Father, to my God and your God'" (John 20:17). The ascension marks the formal return of the Son to heaven, not any time before. However, Jesus could not have been in hell either because, well, hell did not yet exist. In the book of Revelation we learn that at the end of all things, "Death and Hades were thrown into the lake of fire," that is, thrown into hell (Rev 20:14). So Jesus could not descend to a habitation that had not yet been made or at least had not yet been populated with anyone. So where was Jesus? He was in the place called *Hades* (in Greek) or *Sheol* (in Hebrew), the waiting place of the dead. *Hades/Sheol* is the abode of the dead as they wait for the final judgment, while *hell* is the place of everlasting punishment and eternal separation from God. The two are separate places, even though some English translations of our Bibles, like the King James, do not always distinguish them.

More needs to be said about Hades/Sheol (let's just call it "Hades"). In Jewish tradition—as reflected in the parable of the rich man and Lazarus (Luke 16:19–31)—there is a good part of Hades for the saints and a punitive part of Hades for the wicked. When Jesus promised the thief who died with him on the cross that he would join him in paradise, he meant the blessed sanctuary within Hades (Luke 23:43). Importantly, and pushing back on some strands of tradition, Hades is not a purgatorial rehab clinic where old sins can be worked off, nor is it a literal subterranean cavern somewhere in the earth's mantle. Hades simply means the abode of the dead wherever that location happens to be. Old Testament saints who passed away went to the blessed part of Hades where they waited for rescue, while the wicked inhabit the punitive part of Hades where they wait and still wait for the final judgment. When the Creed says that Jesus "descended to the dead," it means that he went to Hades.

Broadly understood, the descent simply unpacks Jesus's death and burial to the effect that Jesus shared in the full and retributive consequences of death conceived as both physical death and the separation of soul from body. Jesus's body was buried, and his soul joined the company of the dead.

In my mind, a better English rendering of the Creed would be something like he "descended to the place of the dead" rather than just "to the dead."[1] Jesus predicted as much when he said that the only sign his generation would be given was the "sign of Jonah," which he explained as meaning that "as Jonah was three days and three nights in the belly of a huge fish, so the Son of Man will be three days and three nights in the heart of the earth" (Matt 12:40). The Son of Man would die, be buried, dwell in the earth like Jonah dwelt in the fish, and then he would rise from the dead. Thus, as part of the atonement, Jesus suffered the same fate as all sinful persons: his body was surrendered to the grave, and his soul entered the domain of death, the world beyond the grave. To use the language of Hebrews, Jesus "suffered death" in its fullest sense "so that by the grace of God he might taste death for everyone" (Heb 2:9).

More specifically, the New Testament witness to the descent arguably points to three particular things.

First, Jesus preached the good news of his victory to the wicked in Hades. Such is implied by some enigmatic verses written by Peter. Jesus "went and made proclamation to the imprisoned spirits—to those who were disobedient long ago when God waited patiently in the days of Noah," and "for this is the reason the gospel was preached even to those who are now dead, so that they might be judged according to human standards in regard to the body, but live according to God in regard to the spirit" (1 Pet 3:19–20; 4:6). While these texts can be interpreted differently,[2] I understand them describing how Jesus went to the place of the dead and declared his victory over the disobedient angels imprisoned there and reminded the wicked of the judgment to come.

Second, Jesus set the saints of old free from Hades and took them up into heaven. In the course of discussing the gifts which the exalted Christ has bestowed upon the church, Paul writes: "This is why it says: 'When he ascended on high, he took many captives and gave gifts to his people' [Ps

---

1. My thanks to Justin Bass for reading and commenting on an earlier version of this section for me.

2. First Peter 3:19 has three basic interpretive options: (1) it refers to the preaching of Christ in the days of Noah; (2) it refers to Jesus preaching to the dead; and (3) it refers to preaching to the dead after Jesus has ascended.

68:18]. (What does 'he ascended' mean except that he also descended to the lower, earthly regions? He who descended is the very one who ascended higher than all the heavens, in order to fill the whole universe)" (Eph 4:8–10). Paul cites Psalm 68, a psalm of victory, and uses the imagery of the psalm to depict Jesus leading captives out of Hades and presenting them as gifts to the rest of the church. The chief idea is that when Jesus rose and ascended to heaven, he took with him departed saints, bringing them out of the bondage of death, and ever since then believers who die go directly to heaven to be with Christ and to join the church triumphant (Acts 7:59; 2 Cor 5:1–4; Phil 1:23; Rev 6:9–11).

Third, Jesus achieved a victory over death and Hades itself. Sometimes death and Hades are treated as virtual synonyms (Rev 1:18; 6:8; 20:13–14). When Jesus said that the "gates of Hades" will not overcome his church, I would paraphrase it as the "doors of death" (Matt 16:18). Peter's Pentecost speech announced that "it was impossible for death to keep its hold on him" (Acts 2:24), and he quoted Psalm 16:8–11 to emphasize that God would not abandon his servant to Hades but raised him up triumphantly (Acts 2:27, 31). John of Patmos experienced a vision of the exalted Jesus and was comforted with the words, "Do not be afraid. I am the First and the Last. I am the Living One; I was dead, and now look, I am alive for ever and ever! And I hold the keys of death and Hades" (Rev 1:17–18). In light of these texts, the descent is part of Jesus's victory over death. Because Jesus descended and rose, the doors of death and the gates of Hades cannot prevail over the church. Because Jesus descended and rose, death could not hold him and Hades could not keep him. Because Jesus descended and rose, he owns the keys to death and Hades. In brief, the descent means that death is defeated and Hades has been subjugated to the will of the risen One.

The Harrowing of Hades

The descent gets a lot of bad press in some quarters. For instance, Wayne Grudem argues that the descent was "a late intruder into the Apostles' Creed that really never belonged there in the first place and that, on historical and Scriptural grounds, deserves to be removed."[3] Let me be clear that this is totally false; it is right that the descent is in the Apostles' Creed, and we are right to profess it. For a start, as we've just seen, there is ample biblical grounds for the descent. What is more, the descent was absolutely unanimous in the church fathers of the second and third centuries. Among the many authors we could cite, Irenaeus reports a tradition he received from a certain presbyter who allegedly knew the apostles and delivered to him this tradition about the descent:

> But the case was, that for three days he dwelled in the place where the dead were, as the prophet says concerning him: "And the Lord remembered his dead saints who slept formerly in the land of the grave; and he descended to them, to rescue and save them" [a saying attributed to Jeremiah/Ps 107:20]. And the Lord himself says, "As Jonah remained three days and three nights in the belly of the whale, so shall the Son of Man be in the heart of the earth" [Matt 12:40]. Then also the apostle says, "But when he ascended, what is it but that he also descended into the lower parts of the earth" [Eph 4:9–10]. This, too, David says when prophesying about him, "And you have delivered my soul from the realm of the dead" [Ps 16:10/ Acts 2:27]. . . . If, then, the Lord observed the law of the dead, that he might become the firstborn from among the dead [Col 1:18], and tarried until the third day "in the lower parts of the earth . . ." [Rev 1:5].[4]

Here we have a very early tradition deriving from the immediate postapostolic period that already knows how the various pieces of Scripture point to the descent of Christ to the realm of the dead. Irenaeus cites this tradition from the presbyter as the well-established teaching of the church about Christ's descent to the place of the dead. To be honest though, that is not all the church had to say on the subject, and the tendency was to elaborate on the details about what Jesus did in Hades. For example, when we get to a fourth-century document like the Gospel of Nicodemus, the

---

3. Wayne Grudem, "He Did Not Descend into Hell: A Plea for Following Scripture instead of the Apostles' Creed," *JETS* 34 (1991): 103.
4. Irenaeus, *Against Heresies* 5.31.1–2.

descent has become highly embellished with all sorts of things going on: Adam gets rescued, John the Baptist paves the way for Jesus, Old Testament saints are released, the gates of Hades are crushed, and Satan is defeated. That might make a good movie for HBO, but it is going way beyond what Scripture says. In any case, the reality of the descent is thoroughly biblical and universally affirmed in the tradition of the church.

The place of the descent in the early creeds is a more complex matter. The problem is that there was no authorized version of the creedal formulas in the early church, so you do get some local variations on precise wording. Some versions omitted the reference to a descent (e.g., the Roman baptismal formula according to Rufinus), while others versions omitted the reference to burial (e.g., the Athanasian Creed). The reason for the elasticity of wording is that a burial implies a descent, and the descent presupposes burial. So omission is not necessarily denial! In any case, the received form of the Apostles' Creed, going back to the Frankish missionary Pirminius, as used in both Catholic and Protestant churches, definitely includes a reference to Christ's descent.

A further matter that has created confusion is the failure to distinguish between Hades and hell in various versions of the Creed. The Latin *inferus* means "lower depths," "underworld," or "place of the dead," while *infernus* means more properly "hell" or "perdition." We find the same distinction in Greek where the underworld is denoted with the words *hadēs* or *katachthonios*, while hell is designated with the word *geenna*. All the earliest versions of the Latin Creed use *descendit ad inferos* with the explicit meaning that Christ "descended to *Hades*." As far as I've discovered in my research, it was the fourth-century monk Rufinus who first changed *inferos* to *inferna* and thereby fostered the misconception that Christ descended to hell rather than to Hades, a misconception that was taken up into the Latin-speaking medieval church (though thankfully the Eastern churches usually maintained a descent to Hades rather than hell in their creeds and liturgies). The problem with a descent to hell is: (1) hell, as stated earlier, does not exist yet, so Jesus could not have descended to hell because it was not there; however, one day Hades will be dumped into hell, which will be made just for that purpose; and (2) it is problematic to say that Christ went to hell since hell is the final and irreversible place of judgment for those who reject God and is thus entirely unfitting for the Son of God. The Reformers were aware of these problems with a descent to hell, and they responded in one of two ways: (1) they simply rejected the doctrine of a descent by restricting Jesus's death to burial (e.g., Martin Bucer; Theodore Beza); or (2) they turned the descent into a metaphor so that Jesus did not literally go down to hell, but rather the fury of hell came upon him on the cross (e.g., Calvin). Such reinterpretations, however well-intentioned, are simply beside the point if we retain the original wording and original meaning of the Creed that Jesus descended to the place of the dead, not to hell.

The descent has found beautiful expression in Christian art and hymnody. In art, among my favorite pieces is the Byzantine fresco in the Chora Church of Istanbul, which depicts Christ pulling Adam and Eve out of their tombs (ca. AD 1315). Romanos the Melodist has a charming chorale piece called "The Victory of the Cross," featuring a musical dialogue between the devil and Hades about the cross. The devil tells Hades that there is nothing to worry about, while Hades panics that he is about to have his stomach ripped open and all the peoples inside him let out. In the hymn we hear:

> *Hades saw the Lord, and said to those in Hell:*
> *"O my priests and O my powers,*
> *who has driven a spike into my heart?*
> *A wooden lance has just pierced me; I am being torn in two*
> *I feel it terribly; my breath is a whirlwind.*
> *My insides burn. My belly churns in pain.*
> *I am forced to vomit forth Adam and Adam's people,*
> *who were deposited with me because of a tree.*
> *But a tree is now leading them*
> *on the return to paradise.*[5]

I am not a big fan of flash mobs. However, the best flash mob I've seen on YouTube took place in Lebanon in Easter of 2011. In a Lebanese

---

5. Romanos the Melodist, "Victory of the Cross," 3.1 (trans. R. J. Schork).

shopping mall a bunch of Greek Orthodox Christians stood up and starting singing in Arabic and Greek a famous hymn about Christ's defeat of death. The words translate to: "Christ has risen from the dead, trampling down death by death, and graciously giving life to those in the grave." If you can grasp that, then you've grasped the meaning of *descendit ad inferos*.

The Terror and Tyranny of Death

The next item in the Apostles' Creed, naturally following Christ's descent to Hades, is his resurrection from the dead. Yet before we can understand the true meaning and significance of the resurrection, we need to wrestle with the terror and tyranny of death. They say that there are two things in life that are certain: death and taxes. With a good accountant and some offshore finances, one can theoretically cheat the tax man. But there is no cheating death. There is no avoiding it and no escaping it since the vestiges of its dark grip eventually take us all. There is no advance in medical science and no doctor however skillful that can indefinitely postpone the inevitable moment when our mortal coil succumbs to the cruel power of death. To quote the Grim Reaper from the movie *Bill and Ted's Excellent Adventure*, "You can be a king or a street sweeper, but sooner or later you dance with the reaper."

Turning to some ancient sources, the Jewish sage Ben Sirach lamented, "Do not rejoice over any one's death; remember that we must all die," and "Remember that death does not tarry, and the decree of Hades has not been shown to you."[6] The Roman moral philosopher Seneca morbidly said, "Death comes for us all. It presses upon our rear. Soon the battle cry will be raised: the enemy is near."[7] The English poet Thomas Gray wrote, "The boast of heraldry, the pomp of power, and all that beauty, all that wealth ev'er gave, await alike the inevitable hour, the paths to glory lead but to the grave."[8] All these people are saying the same thing: death is the inevitable destiny that awaits us all. Death is like a terrifying tsunami that we see on

---

6. Sirach 8:7; 14:12 (NRSV).
7. Seneca, *Ad Marciam de consolatione* 10.5–6 (LCL).
8. Thomas Gray, "Elegy Written in a Country Churchyard," (1750).

the horizon rapidly coming toward us. We know that no matter how far or how fast we might run, we cannot outrun it. We stand on the seashore of mortal existence, playing about in the sands of daily life, knowing that ever so soon the crushing fury of death will fall upon us and upon all whom we love.

I've lived long enough to know that death can be a little scary. The prospect of separation from loved ones and the sheer mystery of the unknown make me shudder once in a while. But I'm glad to know that I'm not alone. Woody Allen once joked, "Death doesn't scare me; I just don't want to be there when it happens." Seneca was less jovial about it. He pointed out that "most men ebb and flow in wretchedness between the fear of death and the hardships of life; they are unwilling to live, and yet do not know how to die."[9] This despair at the prospect of death shapes us, not just individually but culturally as well, to do all sorts of things. The fear of death leads us to segregate the elderly into homes lest their frail and dilapidated bodies remind us of the approaching specter of our own mortality. We bar our doors and windows, build panic rooms, and arm ourselves to the back teeth to avoid a violent death at the hands of violent criminals. Fearing the threat of foreign powers, we drop bombs on them before they can bomb us. We send out drones to hunt down terrorists before they can engage in terrorism on our own soil. Engineers try to build safer cars and safer roads to prevent us from prematurely dying in a traffic accident. We shut down borders with other countries in order to stop people carrying potentially deadly pathogens from entering into our suburbs. We invest huge amounts of money trying to find cures to the incurable diseases that can almost randomly strike us down dead without rhyme or reason. Our culture of safety and our paranoia over security is driven by one single thing: the fear of death.

Looking back at ancient times, you might think that the average Jew, who worshipped the God of creation and covenant, who knew their Hebrew Bible, would have been immune from this fear and felt free to get on with life with the prospect of eternal life before them. Such, however, was not the case. Among the Jews of the Second-Temple period, there was a diverse

---

9. Seneca, *Epistulae morales* 4.6 (LCL).

range of views about the afterlife. The Pharisees obviously believed in the resurrection of the body. Some Jews took a more Hellenistic turn and adopted either the immortality of the soul or believed in the reincarnation of the soul. Others, like the Sadducees, held to some kind of shadowy existence in the underworld. For others, when you were dead you were dead, and the only thing that endured was your memory among those you left behind. Many ancient Jews could despair of death much like any modern person. The author of the Wisdom of Solomon expressed despair and despondence at the irreversible permanence of death:

> *Our name will be forgotten in time,*
> *and no one will remember our works;*
> *our life will pass away like the traces of a cloud,*
> *and be scattered like mist*
> *that is chased by the rays of the sun*
> *and overcome by its heat.*
> *For our allotted time is the passing of a shadow,*
> *and there is no return from our death,*
> *because it is sealed up and no one turns back.*[10]

If that were not sad enough, consider the words of a funeral epitaph left at the grave of a Jewish man named "Jesus," who died at the end of the second century AD.

TRAVELLER, MY NAME IS JESUS, AND MY
FATHER'S NAME IS PHAMEIS;
WHEN DESCENDING INTO HADES I WAS 60 YEARS OF AGE.
ALL OF YOU SHOULD WEEP TOGETHER FOR THIS
MAN, WHO WENT AT ONCE AT THE HIDING PLACE
OF AGES, TO ABIDE THERE IN THE DARK.
WILL YOU ALSO BEWAIL ME, DEAR DOSITHEOS, BECAUSE YOU
ARE IN NEED OF SHEDDING BITTER TEARS UPON MY TOMB.

---

10. Wisdom of Solomon 2:4–5 (NRSV).

WHEN I DIED I HAD NO OFFSPRING,
YOU WILL BE MY CHILD INSTEAD.
ALL OF YOU, THEREFORE, BEWAIL ME,
JESUS THE UNHAPPY MAN.[11]

That is probably not the cheeriest obituary I've read, but it is indicative of the sense of loss, grief, powerlessness, and utter despair that ancient peoples felt at the prospect of death.

The Death of Death

According to the Apostles' Creed death is not the end, and there is a story to tell, and the name of that story is "The Resurrection of the Messiah." Israel's great hope that the God of the covenant would raise up the righteous at the end of history finds incipient fulfillment in the resurrection of the Messiah. God does for Jesus in the middle of history what many Jews had hoped he would do for Israel at the end of history. It is in Jesus, and those who belong to him, that God's promise of covenant love and everlasting life are given.

In a more panoramic horizon, the story of the resurrection is the story of God defeating death and helping his people overcome their fear of death. The dawn of Easter morning lights a beacon of hope against the seemingly invincible darkness of death. The resurrection marks the invasion of God's love and life over a world torn up and turned upon itself by the triumvirate of sin, law, and death. Christians believe that the resurrection is testimony to the goodness of God's power and the power of God's goodness[12]— a power that undoes death, empties the grave, and makes all things new. The resurrection of Jesus demonstrates that God's first-order purposes for creation will come to fruition. Life will yet reign over death, the decay will

---

11. Shemuel Safrai and Menahem Stern, eds., *The Jewish People in the First Century: Historical Geography, Political History, Social, Culture and Religious Life and Institutions*, 2 vols. (Assen: Van Gorcum, 1974–76), 2:1043–44.

12. Leander E. Keck, *Who Is Jesus? History in Perfect Tense* (Columbia: University of South Carolina, 2000), 129.

give way to transformation, and the time is nigh when death itself will work backward, and God will be all in all.

In his resurrection, Jesus's words to Mary, "I am the resurrection and the life," are made good, and so is his promise, "The one who believes in me will live, even though they die; and whoever lives by believing in me will never die" (John 11:25–26). Christians accordingly believe that God raised Jesus to life and will also raise them to life (Rom 8:11; 1 Cor 6:14; 2 Cor 4:14; Phil 3:20–21). Jesus walked through the valley of the shadow of death so that we might follow behind him and join him in his conquest over all that stands opposed to God (Rev 1:18). The life of the risen Son will overflow to those who are united with him by faith. As Paul says, "Since death came through a man, the resurrection of the dead comes also through a man. For as in Adam all die, so in Christ all will be made alive. . . . Thanks be to God! He gives us the victory through our Lord Jesus Christ" (1 Cor 15:21–22, 57). Believers do not spend their days cowering in terror waiting to be victims of death; rather, we are "children of the resurrection" (Luke 20:36), as our identity, mission, and hope are determined by the fact that Jesus is risen and the power of resurrection already flows over to us through the gift of the Spirit. Resurrection means that we are constantly looking forward in faith to the future. According to Peter, God "has given us new birth into a living hope through the resurrection of Jesus Christ from the dead, and into an inheritance that can never perish, spoil or fade" (1 Pet 1:3–4). The resurrection is, to use J. R. R. Tolkien's neologism, a "eucatastrophe," the opposite of a catastrophe, an unexpected triumph amidst the debris of despair, the moment when misery and defeat are turned into inexplicable joy.[13] Because of the resurrection we know that God's most repeated command, "Do not be afraid," can truly be believed.

---

13. J. R. R. Tolkien, *Monsters and the Critics and Other Essays* (London: Harper Collins, 1997), 153.

Raised Immortal

I will not discuss the historicity of the resurrection or the physicality of Jesus's body. Those are tantalizing subjects, and others have covered them far more thoroughly than I can ever hope to do justice to.[14] It will be a better use of our time if we focus on the meaning or significance of the resurrection.

First, the resurrection tells us who Jesus really is. The resurrection is concrete proof that Jesus really, really was the Messiah. He was not a false prophet, not a royal pretender, not a lunatic, not a mere martyr. The resurrection is the divine sign that Jesus was given all authority in heaven and on earth (Matt 28:18), vindicated from false accusations (1 Tim 3:16), marked out as God's Son (Rom 1:4), designated as the heir of all things (Heb 1:2), and installed as Messiah and Lord (Acts 2:36). God's covenant with Israel now has to be interpreted in light of the fact that the resurrection designates Jesus as the Son of God. So when the first Christians proclaimed Jesus's resurrection to outsiders, it wasn't a case of, "Well chaps, you'll never guess what happened last Sunday; our dear friend Jesus of Nazareth, who got a raw deal at his trial, came back to life after his horrible execution. Isn't God really nice!" It was much more than that. The resurrection meant that Jesus was the climax of God's plan. What God was going to do for Israel and for the world, he was going to do through Jesus, Israel's Messiah, the Son of God—and he had already begun to do it!

Second, the resurrection means that the new age has already begun. Our starting point is that many Jews thought that God would resurrect everyone at the end of the age. The final vision of Daniel includes the report that "multitudes who sleep in the dust of the earth will awake: some to everlasting life, others to shame and everlasting contempt" (Dan 12:2). When Jesus told Martha that her dead brother Lazarus would live again, she assumed he was referring to the end of the age, hence her words, "I know he will rise again in the resurrection at the last day" (John 11:24). The strange thing is that what most Jews hoped that God would do for Israel at the end of history, God had

---

14. See N. T. Wright, *The Resurrection of the Son of God*, Christian Origins and the Question of God 3 (London: SPCK, 2003) and Michael R. Licona, *The Resurrection of Jesus: A New Historiographical Approach* (Downers Grove, IL: InterVarsity Press, 2010).

done for Jesus in the middle of history, namely, raised him from the dead. What this means is that Israel's history had reached a definitive moment in the resurrection of Jesus. But if that was the case, then God's whole deal with not only Israel but with the world had now changed. The new age had begun with Jesus's resurrection, since he was the firstfruits of the future resurrection and the firstborn of the new creation (Rom 8:29; 1 Cor 15:20, 23; Col 1:15, 18; Heb 12:23; Rev 1:5). The resurrection shows that history has edged closer to its appointed goal, the future has invaded the present, and the present age will not continue indefinitely. The resurrection is living proof that God invades and disrupts the present order of things by bringing life in the face of death, justification in the midst of condemnation, and rays of hope into the caverns of fear. God's new day arises in the raising of his Son.

Third, the resurrection is the vehicle of our salvation. In the sorts of churches that my family and I usually attend, I lament that while the cross gets a lot of attention, the resurrection is relatively neglected and given much smaller billing. It would not be an exaggeration to say that most Christians think that salvation is what takes place on the cross, and the resurrection is simply God raising big neon lights above it, saying in effect, "Get salvation here." The resurrection is reduced largely to a divine confirmation of what the cross achieved or is treated as little more than proof of life after death. In contrast, I want to make it very clear that we are saved in, by, and through the resurrection of Jesus Christ. Consider what Paul says: "He was delivered over to death for our sins and *was raised to life for our justification*," and "*if Christ has not been raised*, your faith is futile; *you are still in your sins*" (Rom 4:25; 1 Cor 15:17; emphasis added). Paul is saying that we could not be justified or forgiven if it were not for the resurrection of Jesus. To that we can add the testimony of Peter: "Praise be to the God and Father of our Lord Jesus Christ! In his great mercy he has given us new birth into a living hope *through the resurrection of Jesus Christ from the dead*" (1 Pet 1:3; emphasis added). Later, comparing the story of Jesus to the story of Noah's ark, Peter writes, "This water symbolizes baptism that now saves you also—not the removal of dirt from the body but the pledge of a clear conscience toward God. *It saves you by the resurrection of Jesus Christ*" (1 Pet 3:21; emphasis added). All of this is to say that God's justice, forgiveness, new birth, and life are given to us in the crucified *and* risen Jesus. A dead Jesus can be a teacher or a martyr, but he cannot be our Savior. We apprehend life only as it is given to us in the life of the risen Jesus. Here we should probably add that the resurrection proves the Trinitarian nature of salvation. The Father hands over the Son to the cross, the Son obeys the Father, then the Father raises the Son by the Spirit; afterward the Son dispenses the Spirit to believers, and the risen Son continually mediates between humanity and God the Father. Hans Urs von Balthasar summed it up well, "Without the resurrection the whole Trinitarian salvific plan would be incomprehensive, and the work begun in the life of Jesus would remain incomprehensible."[15] To experience the life-giving power of God is to be caught up in the life of the triune God. God has life in himself and communicates that life to believers through the resurrection of Christ, which results first in new birth and then later in the resurrection of the body. Resurrection, then, is the power of God for salvation, a salvation that forgives and renews his people.

Fourth, resurrection is an integral feature of discipleship. There are several things we could say about this, but foremost is that the new life of resurrection forces us to adopt a new way of being human. The resurrection imparts a new ethical paradigm and forces us to adopt a kingdom perspective. Hence Paul's words: "Since, then, you have been *raised with Christ*, set your hearts on things above, where Christ is, seated at the right hand of God. Set your minds on things above, not on earthly things" (Col 3:1–2; emphasis added). Paul is not bidding people to become so heavenly minded that we cease to be of any earthly good. More to the point, the reality of who we are *in Christ* and where *Christ is seated* must surely impact our perspective and praxis in the present. All of Colossians 3 works out what it means in practice to be raised up with Christ. The heavenly perspective on which we are to fix our minds is the truth pertaining to Jesus's exaltation as Lord and the fact that we ourselves are united to him. In addition, resurrection means that we have to get busy with kingdom business. The resurrection means we have the task of proclaiming and embodying before the world exactly what the new creation is and what it looks like. We are a resurrection people and we

---

15. As cited in Graham Cole, *God the Peacemaker: How Atonement Brings Shalom*, New Studies in Biblical Theology 25 (Downers Grove, IL: InterVarsity Press, 2009), 152.

demonstrate how resurrection impacts us when it is lived out in daily work, family life, and community. In 1 Corinthians 15, Paul ends his lengthy and dense discourse about resurrection with an imperative: "Therefore, my dear brothers and sisters, stand firm. Let nothing move you. *Always give yourselves fully to the work of the Lord, because you know that your labor in the Lord is not in vain*" (v. 58; emphasis added). This is Paul telling the Corinthians to hold their ground, to not let up, and to not shut up because the same divine power that God exercised in the resurrection of Christ is now at work in them. The future horizon of resurrection gives purpose and drive to Christian living in the present. If you're contemplating missionary service, adding your name to rosters at church, considering learning to preach, becoming a Sunday school teacher, or wondering what you can do to stop sex trafficking, then do it, and here's the reason why: the resurrection moves us to take risks for God because the resurrection proves that God is behind us, for us, and with us. Our labor in the Lord in this life plants seeds that will sprout forth in the future world, so that what work we do in this age will flower in the coming age of the new creation.

My favorite scene in *The Chronicles of Narnia* has to be the resurrection of Aslan. After his cruel execution by the White Witch and her hordes, the two Pevensie girls later hear a large cracking noise. They turn and see that the stone table has broken in two, and the body of Aslan is gone. It's then that they see the resurrected Aslan emerge against the backdrop of the dawn. The girls are excited but naturally confused, so Aslan explains:

Though the witch knew the Deep Magic, there is a magic deeper still which she did not know. Her knowledge only goes back to the dawn of time. But if she could have looked a little further back, into the stillness and darkness before Time dawned, she would have read there a different incantation. She would know that when a willing victim who had committed no treachery was killed in a traitor's stead, the Table would crack and Death itself would start working backward.[16]

---

16. C. S. Lewis, *The Lion, the Witch, and the Wardrobe* (New York: Harper Trophy, 1994), 178–79.

In the resurrection of Jesus, death works backward, and God's kingdom moves forward, propelling us with it toward the new heaven and new earth that lie ever before us.

The Story Thus Far

We believe that the creator made the world so that he could fill it with his love and glory. Yet humanity fell into sin and rebellion, and so God began his rescue plan to make a people for himself and to rescue his creation from the mire of corruption. His promises to the patriarchs, his covenant with Israel, his election of David—all of this was preparing for the advent of Israel's redeemer and the world's rightful Lord. Jesus, the Son of God, brought Israel the news of God's kingdom, yet he was rejected by the Judean leadership and the Roman authorities, who together conspired to have him crucified. Yet his death was itself a manifestation of the kingdom's saving power by making atonement for sins. Jesus truly died, descended to the grave, and defeated death; the Father raised him up by the power of the Holy Spirit for our justification and to establish a beachhead of the new creation in a world still languishing in the throes of corruption.

Recommended Reading

Bass, Justin W. *The Battle for the Keys: Revelation 1:18 and Christ's Descent into the Underworld*. Paternoster Biblical Monographs. Milton Keynes: Paternoster, 2014.

Bird, Michael F. "The Resurrection of Jesus." Pages 435–48 in *Evangelical Theology: A Biblical and Systematic Introduction*. Grand Rapids: Zondervan, 2013.

Clifford, Ross, and Philip Johnson. *The Cross Is Not Enough: Living as Witnesses to the Resurrection*. Grand Rapids: Baker, 2012.

BELIEVING *That* JESUS REIGNS

He ascended into heaven,
and is seated at the right hand of the Father.
He will come again to judge the living and the dead.

The Ascension Anchor

If you were asked, "What is the one doctrine of them all that is an anchor for your soul?" what might you say? You could of course say the incarnation, God becoming a human being; that'd be a genuinely good answer. Or perhaps the atoning power of the cross, or the hope bequeathed to us in Christ's resurrection. Some might even view the church, with its communion of the redeemed, as a treasured icon of hope in a dying world. Or there again, how about God as Trinity, the most distinctive of Christian beliefs? That would be something definitely worth clinging to in a pluralistic age. However, I find it most curious that the author of Hebrews regarded the ascension of Jesus as the anchor for our souls. He writes: "We have this hope as an anchor for the soul, firm and secure. It enters the inner sanctuary behind the curtain, where our forerunner, Jesus, has entered on our behalf. He has become a high priest forever, in the order of Melchizedek" (Heb 6:19–20). How could he possibly say that? Is he overplaying it a bit? Before anyone glibly dismisses him, note as well that Luke obviously thought the ascension was important since he presents an account of it twice: once at the end of his Gospel (Luke 24:49–53) and then again at the beginning of the book of Acts (Acts 1:9–11). So perhaps the ascension is more than Jesus's return trip to heaven. Just maybe the ascension tells us something about the continuing work of Jesus in the world! Exploring the next item in the Apostles' Creed, the ascension, is what we'll do right now.

Seated at the Father's Right Hand

To be honest, the ascension has struck many people as strange. Some have written it off as a bit of mythology with Jesus flying back up to heaven, which was supposedly only a few hundred meters above the clouds. I've even heard an atheist presenter mock the ascension as the "launching of the Lord." It is important to realize that the ascension is not making a statement about cosmology and how to find heaven on an astronomical map. What we have in the ascension is a mixture of visual marvel, strange metaphor, and utter mystery. We learn first and foremost that Jesus is taken away in such a manner as to leave clear in the minds of observers that he has gone to be with the Father in heaven. The ascension marks the end of the resurrection appearances and the beginning of Jesus's session as the Father's vice-regent. Of course, there are a few more things we can say about it.

First, Jesus ascends to heaven so that he can send the Holy Spirit to his followers. In the Gospel of John, there is a strong emphasis on Jesus departing *so that* the "Advocate" will come: "I will ask the Father, and *he will give you another advocate* to help you and be with you forever—the Spirit of truth" (John 14:16–17; emphasis added); "But the Advocate, the Holy Spirit, whom *the Father will send in my name*, will teach you all things and will remind you of everything I have said to you" (John 14:26; emphasis added); "When the Advocate comes, whom I will send to you from the Father—the Spirit of truth who goes out from the Father—he will testify about me" (John 15:26); and "Unless I go away, the Advocate will not come to you; but if I go, *I will send him to you*" (John 16:7; emphasis added). The ministry of the Advocate (that is, the Holy Spirit) is to continue the witness of Jesus through the witness of the disciples. In Luke–Acts there is a similar emphasis on Jesus's departure to heaven resulting in the giving of the Spirit to the disciples. Prior to the ascension, Jesus promised the disciples that they would receive what the Father had promised them, namely, that they would be clothed with "power from on high" (Luke 24:49). The purpose of such "power" is disclosed in the opening scene in Acts where Jesus told the disciples, "But you will receive power when the Holy Spirit comes on you; and you will be my witnesses in Jerusalem, and in all Judea and Samaria, and to the ends of the earth" (Acts 1:8). What the disciples received was empowerment for mission through the Spirit's enabling. Afterward in Peter's Pentecost speech, the giving of the Spirit is equated with the fulfillment of Joel's prophecy where God said through Joel, "I will pour out my Spirit on all people" (Acts 2:17; Joel 2:28). The visible and spectacular pouring out of the Holy Spirit is proof of three things: (1) It is proof that the "last days" have arrived with the sending of the Holy Spirit in a qualitatively new way (Acts 2:17); (2) it announces the time of salvation since "everyone who calls on the name of the Lord will be saved" (Acts 2:21); and (3), the sending of the Spirit is proof that Jesus in his earthly life was the anointed Spirit bearer and in his exalted state is the Spirit giver: "Exalted to the right hand of God, he has received from the Father the promised Holy Spirit and has poured out what you now see and hear" (Acts 2:33). Importantly, the Spirit is only poured out anew because Jesus has been raised and has ascended; it is he who sends the Spirit.

Second, after Jesus's ascension there is an expectation for the worship of Jesus. The ascension indicates the beginnings of a Trinitarian worship focused on the Lord Jesus and God the Father, operating in the power of the Spirit. The risen Jesus was immediately worshipped as someone who had overcome death and transcends the heaven-earth divide after the resurrection (Matt 28:9, 17). The ascension meant that Jesus was not only assumed to heaven like Enoch or Elijah but also exalted and enthroned beside God; therefore, he was worthy of similar honors given to God. That is why immediately after the ascension the disciples worshipped him (Luke 24:52), and why prayers, baptisms, and healings were performed in his name (Acts 2:38; 3:6, 16; 4:18, 30; 5:40; 8:12, 16). These were forms of devotion to Jesus and the means of receiving benefits from God through Jesus.

Third, Jesus will return in the same manner that he left. The certainty of Jesus's future return is rooted in the reality of his ascension into heaven. Hence the words of the angels to the disciples, "This same Jesus, who has been taken from you into heaven, will come back in the same way you have seen him go into heaven" (Acts 1:11). Jesus will return in the *same* way, but more importantly it is the *same* Jesus. In whatever mysterious way that Jesus ascended into heaven, in the same mysterious way he shall return to reign over the earth and to consummate his kingdom. It certainly appears that for Luke the ascension and return of Jesus belong closely together. As J. A. T. Robinson said, the ascension is "the advance notice of the end."[1]

Fourth, the ascension demonstrates that God has placed a human being at the helm of the universe. It is vital that we remember that when Jesus ascended into heaven, he did not cease to be human and morph into some disembodied state like a humanoid ghost. Jesus ascended as a human being and remains in this glorified human state for the rest of eternity. The significance of this is that God has placed a human person as the head of the universe.[2] This is precisely what God had intended all along. The commission given to Adam in Genesis 1:28 shows that it was humanity's first-order task to rule over creation on behalf of God. The true meaning of the "image of God" is to exercise a royal prerogative as God's representative on the earth. Psalm 8 picks up this theme when it says about human beings, "You have made them a little lower than the angels and crowned them with glory and honor. You made them rulers over the works of your hands; you put everything under their feet" (vv. 5–6). In fact, for the author of Hebrews, Psalm 8 shows that Jesus is the human par excellence, as he is the one whom God crowned with glory and honor because he qualified himself for exaltation by his salvific death for others (Heb 2:5–11). The enthronement of Jesus then constitutes the restoration of the task that God had always intended for humanity: to reign over a created world on behalf of God.

In terms of application, if nothing else, I would love to see churches return to celebrating Ascension Day next to Christmas, Easter, and Trinity Sunday. As to why, consider the words of the great textual critic Bruce Metzger:

---

1. As cited in Arie W. Ziep, *The Ascension of the Messiah in Lukan Christology*, NovTSup 87 (Leiden: Brill, 1997), 196.

2. N. T. Wright, *Surprised by Hope: Rethinking Heaven, the Resurrection, and the Mission of the Church* (New York: HarperOne), 114–16.

Ascension Day proclaims that there is no sphere, however secular, in which Christ has no rights—and no sphere in which his followers are absolved from obedience to him. Instead of it being a fairy tale from the pre-space age, Christ's ascension is the guarantee that he has triumphed over the principalities and powers, so that at his name "every knee should bow, in heaven and on earth and under the earth, and every tongue confess that Jesus Christ is Lord, to the glory of God the Father" (Phil. 2:10–11).[3]

Regent of the Cosmos

I am not much of a comedian, but my favorite Sunday school joke has to be this one: "Why can God the Father only use his left hand?" Answer: "Because Jesus is sitting on his right hand!" Once you calm down after laughing hysterically at that corny joke, a more serious question is this one. What is the Old Testament passage that is most quoted or echoed in the New Testament? That's a tricky one, isn't it! In my experience most students tend to think the answer has to be either Psalm 23 or Isaiah 53. Sadly, Psalm 23 is never once quoted in the New Testament, and while Isaiah 53 is a good guess, it is not the correct answer. The answer is in fact Psalm 110, especially the first four verses:

> *The LORD says to my lord:*
> *"Sit at my right hand*
> > *until I make your enemies*
> > *a footstool for your feet."*
> *The LORD will extend your mighty scepter from Zion, saying,*
> > *"Rule in the midst of your enemies!"*
> *Your troops will be willing*
> > *on your day of battle.*

---

3. Bruce M. Metzger, "The Meaning of Christ's Ascension," in *Search the Scriptures: New Testament Studies in Honor of Raymond T. Stamm*, ed. J. M. Myers, O. Reimherr, and H. N. Bream (Leiden: Brill, 1969), 128.

Arrayed in holy splendor,
    your young men will come to you
    like dew from the morning's womb.
The LORD has sworn
    and will not change his mind:
"You are a priest forever,
    in the order of Melchizedek."
The Lord is at your right hand;
    he will crush kings on the day of his wrath.
He will judge the nations, heaping up the dead
    and crushing the rulers of the whole earth.
He will drink from a brook along the way,
    and so he will lift his head high. (Ps 110:1–7)

This text was top of the billboard charts for Christian preaching.[4] It was popular because it set forth a hugely important claim. Jesus had not only returned to heaven but was in fact now ruling from heaven as well. Jesus had been exalted, and he continues his work from his heavenly throne. This is traditionally known as the "session" of Jesus and refers to his postascension status and activity. There are several pertinent things to take away.

First, Jesus is exalted to God's right hand and is invested with divine authority. Jesus had been formally exalted, that is, installed as God the Father's vice-regent and the one in whom and through whom divine sovereignty is expressed. When the New Testament authors cited Psalm 110 in relation to Jesus's exaltation, they were saying that Jesus had been taken into heaven in order to take control of the affairs of the universe. The person whom Christians worship and bear witness to is the one whom the God of Israel has marked out as the Lord of the universe; he is thus the key agent in its redemption and renewal. As for what Jesus's exaltation means for discipleship, hear the words of the martyr Polycarp in his letter to the

---

4. Cf. citations, allusions, and echoes of Psalm 110:1 in Matt 22:44//Mark 12:36//Luke 20:42; Matt 26:64//Mark 14:62//Luke 22:69; Acts 2:33–35; 5:31; Rom 8:34; 1 Cor 15:25; Eph 1:20–22; 2:6; Phil 2:9–11; Col 3:1; Heb 1:3, 13; 8:1; 10:12–13; 12:2; 1 Pet 3:22; Rev 3:21 (cf. also Mark 16:19). For a good survey of these texts, see Aquila H. I. Lee, *From Messiah to Preexistent Son: Jesus's Self-Consciousness and Early Christian Exegesis of Messianic Psalms*, WUNT 2.192 (Tübingen: Mohr Siebeck, 2005), 202–39.

Philippians: "Therefore, prepare for action and serve God in fear and truth, leaving behind the empty and meaningless talk and the error for the crowd, and believing in the one who raised our Lord Jesus Christ from the dead and gave him glory and a throne at his right hand. To him all things in heaven and on earth were subjected, whom every breathing creature serves, who is coming as judge of the living and the dead."[5] To use a meteorological pun, to be a follower of Jesus means to walk in the "reign" of Jesus. It entails that believers order their lives, finances, relationships, ambitions, and hopes around the most important confession of the faith: Jesus is Lord.

Second, believers embryonically share in the reign of Christ by virtue of their union with Christ. Believers are united with Jesus in his death, resurrection, and exaltation. In the New Testament, reigning with Christ over the earth is held out as an impending hope to be consummated in the future (2 Tim 2:12; Rev 2:26–27; 3:21; 5:10; 20:6; 22:5). However, in Ephesians and Colossians, believers are in a sense already enthroned with Christ. Paul writes that "God raised us up with Christ and seated us with him in the heavenly realms in Christ Jesus" (Eph 2:6), and "since, then, you have been raised with Christ, set your hearts on things above, where Christ is, seated at the right hand of God" (Col 3:1). Obviously this realized aspect of the kingdom, whereby believers can already count themselves as reigning with Christ, can lead to an unhealthy spiritual triumphalism. Lest we feel tempted to seize power, as the church across the ages has often done, we need every once in a while to pinch ourselves and remember that this is not the kingdom of heaven and we cannot usher it in with our own political craft. We are not on the throne yet, but the message of the exaltation is that our Man is, our Messiah is, our Master is, and where he is, there we shall also be! What that should lead to is neither triumphalist political ambition nor a disdain for all other earthly authorities. Rather, the prospect of reigning with Christ should cultivate a deep desire to live lives worthy of our royal calling (Col 3:2). It should promote a sense of awe at the grace of God that turned rebellious sinners who raged against the kingdom into royal heirs of the glorious king (Eph 2:7).

Third, Jesus remains our high priest even from his heavenly throne. The priestly office of Christ is expressed in his mediation between God

---

5. Polycarp, *To the Philippians* 2.1.

and humanity. That mediation is demonstrated supremely in his atoning death but is not limited to it. The exalted Jesus is the mediator who gives us access to God and continues to make intercession on behalf of his people. A recurring theme in Hebrews is that Jesus has entered the heavenly sanctuary ahead of us as our forerunner, and we have assurance that we too will be accepted there (Heb 6:20; 10:19–22). Because of Jesus's ascension and exaltation, believers have a brazen confidence to presume upon God's favor and a shameless sense of security that God's door is always opened to them. In addition, Jesus continues to make intercession to the Father on our behalf. Jesus's high priestly prayer recorded in John 17 promises that Jesus will continue to intercede for his followers after he returns to heaven. This is the same reason why Paul asked, "Who then is the one who condemns? No one. Christ Jesus who died—more than that, who was raised to life—is at the right hand of God and is also interceding for us" (Rom 8:34). The author of Hebrews celebrated that Jesus "is able to save completely those who come to God through him, because he always lives to intercede for them" (Heb 7:25). This intercession should not be conceived of as Jesus constantly requesting a reluctant Father to be merciful. Rather, it is more like Jesus presenting his brothers and sisters to the Father, pleading their prayers for them, and turning his Father's gaze upon them. And when the Father looks down at his churchly children, he sees them as one with his beloved Son who is seated beside him.

In Christian pop culture, it is common for folks to ask, "WWJD?" that is, "What would Jesus do?" However, because of the exaltation of Jesus and his continual priestly work on our behalf, we can legitimately ask, "WIJD?" that is, "What is Jesus doing?" We can try to discern what Jesus is up to, what he is pushing ahead with, and what he is trying to accomplish through us; then we can think about how we can advance Jesus's kingdom in this world. The Spirit of Christ compels us to continue our mission, watching in prayer, waiting in faithfulness, and working hard for the kingdom until the day when our king returns and all things are renewed under the rule of the Son and the reign of his saints.[6]

---

6. See similarly Graham Cole, *He Who Gives Life: The Doctrine of the Holy Spirit* (Wheaton: Crossway, 2007), 243.

Return of the King

Can you imagine a big fat ancient Jewish wedding? According to several sources, it went something like this. After a formal betrothal, it would be up to a year or more that a bride had to wait for her future husband and his friends to come and formally fetch her for the wedding ceremony.[7] When the time of the wedding approached, the bride with her attendants would wait in anticipation each evening for the bridegroom's party to arrive in jubilant fanfare to take the bride to the groom's house. The bride would be carried from her father's house to the bridegroom's house in a carriage, while people played musical instruments, sang, and danced under the glow of torches and lamps. The bridegroom would receive the bride into his house, there would be a reading of the marriage contract, a blessing would be prayed, and then the couple would consummate the marriage.[8] Thereafter it was up to a week of feasting and merriment.[9] It was a public, celebratory, and judicial event, signifying the marriage of the couple, who would be adorned in garlands, making them "royalty" for the day.[10]

You might be wondering what this has to do with the second coming of Jesus. Well, the return of Jesus is likened to a bridegroom coming to fetch his bride and to take her to their new home, followed by a massive wedding feast. Listen to the parable of the unprepared virgins:

> At that time the kingdom of heaven will be like ten virgins who took their lamps and went out to meet the bridegroom. Five of them were foolish and five were wise. The foolish ones took their lamps but did not take any oil with them. The wise ones, however, took oil in jars along with their lamps. The bridegroom was a long time in coming, and they all became drowsy and fell asleep.

---

7. See m. Ketubbot 5.2.

8. See the account of an Arab wedding that was ambushed by the Maccabean brothers in revenge for the death of their brother: 1 Maccabees 9:37–41; Josephus, *Jewish Antiquities* 13.20.

9. Cf. Gen 29:27; Judg 14:12, 17.

10. See Craig S. Keener, "Marriage," in *Dictionary of New Testament Background*, ed. C. A. Evans and S. E. Porter (Downers Grove, IL: InterVarsity Press, 2000), 685–87; Michael L. Satlow, *Jewish Marriage in Antiquity* (Princeton: Princeton University Press, 2001), 168–81.

At midnight the cry rang out: "Here's the bridegroom! Come out to meet him!" Then all the virgins woke up and trimmed their lamps. The foolish ones said to the wise, "Give us some of your oil; our lamps are going out."

"No," they replied, "there may not be enough for both us and you. Instead, go to those who sell oil and buy some for yourselves." But while they were on their way to buy the oil, the bridegroom arrived. The virgins who were ready went in with him to the wedding banquet. And the door was shut.

Later the others also came. "Lord, Lord," they said, "open the door for us!" But he replied, "Truly I tell you, I don't know you." Therefore keep watch, because you do not know the day or the hour. (Matt 25:1–13)

This parable is a warning for people to be ready for the return of Jesus. While not knowing the hour of his return, they must make sure that the oil lamps of their faith are fully lit, lest they miss the return of the bridegroom for his bride!

In the book of Revelation, the prelude to the return of Jesus is described in highly charged language and with symbolically layered imagery, looking forward to Jesus bringing heavenly justice down on God's earthly enemies (Rev 19:1–10). But take notice of the news of celebration that comes from the multitude in heaven and from the report of the angel (vv. 6–9):

"Hallelujah! For our Lord God Almighty reigns. Let us rejoice and be glad and give him glory! For the wedding of the Lamb has come, and his bride has made herself ready." . . . Then the angel said to me, "Write this: Blessed are those who are invited to the wedding supper of the Lamb!" And he added, "These are the true words of God."

All this is to say that the primary biblical metaphor for the second coming is a wedding feast! A wedding feast is such a poignant and powerful image for Christ's return because it conveys notions of celebration and consummation as well as feasting, family, festivity, and fellowship all rolled in one. Whatever we might say about the return of Jesus, and we could say a lot—the importance of faithful readiness, the fate of Israel, the portentous events leading up to it, the final judgment, the wonder of the new heaven and the new earth—we should never forget that Jesus's return is the fulfillment of our longing for divine intimacy, our being with God and enjoying him forever. That is the blessed hope that the second coming sets before us. What we need to do now is briefly outline what the second coming is about, what it means, and how we live in light of it.

The return of Jesus really matters. Yes, I know some people get a little obsessed with the second coming. They have all sorts of crazy charts, make strange and speculative predictions about exactly when Jesus will return, try to dissect the minutia of detail in the book of Revelation, and argue over the tribulation and a millennium. Even so, we cannot afford to gloss over this part of our faith. While Paul would not want his churches to become end-time maniacs, he often exhorts them not to be "ignorant" about the final things either (Rom 11:25; 1 Thess 4:13). That is because the ending of a story matters. It is the end of the story that tells you what the story was really about in the first place. To give my favorite example as a Gen Xer, we learn from the ending of *The Return of the Jedi* that the original *Star Wars* trilogy was really about the redemption of Anakin Skywalker. We learn from the ending of C. S. Lewis's *The Lion, the Witch, and the Wardrobe* that the story is not about three English children in a magical world but about Aslan bringing liberation to Narnia and setting humanity as regents over it. What the second coming tells us is that the end, the end as God intends it, is about God bringing his justice and peace to earth and healing the pain of the world by uniting himself to his creation through the Son, so that God may be "all in all" and fill all things in every way (1 Cor 15:28; Eph 1:23).

The Christian story of the end is all the more important because it competes with other accounts of the end of the world. Islamic versions of the "last things" are very similar to Christian accounts, except that in Islamic doctrine a figure called the Mahdi (i.e., an Islamic teacher) partners with Isa (i.e., Jesus) to rule the world before the final day of reckoning. Buddhist beliefs generally tend to focus on the annihilation of the individual soul in nirvana without too much recourse to the future state of the universe. Secular futurists see the end of the world in an ecological disaster caused by overpopulation, overpollution, and overuse of natural resources. Yet the Christian story of the end is much different. In the Christian view, it is not annihilation or ecological catastrophe that is the final moment of human history. God's story according to the gospel requires a final divine act to bring a rebellious world into order and to put it under the power of our heavenly king. The final chapter in this saga includes the glorious return of Jesus Christ to establish his kingdom fully and finally. It is the moment when, as N. T. Wright likes to remind us, "He will put the world to rights."[11] Jesus is not coming back to inflict apocalyptic carnage on a bunch of innocent agnostics; rather, he is coming to bring heavenly justice to a world that is submerged in wickedness and mired in corruption. That is why the Apostles' Creed affirms that "he will come again to judge the living and the dead." His first coming was in humility to bring redemption; his second coming will be in glory to bring God's redemptive purposes to a majestic consummation. Jesus returns to save his people, to rule in righteousness, and to usher in a new heaven and a new earth. Jesus is Lord, and at his return he will make his lordship fully known. He will be by might what he is by right: the king of heaven and earth. Thus, the return of Jesus is not a dispensable afterthought or an appendix at the end of the book that we can skip over; rather, it is the distinctive belief of Christians and the vital final act of our hope. That is why it was embedded in Christian creeds because it is so part and parcel to what it means to believe in God and to hope in Jesus.

There is ample biblical witness to the reality and nature of Jesus's return. The Gospel of John, for all its focus on the end as already begun with Jesus's appointed "hour," does not lose sight of the fact that Jesus made a promise to all of his disciples that "if I go and prepare a place for you, I will come back and take you to be with me that you also may be where I am" (John 14:3). Paul's most lucid account of the second coming comes from his first letter to the Thessalonians: "For the Lord himself will come down from heaven, with a loud command, with the voice of the archangel and with the trumpet call of God, and the dead in Christ will rise first. After that, we who are still alive and are left will be caught up together with them in the

---

11. N. T. Wright, *Simply Christian: Why Christianity Makes Sense* (New York: HarperOne, 2006), passim.

clouds to meet the Lord in the air. And so we will be with the Lord forever" (4:16–17). Paul wrote to the Philippians, "We eagerly await a Savior from there [heaven], the Lord Jesus Christ, who, by the power that enables him to bring everything under his control, will transform our lowly bodies so that they will be like his glorious body" (Phil 3:20–21). Similar ideas are found in Colossians: "When Christ, who is your life, appears, then you also will appear with him in glory" (Col 3:4). Paul sums up the second coming as our "blessed hope—the appearing of the glory of our great God and Savior, Jesus Christ" (Titus 2:13). In Hebrews we find a similar belief expressed: "He will appear a second time, not to bear sin, but to bring salvation to those who are waiting for him" (Heb 9:28). Arguably the most vivid description of the second coming is Revelation 19:11–21 which depicts "heaven standing open" and Jesus appearing as a mighty warrior ready to destroy his enemies. Revelation is emphatic that Jesus's coming is imminent (Rev 1:7; 2:5, 16; 3:3, 11; 16:15; 22:7, 12, 20), and Jesus repeatedly declares "I am coming" (Rev 2:5, 16; 3:11; 16:15; 22:7, 12, 20).

The best summary of the biblical teaching about the return of Jesus, which I think Christians of all types could affirm, is summarized by article fifteen of the Lausanne Covenant which expounds this tenet of the faith as follows:

We believe that Jesus Christ will return personally and visibly, in power and glory, to consummate his salvation and his judgment. This promise of his coming is a further spur to our evangelism, for we remember his words that the gospel must first be preached to all nations. We believe that the interim period between Christ's ascension and return is to be filled with the mission of the people of God, who have no liberty to stop before the end. We also remember his warning that false Christs and false prophets will arise as precursors of the final Antichrist. We therefore reject as a proud, self-confident dream the notion that people can ever build a utopia on earth. Our Christian confidence is that God will perfect his kingdom, and we look forward with eager anticipation to that day, and to the new heaven and earth in which righteousness will dwell and God will reign forever. Meanwhile, we rededicate ourselves to the service of Christ and of people in joyful submission to his authority over the whole of our lives.[12]

Let me stress that this is not a pie in the sky. There is a deeply practical side to our future hope for Christ's return. How we act in the present is deeply impacted by what we think of the future. What we think about evangelism, justice, ecological responsibility, pastoral care, budgets, the church, and ethics is based on what God *has done* and *will yet do* for his people *through Jesus Christ.* If our actions echo into eternity, if we contribute anything to God's coming kingdom, then we will be constrained to operate with a kingdom perspective.

But what does this mean for us? How does it challenge us and even change us? Well, a number of implications come to mind.

First, there is the outstanding mission to evangelize the nations. In light of Jesus's impending return, the church is to set themselves the task of announcing the good news that the Lord Jesus has died and risen and will come again as judge. In Jesus's name, the church is to preach the forgiveness of sins and to declare that the sufferings and injustices of this age are set to end. In Matthew's Olivet discourse, Jesus said that "this gospel of the kingdom will be preached in the whole world as a testimony to all nations, and then the end will come" (Matt 24:14). The evangelistic mission is an imperative task because its completion will herald in the return of the Lord Jesus.

Second, we are called to endure and persevere ahead of Christ's return. Paul constantly exhorted his network of house churches to endure their trials because they had assurance that their God would vindicate them from accusation and take them into his presence. He tells the Corinthians that both he and they must show "patient endurance" and do so knowing that they have the Spirit, which is a deposit "guaranteeing what is to come" (2 Cor 1:6–22). He reminded the Thessalonians of their "endurance inspired by hope in our Lord Jesus Christ" (1 Thess 1:3). The Thessalonian believers were even a model to others: "Therefore, among God's churches we boast about your perseverance and faith in all the persecutions and trials you are

---

12. "Lausanne Covenant," https://www.lausanne.org/content/covenant/lausanne-covenant.

enduring. All this is evidence that God's judgment is right, and as a result you will be counted worthy of the kingdom of God, for which you are suffering" (2 Thess 1:4–5). Endurance under intense duress from religious, social, and political pressures is paramount in Revelation. John describes himself as a "brother and companion in the suffering and kingdom and patient endurance that are ours in Jesus" (Rev 1:9). Twice the seer repeats the exhortation, "This calls for patient endurance and faithfulness" on the part of God's people (Rev 13:10; 14:12). We become steadfast in our faith by abiding, remaining, and keeping ourselves in the love of God.

Third, arguably the most crucial outcome of our blessed hope is the reminder to be encouragers. One of the purposes of prophecy in the early church was so that everyone would be "instructed and encouraged," especially if that prophecy had a forward-looking element toward Christ's return (1 Cor 14:31). After detailing the events set to transpire at the Lord's return (1 Thess 4:15–17), Paul then immediately tells the Thessalonians, "Therefore encourage one another with these words" (1 Thess 4:18). In Hebrews, the audience is told, "And let us consider how we may spur one another on toward love and good deeds, not giving up meeting together, as some are in the habit of doing, but encouraging one another—and all the more as you see the Day approaching" (Heb 10:24–25). As Christians live under the thunderous clouds of mortality and persecution, they keep each other from falling or failing as they set their faces toward the return of Christ. Until that day they pray, "Come, Lord!" (1 Cor 16:22; cf. Rev 22:20; Didache 10.6).

When do you long the most for the Lord's return? It might be when you see the horror and suffering of humanity on television. Or perhaps it is when dealing with the frustration or even the sin of people in the church. All that and more can make us raise our eyes to heaven and pray for the Lord's instant return. I have to confess that I most feel the sense of anticipation at Jesus's return when I share in the Lord's Supper. I've always found it interesting that Paul concludes his description of the Lord's Supper with the words, "For whenever you eat this bread and drink this cup, you proclaim the Lord's death until he comes" (1 Cor 11:26). For me, the Lord's Supper is really the hors d'oeuvres for the messianic banquet. The Lord's Supper reminds me that no matter how hard a week I've had that there is a feast waiting for me, and I've only had a small taste of the good things still to come.

No wonder then that the image of sharing food and fellowship with God appears throughout Scripture as a recurring way of imagining our hope to dwell in God's presence. One of the most blessed words in Scripture comes from Exodus where it is reported that the Israelites "saw God, and they ate and drank" (24:11), which I think is as true an anticipation as any of the future life ahead of us. According to Isaiah, the new creation will be like the gentiles flocking to a holy mountain to come and banquet with God (Isa 25:6–8). Jesus said that in the kingdom of heaven "many will come from the east and the west, and will take their places at the feast with Abraham, Isaac and Jacob" (Matt 8:11). And John's vision of the "wedding supper of the Lamb" is arguably the richest of them all (Rev 19:9). I take great pleasure in imagining what that wedding supper will be like. I can imagine Southern Baptists making the fried chicken, Aussie Anglicans grilling up some shrimp, maybe some Korean Presbyterians making BBQ, Methodist Mexicans preparing fish tacos, and French Pentecostals baking the pastries. That's what I imagine! But lest we get too lofty minded, we need to remember that we are not there yet! When we break the bread of communion, we are reminded of Jesus's body broken for us and we reinscribe our hearts with the hope for his bodily return. But in the interim, we are called to imitate the one whom we anticipate and to remain ever watchful for the dawn that will one day break upon us. We may hope for many things in the future, like getting a driver's license, going to college, graduation, marriage, children, or retirement. Yet our deepest longings should be for the return of the bridegroom to take us, his bride, into his home. For where our deepest longings are, there our heart is also.

The Story Thus Far

We believe that the God who is love made the world to be the object of his love. Yet rebellion, corruption, and death consumed human existence, and so God launched his rescue plan through Abraham and Israel to bring peace to the sin-cursed earth. There would be a man from Abraham's lineage, from the house of David, who would execute the Father's plan for salvation by the power of the Spirit. The Word became a man, the man for whom it was determined before the foundation of the world that he would reconcile God and humanity. The man Christ Jesus was crucified under Pontius Pilate and descended to the grave. Yet he conquered death; the Father raised him up by the power of the Holy Spirit, and he ascended to heaven to reign as God's vice-regent. Now he continually intercedes for believers as their high priest and one day will come again to put the world to rights.

Recommended Reading

Bird, Michael F. "The Ascension and Session of Jesus." Pages 449–59 in *Evangelical Theology: A Biblical and Systematic Introduction*. Grand Rapids: Zondervan, 2013.

Chester, Tim, and Jonny Woodrow. *The Ascension: Humanity in the Presence of God*. Fearn: Christian Focus, 2013.

Hoekema, Anthony A. *The Bible and the Future*. Grand Rapids: Eerdmans, 1979.

Plevnik, Joseph. *Paul and the Parousia: An Exegetical and Theological Investigation*. Peabody, MA: Hendrickson, 1997.

12

BELIEVING *in the* SPIRIT

I believe in the Holy Spirit.

A Spiritual People

The next lines of the Apostles' Creed lead us to reflect on God's Spirit and God's people. These two naturally go together in the biblical story. God's Spirit was always with and around God's people. God's Spirit would rest on particular leaders like Moses, Joshua, the elders of Israel, the judges of Israel, and especially the prophets, whom the Spirit of the Lord specially animated so that they engaged in both foretelling and forthtelling on God's behalf. In which case, receiving the Spirit meant a commission for a particular task, one with great responsibility and often fraught with danger.

Interestingly enough in the exodus story, there was a moment when the Spirit bestowed upon Moses was also shared with Israel's elders. When two particular elders were found prophesying in the camp, Moses was informed about it, with the underlying assumption that he would be jealous. Yet Moses's response was quite the opposite: "I wish that all the LORD's people were prophets and that the LORD would put his Spirit on them!" (Num 11:29). Moses hoped for a day when all of God's people would receive God's Spirit and prophesy in his power. It was the prophet Joel who prophesied that such a day would indeed come. Speaking to the people of Judah in the aftermath of a national disaster, he told them God's promise that "I will pour out my Spirit on all people. Your sons and daughters will prophesy, your old men will dream dreams, your young men will see visions. Even on my servants, both men and women, I will pour out my Spirit in those days" (Joel 2:28–29). One of the signs of restoration and blessing was that God would bestow his Spirit in a whole new way. It would be given to all—not just royal leaders, priests, or prophets—but to everyone.

Fast-forward now to the day of Pentecost when the disciples were all gathered together in a room somewhere in Jerusalem, and just as Jesus promised, God's Spirit fell upon them. Something like "tongues of fire" rested on each of them and they began to speak in foreign languages which they did not otherwise know (Acts 2:3–4). The cacophony of voices made a spectacular noise, so much so that outsiders assumed that there was a drunken gaggle upstairs babbling on about something. Yet Peter's response is direct and dramatic. He famously explained, "These people are not drunk, as you suppose. It's only nine in the morning! No, this is what was spoken by the prophet Joel" (Acts 2:15–16). What is remarkable is not merely the fact that God had now poured out his Spirit (it had been a long time since Joel made his prophecy), but upon whom the Spirit was given! The Spirit was not given to Herod Antipas and his entourage, not to the high priests, not to scrupulous Pharisees, nor to any other religious leader of the day. It was Jesus's followers who were the recipients of God's long-promised gift of the Spirit, who now prophesied his praise and performed his deeds of power. What this meant was as momentous as it was contentious: Jesus is the one who gives the Spirit; it is through him and in his name that the Spirit comes, and it is for his kingdom that the Spirit embraces and empowers people.

Thereafter in the book of Acts, the Spirit keeps filling the apostles and other believers to preach, prophesy, and perform amazing works. What was even more world-shaking was that the Spirit was not only given to Jews but also to Samaritans and even to gentiles. The Jesus movement was not simply going to be an in-house Jewish thing, confined within the borders of Israel, but would embrace the whole world. The spiritual renewal of Israel would lead to the renewal of the nations. All people, whether Jew or gentile, Greek or Roman, barbarian or Scythian, male or female, slave or free—everyone without distinction—could know the grace of God, the love of the Messiah, and the blessing of God's Spirit.

What the Apostles' Creed is pointing us to and reminding us of at this point is this. God's Spirit, as given through Jesus, plunges us into a river of blessing; he gives life, saves and sanctifies, unites believers with Jesus and with each other, and equips and empowers them to be a spiritual people ready for earthly labor as much as eternal life.

Sadly though, the Holy Spirit, particularly his giftings and manifestations, has courted much controversy in recent ages. Whereas the Spirit compels us to come together, more often than not the mere mention of the Spirit compels us to crawl into our own factional corners where we mutter criticisms about certain peoples' claim to spiritual prowess or some group's lack of spiritual life. So we must carefully and cautiously examine the issues inside this tinderbox of theological controversy when we talk about the Spirit and his role in the church.

The Spirit Aggrieved

At a ministers' fraternal, a number of clergy were discussing the denominational identity of the members of the Trinity. Concerted debate took place over whether Jesus was a Baptist (because he was baptized as an adult) or Presbyterian (because he instigated the new covenant) or Methodist (because he liked preaching outdoors) or Catholic (because he really loved his mother). The only thing the fraternal could agree on was that the Father was probably Anglican and the Spirit was definitely Pentecostal! As much as we like to joke about denominations, this joke masks a sad underlying reality. Over the last hundred years, the Holy Spirit has been the subject of intense and torrid debates, usually accompanied with accusations of heresy and counteraccusations of spiritual barrenness. Such debates, I imagine, leave the Spirit deeply grieved.

The spread of Pentecostal churches and the rise of charismatic congregations all over the globe in the last hundred years has ushered in a blessing of spiritual renewal and is a much-needed reminder that God's Spirit blows afresh in every generation. I am not afraid to call the rise of Pentecostal and charismatic churches, especially in the Global South, a mighty movement of the Holy Spirit. Unfortunately, this Pentecostal explosion has also brought with it painful divisions over the form of spiritual gifts and the manifestation of the Spirit's power. Tragically, the Pentecostal phenomenon has incited debates and caused disunity over speaking in tongues, the meaning of Spirit baptism, the nature of spiritual gifts, and especially over prosperity doctrine. These days the Holy Spirit has been more a topic of theological conflict than a source for spiritual renewal. Pentecostal theologian Jack Levison worries that if divisions proliferate, then the global church might effectively split into two Christianities, with one version that thinks the Spirit manifests itself in spectacular fashion and another that seeks a more austere and steady spirituality.[1]

If perennial debates over the Spirit were not bad enough, I must confess that I am habitually mortified when I learn about many of the unorthodox things that professing Christians believe about the Spirit. I say with no exaggeration that I have met Christians who seem to think of the Holy Spirit as something like Jesus's vapor trail, or a mysterious and impersonal "force" that conveys God's presence, or even a kind of heavenly buzz that falls on people when some funky psychedelic worship music is played. The way some people describe the Holy Spirit could just as well describe magnetism, mood rings, or Motown records from the 1960s. Then there are other churches that are positively petrified of anything to do with the Holy Spirit lest they themselves get too enthusiastic in their faith that they might start dancing in the aisles or begin muttering, "Untie my bow tie. . . . Who stole my Honda?" In some places, this has led to a kind of "don't ask, don't tell" policy when it comes to one's experience of the Holy Spirit. Churches of this kind have purposely retreated from making the Holy Spirit an object of theology, worship, and spirituality with the result that they've basically adopted a Trinity of Father, Son, and Holy Bible. That is catastrophic on so many levels, because if you don't have the Spirit then you don't have Christ. We need the Spirit like we need air in our lungs. The recent patriarch of the Greek Orthodox Church of Antioch, Ignatius Hazim, argues, "Without the Holy Spirit, God is distant, Christ is in the past, the Gospel is a dead letter, the Church is simply an organization, authority is domination, mission is

---

1. Jack Levison, *Inspired: The Holy Spirit and the Mind of Faith* (Grand Rapids: Eerdmans, 2013), 222.

propaganda, worship is the summoning of spirits, and Christian action is the morality of slaves."[2] All I can say in response is, "Whoa and wow!" You cannot put it clearer than that! We need the Spirit. Charismatic debates or not, we need the Spirit moving in our churches and filling our bodies with heavenly fire.

Advocating for the Advocate

So how do we chart a path through this dark forest of ignorance, fear, and mania that seems to dog contemporary churches when it comes to the Holy Spirit? How do we seek the Spirit's presence and power without descending into a charismatic chaos? How can we be open as well as discerning toward the things of the Spirit? Well, I suggest that a good starting point will be making explicit the connection between the Holy Spirit and the gospel. This will prove to be the ballast to our ecclesiastical ship as we try to navigate our way through a sensitive topic.

My proposal is that we should expect the Holy Spirit's work to be something we experience since spiritual experience is part of the promise of the gospel. Jesus promised his disciples that he would send them the Spirit to clothe them with "power from on high" (Luke 24:49; Acts 1:4–5). The day of Pentecost was the moment when the disciples received this gift of fresh wind and fresh fire that moved in their hearts to lead them in their apostolic mission. The apostle Peter told the Jerusalem crowd, "Repent and be baptized, every one of you, in the name of Jesus Christ for the forgiveness of your sins. And you will receive the gift of the Holy Spirit" (Acts 2:38). According to Paul, the Spirit is sent into the hearts of believers so that they can address God as "*Abba*, Father" (Gal 4:6). The Spirit is closely connected to our experience of God's love since Paul told the Romans that "God's love has been poured out into our hearts through the Holy Spirit, who has been given to us" (Rom 5:5). Paul reminded the Corinthians that "we were all baptized by one Spirit so as to form one body—whether Jews or Gentiles,

---

2. As cited in Graham Cole, *He Who Gives Life: The Doctrine of the Holy Spirit* (Wheaton: Crossway, 2007), 283.

slave or free—and we were all given the one Spirit to drink" (1 Cor 12:13). The New Testament emphasizes repeatedly the experience of joy that comes upon those who are nourished by the Holy Spirit's presence. Jesus himself prayed when he was "full of joy through the Holy Spirit" (Luke 10:21). Luke recounts how the disciples in Pisidian Antioch, even after Paul and Barnabas were expelled from the city, were "filled with joy and with the Holy Spirit" (Acts 13:52). Paul praises the Thessalonians because they "welcomed the message in the midst of severe suffering with the joy given by the Holy Spirit" (1 Thess 1:6). We can hardly forget either that Christians are recipients of the "gifts of the Holy Spirit distributed according to his will" (Heb 2:4). Christians are told to "eagerly desire" the spiritual gifts (1 Cor 12:31; 14:1) and commanded to "be filled with the Spirit" (Eph 5:18). Taking all this together, the blessings of the gospel include new experiences such as new birth, Spirit baptism, the filling of the Holy Spirit, spiritual gifts, and everlasting joy. Hard not to get a little excited about that!

On top of that, we should remember that the Holy Spirit applies the work of Christ recounted in the gospel to us. The Spirit testifies to Christ because he wants to draw people into a relationship with Christ (John 15:26). The Holy Spirit is also the Spirit of Christ and as such is the glue that connects us to the Son (Rom 8:9; Phil 1:19; 1 Pet 1:11). Jesus taught that the life that he promises is given by the Spirit since "the Spirit gives life; the flesh counts for nothing" (John 6:63). Paul is similar when he says that the reason that there is no condemnation for those in Christ Jesus is because "through Christ Jesus the law of the Spirit who gives life has set you free from the law of sin and death" (Rom 8:2). We are even "justified in the name of the Lord Jesus Christ and by the Spirit of our God" (1 Cor 6:11). What this means, as John Calvin saw with unsurpassed clarity, is that the Holy Spirit is the bond of our union with Christ. It is through the agency of the Holy Spirit that the benefits of Christ's death and resurrection flow to us. When we are in the Spirit, then Christ is alive in us.[3]

Accordingly, life in the Spirit cannot be pursued apart from first apprehending the life given to us in Christ. The upshot is that it is very difficult to

---

3. John Calvin, *Institutes of the Christian Religion*, 3.1.1.

move in the Spirit without making much of Jesus Christ. In fact, a healthy account of life in the Holy Spirit must necessarily take into account the Trinitarian dimensions of the Spirit's work as he relates to the Father and to the Son. Anything less might reduce the Spirit to the Father's energy or the Son's ambiance, or else risk thinking of the Spirit in isolation altogether from the Father's purposes and the Son's mediatorial work. A biblically and theologically coherent doctrine of salvation will be authentically Pentecostal and will focus on the Spirit's witness to Christ and the Spirit's role in bringing us into union with Christ, and will locate these things as part of the wider Trinitarian reality of God's being and work. It would be very wrong not to stress such biblical truths about the Spirit in any church that strives to be a Spirit-filled congregation.

Thus the safety rope tied firmly around our waist, stopping us from falling over the cliffs of spiritual eccentricities, is recognizing that the Holy Spirit is the gift of the gospel and the agent of our union with Christ. We should never want to duck or brush over the study of the Holy Spirit; it is just too important a topic to neglect. Yet it must be handled with responsibility and maturity lest we focus on the Spirit's manifestations and thus diminish the Spirit's role as the material cause of all our riches in Christ. With that in mind, we can explore anew the person and work of the Holy Spirit.

The Divine Personhood of the Holy Spirit

R. A. Torrey, the great American evangelist and Bible teacher of the late 1800s and early 1900s, put the issue of the Spirit's divine personhood in very stark terms:

> It is of the highest importance from the standpoint of worship that we decide whether the Holy Spirit is a Divine Person, worthy to receive our adoration, our faith, our love, and our entire surrender to Himself, or whether it is simply an influence emanating from God or a power or an

illumination that God imparts to us. If the Holy Spirit is a person, and a Divine Person, and we do not know Him as such, then we are robbing a Divine Being of the worship and the faith and the love and the surrender to Himself which are His due.[4]

I think Torrey is right on the money; grasping the divine personhood of the Holy Spirit is absolutely vital if we are to have a proper understanding of God the Holy Spirit, the third member of the Trinity.

First, we should begin by noting that the Holy Spirit is a genuine person. Personhood is a complex matter; what makes one an actual person is something psychologists, sociologists, ethicists, and neurologists debate amongst themselves. To put it simply, I think we could agree that a person is someone who is self-aware, capable of cognition, has a capacity to relate to other beings, and possesses recognizable traits of character. A person is someone who can distinguish "I" from "you." The Holy Spirit meets this criterion as he speaks with an "I" on at least one occasion when he spoke through a prophet, "Set apart for me Barnabas and Saul for the work to which I have called them" (Acts 13:2). He also "testifies" about Jesus (1 John 5:6) and continually "speaks" to the churches (Rev 2:7, 11, 17, 29; 3:6, 13, 22). On other occasions, the Holy Spirit is said to be the one who speaks in Scripture by inspiring human authors (Acts 28:25; Heb 3:7; 10:15; 2 Tim 3:16; 2 Pet 1:21) or by animating prophecy (2 Sam 23:2; Ezek 11:5; Zech 4:6; Acts 21:11; 1 Cor 12:3; 1 Tim 4:1; Rev 14:13). The Holy Spirit is obviously a communicative agent who speaks from within the Godhead and speaks to and through people with an important message.

We find in the New Testament evidence of various activities and roles attributed to the Spirit that further imply that the Spirit is a personal agent. Jesus promised to send the Holy Spirit who would come as another *paraklētos* (from which we get the English word "Paraclete"). The translation of this word is notoriously complex and can mean something like "comforter," "advocate," or "helper" (John 14:16; 15:26; 16:7). The Holy Spirit is said to be another *paraklētos* who continues the ministry of Jesus in the midst of the

---

4. R. A. Torrey, *The Person and Work of the Holy Spirit* (New York: Revell, 1910), 2.

disciples as sent by the Father (John 14:16). His role is to witness, convict, guide, hear, speak, glorify, and declare (John 16:8–15). Paul's discourse in Romans 8 contains further images of the Spirit as an active person. There is the leading of the Holy Spirit as a privilege of being children of God (Rom 8:14), the witness of the Spirit to our own spirit (Rom 8:16), the help of the Spirit in prayer (Rom 8:26), and the intercessory work of the Spirit as linked to the "mind of the Spirit" (Rom 8:27). We also learn that the Spirit of God knows the thoughts of God (1 Cor 2:11), and it is the Spirit who decides how the grace gifts are to be distributed among the churches (1 Cor 12:4, 11; Heb 2:4). The Spirit can be insulted (Heb 10:29) and blasphemed (Matt 12:31–32). There is an encouragement that also comes from the Spirit of God (Acts 9:31), and the "Spirit of Jesus" also prevented Paul from going into Bithynia (Acts 16:7). Elsewhere Paul speaks of "grieving" the Holy Spirit (Eph 4:30) much in the same way that Isaiah referred to Yahweh's Holy Spirit being grieved by Israel's rebellion (Isa 63:10). Bruce Milne says that one can resist a power, but you can only grieve a person.[5] Thus, the Holy Spirit is not an impersonal force that descends from heaven. He is a person with personality, purpose, and prerogatives.

We should understand, secondly, that the Holy Spirit is not just any person but is a fully divine person. In the church fathers, consensus over the divine nature of the Holy Spirit was established relatively slowly, mainly because it took a backseat to christological debates about Jesus's deity and how his human and divine natures relate together. While some like Arius and Macedonius thought the Spirit was a lesser "god" than the Father and the Son, the Council of Constantinople affirmed the full and equal deity of the Holy Spirit, adding to the Creed of Nicaea that the Holy Spirit is "the Lord, the Giver of Life, who proceeds from the Father; with the Father and the Son he is worshipped and glorified." Such a theological claim is more than defensible since there is ample biblical justification for regarding the Holy Spirit as part of the divine identity. The Christian God must be defined in relation to the persons of the Father, Son, and the Holy Spirit.

There are references to the Holy Spirit in the New Testament that are

---

5. Bruce Milne, *Know the Truth*, 3rd ed. (Downers Grove, IL: InterVarsity Press, 2009), 222.

interchangeable with references to God. For instance, Peter told Ananias that by lying about the property he and his wife sold, they were lying to the Holy Spirit, yet in the next verse Peter adds that Ananias was lying to God (Acts 5:3–4). Similarly, Paul told the Corinthians that the body of believers is a "temple of God" (1 Cor 3:16–17); a bit later in the same letter he wrote that the body of believers is a "temple of the Holy Spirit" (1 Cor 6:19–20). At one point Paul even says that the "Lord is the Spirit" (2 Cor 3:17). It is commonly said that God raised Jesus from the dead (Acts 2:24, 32; 3:26; 4:10; 5:30; 10:40; 13:30, 37; Rom 10:9; Gal 1:1; 1 Pet 1:21), and yet it is stated elsewhere that the Spirit raised up Jesus (Rom 8:11). In the Gospels it is possible to commit blasphemy against the Holy Spirit, and this only makes sense if the Spirit is in some sense identifiable with God (Matt 12:28–31).

The Holy Spirit also possesses the qualities and attributes of God. The Holy Spirit is omniscient to the point that no one comprehends the thoughts of God except the "Spirit of God" (1 Cor 2:10–11). The Holy Spirit is also regarded as the presence of divine power when described as "the power of the Most High" (Luke 1:35). The Holy Spirit is described as the "eternal Spirit" (Heb 9:14). The Spirit is also the key agent in the act of creation (Gen 1:2; Job 33:4; Ps 104:30). The Holy Spirit is omnipresent and can be found in heaven, earth, and even in Sheol (Ps 139:7–10). God speaking to and through human subjects is often attributed to the agency of the Holy Spirit as the divine voice heard through speakers (Acts 4:25, 31; 28:25–27). It would appear then, as Cole puts it, that "The Holy Spirit is as much deity as is the Father as is the Son, but distinct as a person from both."[6]

The Holy Spirit's Work

That brings us to the work of the Holy Spirit. This is a big topic, and we shall have to zero in on the most salient aspects of it if we are to keep matters at a readable length. It will be clear that the Holy Spirit is a key agent in the various economies of God's work in the world. In short, we can point out

---

6. Cole, *He Who Gives Life*, 70.

that the Holy Spirit actively takes part in creation, revelation, salvation, and empowerment in fulfillment of God's plan to call a people to himself.

We see in the Old Testament that the Spirit is active in the creation of the world and in giving breath to all living things (Gen 1:1–2; Job 33:4; Ps 104:29–30). The Spirit gives gifts of intellect, skill, and artistry to equip God's people for the tasks that they are given (Exod 31:1–11). God's renovation of the world will be ushered in and through the power of the Spirit to unite the old earth with heaven in order to produce a new heaven and a new earth (Rev 21–22). The Holy Spirit is the architect of the new Jerusalem that the glorified saints will inhabit (Rev 21:1–3). The Holy Spirit is then intimately involved in bringing the world into existence, imparting life to men and women, giving them spiritual life, and renewing creation into its glorious and magnificent end state. We can surmise from this that the Holy Spirit is God's creative self, vitalizing and inventive, authorial and artistic. The Spirit is, dare I say, the arty side of God.

The Holy Spirit is crucial to our understanding of divine revelation. The Holy Spirit can be likened to the sound waves of the divine voice that echo forth into the world. The Holy Spirit reveals God's purposes to human creatures by inspiring prophets and apostles to speak forth the words of God in human speech, what we traditionally call divine inspiration. In the Old Testament, the prophetic message was a word from God given to the prophets by the Spirit. For instance Ezekiel writes, "Then the Spirit of the LORD came on me, and he told me to say . . ." (Ezek 11:5). This testimony is affirmed in the New Testament that the prophets spoke from God as carried along by the Holy Spirit (2 Pet 1:21). This prophetic ministry is also apparent in the early church with the office of "prophet" (Acts 13:1; 21:10; 1 Cor 12:28–29; Eph 2:20; 3:5; 4:11). Later we find that inspiration is also extended to *inscripturation*, committing the prophetic word and apostolic instruction to writing, where it becomes Scripture (2 Tim 3:16). Of course there is no point in giving a message unless it is understood. The Spirit not only reveals things but also ensures the effectiveness of the revelation itself. So the Holy Spirit performs an illuminating work so that the divine message is effectively understood by hearers. This is why the psalmist desires the Spirit to lead and teach him to do God's will (Ps 143:10). The role of the Spirit according to John is to teach

Jesus's disciples the things they need to know to follow him (John 14:26; 16:13). The Spirit is given specifically so that God's people "may understand what God has freely given us" (1 Cor 2:12–14).

Our conception of salvation should recognize the shape of the Spirit's work in us. The Spirit is the one who "gives life" (John 6:63; Rom 8:10–11; 2 Cor 3:6) principally by uniting us with Christ (Rom 8:2; 1 Cor 6:11; Eph 1:13). Our first experience of the Spirit's life-giving power is regeneration or new birth. Regeneration pertains to the spiritual change wrought in the heart of a person by the Holy Spirit. In this infusion of new life, the sinful heart is changed so that a person can respond to God in faith and live in accordance with God's will (John 3:3, 5, 7; Titus 3:5). He enlightens the darkened mind to behold spiritual realities (1 Cor 2:14–15; 2 Cor 4:6; Col 3:10) and liberates the enslaved soul for free obedience to God (Rom 6:14, 17–22; Phil 2:13). Daniel Migliore sums it up well: "The Spirit is the power of transformation from non-being to being, from the old to the new, from enslavement to the powers of sin and death to a new life in communion with God and others."[7]

Finally, in our brief survey of the Spirit's work we can consider the Spirit's empowering role. In the Old Testament the Holy Spirit often empowered people for ministries that served God's purposes. God empowered Joshua with leadership and wisdom (Num 27:18; Deut 34:9) and enabled the judges to deliver the nation from peril (Judg 3:10; 6:34; 11:29; 13:25; 14:6, 19; 15:14). The Holy Spirit was with Saul and David as part of their kingly office (1 Sam 11:6; 16:13). Jesus was uniquely empowered by the Spirit (Luke 4:14) and preached with the Spirit actively upon him (Luke 4:18–19). The prophecy about the abundant fullness of God's Spirit being poured out on "all people" in Joel 2:28–29 is fulfilled at Pentecost (Acts 2:16–18). We also find that the Spirit empowered Christians to work miracles like we see with Stephen (Acts 6:5, 8), Paul (Rom 15:19; 1 Cor 2:4), and others (Heb 2:4). But what is most noticeable of all is that the Holy Spirit empowers apostolic preaching of the gospel throughout Acts. The Spirit's empowerment also consists of equipping the church with spiritual offices of pastors, teachers,

---

7. Daniel L. Migliore, *Faith Seeking Understanding: An Introduction to Christian Theology*, 3rd ed. (Grand Rapids: Eerdmans, 2014), 237.

and evangelists (Eph 4:11), with a bounty of spiritual gifts (Rom 12:6–8; 1 Cor 12:7–11), and with the ability to fight spiritual struggles against the present evil age (Eph 6:17). It is true to say, as Gordon Fee put it, that the Holy Spirit is "God's empowering presence."[8]

Keeping in Step with the Spirit

The Holy Spirit can easily get neglected, and yet it is only to our own impoverishment. If we are serious about seeking the Spirit and being filled with the Spirit, then we have to cultivate a spirituality that has a big place for the Holy Spirit. A big task of discipleship is to "keep in step with the Spirit" (Gal 5:25), which means knowing him, following him, and growing in him.

Here's what we need to know: As a divine person, the Spirit is coeternal and coequal with Father and Son. He is the love between Father and Son. He is the grace between Christ and the believer. He is the presence of God's power and the power of God's presence on the earth. In salvation the Holy Spirit is both giver and the gift itself. What the gospel promises, the Holy Spirit actualizes: life, love, joy, and peace. In our spiritual life, the Spirit speaks, leads, helps, witnesses, and even inhibits where necessary. He raises us to a godly standard of virtue, illuminates our interpretation of Scripture, and hastens our feet to bring tidings of good news to the nations. Theological study without the Holy Spirit behind it would be drier than a James Bond martini. The Holy Spirit reminds us that we are not studying divine ideas but encountering divine persons, that faith is cognitive as well as charismatic, and that exegesis and experience go together. As we explore the meaning of our faith in God, the Holy Spirit quickens our minds so that our minds give the Spirit more to work with in terms of directing our actions, prayers, energy, and mission toward glorious and Godward ends.

---

8. Gordon D. Fee, *God's Empowering Presence: The Holy Spirit in the Letters of Paul* (Peabody, MA: Hendrickson, 1994), 5–9.

The Story Thus Far

When Christians confess their belief in God, they mean the triune God—Father, Son, and Holy Spirit. The Spirit is the member of the Trinity whose unique job it is to impart life, to quicken, and to provide breath to every living thing. All men and women, if they are to live to God, need the Spirit's regenerating work to bring them from darkness to light, to change their heart of stone to a heart of flesh, and to open their eyes to see the God who is there. Throughout redemptive history we find testimony to the Spirit's work in leading and guiding a people through the divine word that came upon prophets and kings. The climax of that history was of course Jesus Christ. Jesus himself was the anointed Spirit bearer and now also the exalted Spirit giver. The Spirit is a fully divine person, not an impersonal force, even though he comes in power like wind and fire. He reveals, rebukes, and rejoices. The Holy Spirit crafts and forms a spiritual people, advocates for them, and dwells within them as a deposit of the good things still to come. All of the Christian life, then, is the attempt to keep in step with the Spirit, to pursue his giftings, and to produce the fruit of the Spirit.

Recommended Reading

Burke, Trevor J., and Keith Warrington, eds. *A Biblical Theology of the Holy Spirit*. London: SPCK, 2014.

Carson, D. A. *Showing the Spirit: A Theological Exposition of 1 Corinthians 12–14*. Grand Rapids: Baker, 1987.

Cole, Graham. *He Who Gives Life: The Doctrine of the Holy Spirit*. Wheaton: Crossway, 2007.

Packer, J. I. *Keep in Step with the Spirit*. Old Tappan, NJ: Revell, 1984.

13

BELONGING
to the CHURCH

I believe in ... the holy catholic Church,
the communion of saints.

Introducing the Jesus People

The Apostles' Creed was written by the church and for the church and even mentions the church as one of the main beliefs of the faith to be confessed. Ironically though, the church is often one of the things forgotten or left out when we talk theology. The doctrines of the Trinity, the person of Christ, the atonement, and even the Holy Spirit are big players on the theological team, while the doctrine of the church often gets left on the sidelines to carry the water. That is because, sadly, the church usually is treated more like the packaging of theology rather than part of its content. Many folks have a view of the church that is so impoverished that they could probably qualify for theological food stamps.

Nick Perrin once wryly commented that for many people the church is little more than the weekly meeting of Jesus's Facebook friends.[1] It is merely a gathering of religious consumers with a common interest, much like a group of people gathered together at an Apple Store or those waiting

---

1. Nick Perrin, "Jesus's Eschatology and Kingdom Ethics: Ever the Twain Shall Meet," in *Jesus, Paul, and the People of God: A Theological Dialogue with N. T. Wright* (Downers Grove, IL: InterVarsity Press, 2011), 102.

for their connecting flight in the lounge of an airport. It is too easy to view the church as a convenient location to have one's spiritual needs satisfied. Church becomes the place where *I* go to get *my* God fix for the week. A place where *I* can get some encouragement from *my* favorite preacher. Somewhere *I* can attend to enjoy the worship music that *I* find uplifting. A convenient place where *I* can meet up with *my* Christian friends. A provider who exists primarily for *my* spiritual satisfaction and *my* religious pleasure. Whatever we might call that entity, consumerist religion or even McChristianity, it is certainly not church as Christians have ordinarily understood it. The church is not a local religious franchise with a mission statement to cater for *my* spiritual needs. The church is not a business, selling snack-sized portions of religion to the muddled masses who crave a few ounces of transcendence in their ordinary lives.

So what is the church? I would say that the church is the visible gathering of the faithful for the representation of Christ's presence to the world. This definition rules out a few things. For a start, the church is the people, not the steeple. The church is not the pews nor the pulpit, not the podcasts nor the programs. What I'm trying to stress is this: the church is not where we meet or what we do; it is who we are!

When believers meet together, they are recognizing each other as part of the Messiah's family of called out, baptized, sanctified, holy, Spirit-filled God lovers. They become something together that they are not themselves individually. There is no church of "me," only a church of "us." Paul reminds us and all who come after us that "you are the body of Christ, and each one of you is a part of it" (1 Cor 12:27). We are Christians only if we are churchians. A churchless Christianity is a contradiction like Christ without a body. That is why Augustine said, "He cannot have God for his father who has not the church for his mother!" To which John Calvin adds, "For there is no other way to enter into life unless this mother conceives us in her womb, gives us birth, nourishes us at her breast, and lastly, unless she keeps us under her care and guidance until, putting off mortal flesh, we become like the angels."[2] That is because our identity in Christ cannot be understood apart from our membership in the corporate body of Christ. As the African

---

2. Calvin, *Institutes of the Christian Religion*, 1.1.3–4.

theologian John Mbiti once said, "I am because we are; and since we are, therefore I am."[3] Our identity, individually and corporately, is bound up with the church as the living body of Christ on earth.

The doctrine of the church should not then be treated as an optional extra, like ordering a side salad with your christological main course. God's electing purposes have always been about calling and creating a bride for the Son (Isa 49:18; 61:10; Rev 19:7; 21:1–9). The story of Israel has been one of redemption, judgment, and renewal within God's plan to create a worldwide family to worship him (Isa 5; 27; Ezek 16; Amos 9; Zech 8; Mark 6–8; Rom 4; 9–11; Heb 11; Rev 7). At the center of God's kingdom is not only the king but the people ruled by the king, his royal subjects (Exod 19:5–6; 1 Pet 2:9). Jesus laid down his life and shed his blood not merely to make salvation possible but to actually save his flock, his church (John 10:11, 15; Acts 20:28). Paul could describe the church as those upon whom "the culmination of the ages has come," as they are the vanguard for the new creation (1 Cor 10:11). The church is a major player in God's plan to put the world to rights and to establish his sovereign reign over the nations. Kevin Vanhoozer has fittingly argued that the church is the "company of the gospel," a cast of actors who perform the redemptive drama of the gospel. The church gathers together, scripted by Scripture, under the direction of the Holy Spirit, illuminated by our traditions, in order to be built up into Christ. We go to church to rehearse, to celebrate, and to better understand the drama of redemption that reaches us in the gospel of Jesus Christ.[4]

One God, One People

When it comes to talking about the church, there is as always much we could haggle over, such as visible church vs. invisible church, church vis-à-vis kingdom, the sticky topic of the church and political power, the church in relation to ethnic Israel, and the church as local or universal. And this list does not even include debates about church sacraments and forms of church

---

3. John S. Mbiti, *African Religion and Philosophy*, 2nd ed. (Oxford: Heinemann, 1989), 141.
4. Kevin J. Vanhoozer, *The Drama of Doctrine: A Canonical-Linguistic Approach* (Louisville: Westminster John Knox, 2005), 399–444.

governance. But in mapping out a doctrine of the church, first and foremost we must remind ourselves that the one God has one plan for his one people.

When we talk about the church as the "people of God," we are referring to a constellation of images across both testaments that denote the believing community.[5] This includes images referring to this people as the "elect," God's "flock," "a kingdom of priests," and a "remnant." This is the people called by God into covenant with himself, and their origins lie in God's desire to have a people of his own (Deut 7:6). This people lives under the one covenant of grace across the various dispensations of redemptive history from Eden to the new Jerusalem. In the new covenant, Israel is expanded from an ethnic group into a fellowship of people of different nationalities and races. Israel is not replaced by gentiles; rather, Israel is expanded to include gentiles into its ranks. The "Israel of God," as Paul calls it, is the united commonwealth of Jews and gentiles sharing in one body (Gal 6:16; Eph 2:12–3:21). The church in its new covenant appearance is formed by the Holy Spirit, who unites persons with Christ (1 Cor 3:16; Eph 4:4) and joins them together in a shared confession of the lordship of Jesus Christ (Rom 10:9; 1 Cor 12:3).

To sum up the biblical images for the church, we could say that the church is one people under God, part of the story of God's plan to repossess the world for himself, living in union with Christ and nourished by the Spirit and projecting God's salvation into the world.

The Marks of the Church

In every family there are certain telltale signs of someone belonging to it. It might be children who look like their parents with the same hair or eye color, or share a particular way of talking, or follow a particular sports team, or like certain foods, or who share certain habits. Similarly, there are several characteristics shared by all churches, features which show a family resemblance and indicate that this group of people is part of Jesus's family, the church.

---

5. Paul S. Minear, *Images of the Church in the New Testament* (Philadelphia: Westminster, 1960), 67.

The first thing the Apostles' Creed says about the church is that we believe in "the holy catholic Church." The words "holy" and "catholic" are adjectives used to describe the nature of the church. The Nicene Creed expands this into "one holy catholic and apostolic church." Those four adjectives—one, holy, catholic, and apostolic—have traditionally been known as the marks of the church by which you can know that you have the true church. These marks are easily the best headings to use to parse what we mean when we use the word *church*.

Oneness

The *oneness* of the church derives from the electing purpose of God, who calls one people to be his treasured possession. God brought a people into being through the patriarchs by rescuing Israel and making a covenant with them, and the story of Israel is continued in the story of the church. The church has one head in Christ (1 Cor 11:3; Eph 4:15; 5:23; Col 2:10) and so it has only one body (Eph 5:23; Col 1:18, 24). This oneness entails the importance of unity among those who profess faith in God. Just as unity was vital for Israel (2 Chr 30:12; Ps 133), so it is also important for the church (John 17:23; Eph 4:13). Jesus prayed that his followers would be "one," just as the Father and the Son are one (John 17:11, 21). For Paul, the unity of the Spirit and the bond of peace is something to be earnestly pursued because "there is one body and one Spirit, just as you were called to one hope when you were called; one Lord, one faith, one baptism; one God and Father of all, who is over all and through all and in all" (Eph 4:4–6). The oneness of the church is beautifully symbolized in the one loaf of bread that we all share at the Lord's Supper (1 Cor 10:17). No wonder that many Christians prayed these words during the Lord's Supper: "As this broken bread was scattered upon the mountains and being gathered together became one, so may Thy Church be gathered together from the ends of the earth into Thy kingdom; for Thine is the glory and the power through Jesus Christ forever and ever."[6]

---

6. Didache 9.4 (J. B. Lightfoot and J. R. Harmer, eds., *The Apostolic Fathers* [London: Macmillan, 1891; repr., Grand Rapids: Baker, 1962], 126).

Sadly though, the church is not always unified or at one mind. The multiplicity of denominations is testimony to how badly the body of Christ has been rent into innumerable fellowships, with each thinking of itself as the only or truest part of Christ's people. As much as we can lament the division and disagreement between the various Christian groups, it is worth remembering that diversity has always been part of the church's life. You only have to read Luke's account of the Jerusalem council (Acts 15), listen to Paul recount the painful incident at Antioch (Gal 2:11–14), read Paul's plea to the Corinthians against factionalism (1 Cor 1:10–17), and notice Paul's attempt to reconcile two colleagues at odds with each other (Phil 4:2) to know that even the best of saints do not always get along and agree on important matters.

Diversity in the church has been an ever-present reality, yet often a good one since diversity brings together a multiplicity of gifts and graces. Christ's one body has many parts (1 Cor 12:12, 18, 20). Diversity, even theological diversity, can mean riches for the body of Christ since we are forced to expand our horizons beyond our own faith and practices. Other traditions can help us overcome the blind spots in our own tradition. Catholics remind us of the ancient roots of the church. Baptists remind us that Christians are Bible people and the church is for believers. Methodists remind us about the importance of piety and personal holiness. Presbyterians remind us about God's sovereignty and God's covenant promises. Pentecostals remind us that God's Spirit is still with us and not on sabbatical. Anglicans remind us to hold together the catholicity of our ancient faith with the protest of our Protestantism. Lutherans remind us to remain true to justification by faith. Even among these diverse fellowships, the fact that they can all recite the Apostles' Creed is proof that there is still one church professing a common faith in one God, through one Lord, in the power of one Spirit. While the church's oneness is invisible and created by the Holy Spirit, even so we are called to translate our invisible unity into visible expressions. Thus the challenge for the churches is, as Paul told the assemblies in Rome, to "make every effort to do what leads to peace and mutual edification" (Rom 14:19).

Holy

A further mark of the church is its *holiness*. The idea of holiness here does not mean that the church is entirely free of sin. I've visited enough churches to know that such is far from reality. The holiness that marks out the church is something that is both a divine gift and an urgent task. Holiness is first of all bestowed by God's consecration of the church to be his treasured possession. Then, secondly, God also calls his people to live in holiness before him. So on the one hand, believers are sanctified by virtue of their union with Jesus Christ, the Holy One (Acts 26:18; 1 Cor 1:30; 6:11; Eph 5:26; Heb 2:11; 10:29). Then on the other hand, Christians are to pursue holiness, to be holy just as God is holy (Lev 11:44; 19:2; Eph 1:4; 1 Thess 4:3, 7; 2 Tim 1:9; Heb 12:14; 1 Pet 1:15–16). A good example of this dual focus of holiness as gift and task can be found in the opening of 1 Corinthians where Paul writes, "To the church of God in Corinth, to those *sanctified in Christ* Jesus and *called to be his holy people*" (1:2; emphasis added). The holiness that Paul refers to here is both a position we have in Christ and also a calling to be appropriately lived out. Holiness is central to the mission of church. If the church is to make a difference, then it must be different. At the core of the church's difference from the world we find its holiness.

Catholic

Another mark of the church is its *catholicity*. No, not *Catholic* in the denominational sense of belonging to the Roman Catholic Church, but *catholic* in the technical sense of there being a universal church. One interesting thing about the early church is that they considered themselves to be a worldwide movement through a network of assemblies spread throughout Palestine, Syria, Asia Minor, Greece, and Italy. When Paul addressed the Corinthians, he referred to them as one chapter among those "everywhere who call on the name of our Lord Jesus Christ—their Lord and ours" (1 Cor 1:2). He lauded the Romans because their "faith is being reported all over the world" (Rom 1:8). Writing to the Colossians, he celebrates the fact that just as they received the gospel, so also "the gospel is bearing fruit and growing throughout the whole world" (Col 1:6). This is what is meant by the catholic or universal church. The church is not restricted by geography, ethnicity, gender, class, or status. It is a universal assembly that is made up of people from every tribe, language, culture, and place. There is one church that exists in all places, and yet it adheres to one faith. In the end, the catholicity of the church is simply the universal expression of its oneness. All believers, wherever they are, are one in Christ and therefore one with each other. The concept of "independent" churches then is an oxymoron. One cannot be "independent" of other churches any more than one can be independent of Christ. The mark of catholicity means recognizing that God is at work in other places, in other assemblies, drawing men and women to himself and drawing them together under the banner of Jesus Christ.

Apostolic

The mark of *apostolicity* designates the churches in their faithfulness to the apostolic message about Jesus Christ. You know when you buy a product that it will sometimes have a tag to indicate that it is a genuine product produced by Gucci, Apple, or the NFL. Similarly, apostolicity is the tag that indicates that you have a true church. The mark of an authentic church is holding to the teaching of the apostles about the gospel. This is what Paul meant by the gospel and the pattern of instruction that he himself received and passed on (1 Cor 11:2; 15:1–3; 1 Thess 2:13; 2 Thess 2:15; 3:6). Elsewhere in the New Testament there is a similar emphasis on receiving and transmitting apostolic tradition about Jesus (Luke 1:1–4; Phil 4:9; 2 Tim 1:13–14; Heb 10:32; Rev 3:3). The most lucid expression of this comes from Jude where we hear about "the faith that was once for all entrusted to God's holy people" (Jude 3). Apostolicity entails that the church is built on the foundation of the apostles and prophets (Eph 2:20). The church maintains the apostolic faith by guarding the good deposit of the gospel (2 Tim 1:14) and is constantly sending out messengers to declare the good news of the gospel (Matt 28:19–20; Luke 24:46–48; Acts 1:8). As Karl Barth said, "The Real Church is the assembly which is called, united, held together and governed by the Word of her Lord, or she is not a Real Church."[7]

---

7. Karl Barth, "The Real Church," *Scottish Journal of Theology* 3 (1950): 342.

Thus, we may conclude that the real, true, and genuine church consists of one, holy, catholic, and apostolic church. What this means in a nutshell is that: (1) The church is one since it lives under one Lord and heeds Jesus's command for unity; (2) the church is holy since it receives God's consecration by the Spirit of holiness and then calls its members to be led by the Spirit and to pursue Christlikeness; (3) the church is catholic since its borders are open and it resists any attempt at tribalism; and (4) the church is apostolic since it orients itself toward the first-century message of the apostles and the promotion of the gospel of Jesus Christ.[8]

A Common Union for a Common Good

The Apostles' Creed mentions the church as the "communion of saints." To say that the church is a communion simply means that it is a common union of believers. This communion exists *horizontally* among Christians who live and sometimes languish upon the earth and *vertically* with the departed members who are alive with Christ in heaven. In other words, neither geography nor death can fracture the church from its union with one another and affection for each other. Importantly, the New Testament assumes that Christians will share in the life of a local fellowship, meeting for worship and encouragement, engaging in preaching and teaching of the Word, submitting themselves to accountability and discipline, and sharing in the work of a common mission. Going to church does not make you a Christian any more than going to McDonald's makes you a hamburger. But it is hard to imagine a Christian without a love for God's people or without an enjoyment of the corporate worship of God when they gather together. A Christian should be committed to serving the church and his or her community, to nurturing themselves on the sacraments or ordinances of the gospel, and to hungering for a regular diet of biblical instruction. The common life of the church is the place where God's gifts and graces are most acutely manifested and where sick and weary souls go to be fed,

---

8. Cf. Matt Jenson and Dave White, *The Church: A Guide for the Perplexed* (London: T&T Clark, 2010), 79–82.

healed, strengthened, encouraged, and equipped to be the people God has called them to be.

A Peculiar People in a Postmodern World

I rather like how the old King James calls God's people—both Israel and the church—by the name "a peculiar people" (Deut 26:18; Titus 2:14; 1 Pet 2:9). Now I know that this is Elizabethan language for "treasured/special people"; however, there is something very true about the church as peculiar in the sense of "odd" or "strange." I mean, Christians really can be peculiar or weird if you listen to anything they say and watch stuff that they do. To a visitor from out of town or from outer space with no knowledge of Christianity, visiting a church would lead to all sorts of puzzled looks. Why is everyone wearing a mathematical plus sign around their necks? Why sing "hims" rather than "hers"? Why does everyone refer to the head honcho as "pasta"? Can we eat him the same way we eat the body of Jesus and drink the blood of Jesus (which is not actually flesh and blood but just bread and wine in case nobody has noticed)? Is this "Jesus" related to the Puerto Rican boxer I heard about on the radio? "Father, Son, and Holy Spirit"? Exactly how many gods are in this crazy religion? Why does that guy suddenly sound like he's reading Shakespeare when he prays by reverting to "thy" and "thou"? Why is a baby getting a bath such a big deal; have you never seen a baby bathed before? And what is this NIV book that I see everyone reading? And why, oh why, do you people insist on pronouncing "job" with a long "o" to make "j-oh-b"? Let me add that this is not stuff I'm making up. This is the kind of thing I've had non-Christians ask me when they observed a Christian worship service for the first time. Christian language, behavior, and worship look weird to outsiders.

Of course, the peculiarity of Christians is nothing new. Christians have always looked peculiar to outsiders. In the ancient world, Christians appeared strange because they were very Jewish, they read the Jewish Scriptures, they worshipped the one God of the Jews, and they believed in Israel's Messiah. Yet they had none of the ethnic symbols of the Jews like circumcision and Sabbath keeping, and they opened their ranks to non-Jews as full members. Christians claimed to have a "religion," but they did not have a dedicated temple or priesthood, and didn't make sacrifices like other Greco-Roman religions did. How can you do "religion" without all that? In addition, how can a good Roman citizen stoop down to wash the feet of someone of a lower station like a slave or break bread with a barbarian? Worshipping a crucified criminal was deplorable and believing in the resurrection of the dead was like hoping for a zombie apocalypse. To outsiders, all of this was weird, whacky, and even a little wrong. Yet in my mind, the church needs more than ever to pursue its peculiarity as a missional imperative.[9] The motto of the city of Austin, Texas is "keep Austin weird"; so too we need to work and to act to keep Christianity weird. If we are going to make a difference, then we need to be different.[10]

Know this: the world of our parents and grandparents is no more. We have to realize that the Western world has changed; it either already is or else is very quickly becoming decidedly post-Christian and radically secular. The church is no longer the chaplain for Christendom; it is now a recalcitrant resistance to the secularizing agenda. The church is no longer the moral majority; it is now the immoral minority with offensive views on everything from family to religious pluralism and sexuality. The church is no longer the first estate but more like an enemy of the state through its unflinching devotion to God and its uncompromising refusal to bow the knee to the cultural and political lords of the land.

As the church of the twenty-first century enters its adolescence, we have to prepare, culturally and politically speaking, to be exiled within our own cities and to be aliens in our own lands. The church's previously privileged position as a religious and moral authority is gradually being eroded as Western countries become more culturally diverse and highly secularized.

---

9. On this, see Rodney Clapp, *A Peculiar People: The Church as Culture in a Post-Christian Society* (Downers Grove, IL: InterVarsity Press, 1996).

10. See Sarah Pulliam Bailey, "Russell Moore Wants to Keep Christianity Weird," *Christianity Today*, 08 September 2015, http://www.christianitytoday.com/ct/2015/september/russell-moore-wants-to-keep-christianity-weird.html.

While there are some grounds for lament here, this move to the margins might not actually be a bad thing. Stanley Hauerwas and Will Willimon comment that as we enter the twilight of the old Constantinian world, "We have an opportunity to discover what has and always is the case—that the church, as those called out by God, embodies a social alternative that the world cannot on its own terms know."[11] This is our chance to be the "salt of the earth" and "the light of the world" (Matt 5:13–14), to turn "the world upside down" (Acts 17:6 ESV), to "shine . . . like stars" (Phil 2:15), and to demonstrate that "in this world we are like Jesus" (1 John 4:17). What the church has to offer the world is not our architecture, our programs, our press releases, our politics, our clergy, or even our potlucks. The best thing and really the only thing we have to offer is Jesus Christ. The one thing that the church can offer that no other organization or institution can is Jesus as Lord and Savior of all peoples. The mission of this peculiar people called the church is to live and love, serve and sing, preach and teach that Jesus Christ is Lord.

The Story Thus Far

Christians believe in God—Father, Son, and Holy Spirit—who together made the heavens and the earth. The human race was God's crowning achievement, and yet they tried to usurp God's sovereign power by their disobedience, leading to the introduction of corruption, guilt, and death into the world. Yet God has been working through his people, the patriarchs and Israel, to rescue the world. The climactic moment of that rescue happened with the coming of Jesus of Nazareth. This Jesus, human in every way and divine in every way, proclaimed the kingdom, died an atoning death, was raised in glory, and has ascended to God's right hand to rule as humanity's vice-regent at the Father's side. It is the ascended Jesus who pours out the Spirit upon his people, equipping them to be witnesses to him and to build for the kingdom on earth. This spiritual people serves as a billboard,

---

11. Stanley Hauerwas and William H. Willimon, *Resident Aliens: Life in the Christian Colony* (Nashville: Abingdon, 1988), 17–18.

pointing ahead to the day when God will usher in his new creation and wipe every tear from their eyes so that the world will be reborn into God's resplendent glory.

Recommended Reading

Basden, Paul A., and David S. Dockery, eds. *The People of God: Essays on the Believers' Church*. Nashville: Broadman & Holman, 1991.

Bird, Michael F. "Part Eight: The Community of the Gospelized." Pages 697–805 in *Evangelical Theology: A Biblical and Systematic Introduction*. Grand Rapids: Zondervan, 2013.

Harper, Brad, and Paul Louis Metzger. *Exploring Ecclesiology: An Evangelical and Ecumenical Introduction*. Grand Rapids: Brazos, 2009.

Horton, Michael S. *People and Place: A Covenant Ecclesiology*. Louisville: Westminster John Knox, 2008.

BELIEVING *in* SALVATION, WAITING *for* GOD'S NEW WORLD

I believe in . . . the forgiveness of sins,
the resurrection of the body,
and the life everlasting.
Amen.

Forgiveness and Forever

As we approach the close of the Apostles' Creed, we see that this short little syllabus of Christian teaching ends by affirming our reconciliation to God and our hope for eternal life through Jesus Christ. God's people can be assured that they are forgiven on account of Christ; they can rest knowing that they will be resurrected by the Spirit of God and will inhabit the Father's new world. And so we reach the climax of the Creed with mention of salvation, resurrection, and eternal life. These tenets, I suspect, are deliberately placed here to specifically remind Christians of the hope upon which we have put our faith, namely, that God accepts us, God will rescue us from death, and God promises to be with us forever.

When Did You Get Saved?

There was once an evangelist who would walk around airports, go up to travelers, and ask them, "When did you get saved?" His operating assumption was that these people were not "saved," and his job was to tell them how to get saved and avoid the flames of hell. But one day the evangelist got quite a surprise. On one occasion the person he asked was a retired pastor. The evangelist went up to him and asked rather abruptly, "Are you saved? When did you get saved? Can you tell me when you got saved?" The pastor stopped in his tracks, feeling a bit accosted by the well-intentioned though somewhat intrusive evangelist. He paused for a moment, scratched his head, and replied, "I got saved two thousand years ago, but I only found out about it recently!" Then promptly walked off! The evangelist equated salvation with making a decision to accept Jesus. That is true in a sense, as the moment when one first believes is a defining event in one's salvific journey. In contrast, the pastor referred to events that took place at Easter some two thousand years earlier, the cross and resurrection, as the moment when his salvation occurred. Again, that is true; the cross and resurrection are the fulcrum on which our salvation hinges because it is where atonement for sins is made and new life is launched into our world. Although the airport evangelist and traveling pastor were both correct, they emphasized different aspects of salvation. The evangelist was interested in the subjective side of salvation, where and when a person made a faith response to the gospel, while the pastor emphasized the objective side of salvation, when and where God's act of salvation was made manifest. In the interests of keeping it simple, we could say that salvation has three tenses: past, present, and future. According to oral tradition, the British biblical scholar B. F. Westcott was once asked if he was "saved," to which he replied to the effect, "I was saved, I am being saved, I will be saved."[1] It is these three tenses of salvation that we will explore below.

---

1. See B. F. Westcott, *St. Paul's Epistle to the Ephesians: The Greek Texts with Notes and Addenda* (London: Macmillan, 1906), 32.

Saved before the Foundation of the World

For a start, we could say that salvation is a prior event, going all the way back to eternity past and God's decision "before the creation of the world" to be the God who calls and redeems a people through the sacrificial death of Jesus Christ (Eph 1:4; 1 Pet 1:20; Rev 13:8). The cross, resurrection, and giving of the Spirit are likewise past events that determine salvation for everyone. Salvation, then, includes the series of past events in redemptive history that God has wrought to reconcile us to himself. We were saved in eternity past, at Golgotha, and on the day of Pentecost!

I Have Decided to Follow Jesus!

Next we have to add that salvation is a present experience, even a process that begins with our decision to receive Christ and that continues in our Christian life. Luke records how God's Spirit moved in the early church so that "the Lord added to their number daily those who were being saved," emphasizing the present and ongoing nature of salvation (Acts 2:47). Paul instructed the Philippians "to work out your salvation with fear and trembling, for it is God who works in you to will and to act in order to fulfill his good purpose" (Phil 2:12–13)—that is, work out what God has worked into you. The process of salvation is a series of events, encompassing transformation, growing in holiness, imitation of God, and conformity to the image of Christ. God does not save us and then leave us be; instead, he continues to work in us and through us to make us little replicas of his Son. That is what it means to be counted among those who are "being saved."

Patiently Waiting

Finally, salvation is future; it is "not yet" and awaits a future point of completion. This is why Paul and Barnabas encouraged all the believers in the churches they visited with the words, "We must go through many hardships to enter the kingdom of God" (Acts 14:22). Peter exhorted the churches in Asia Minor, "This inheritance is kept in heaven for you, who through faith are shielded by God's power until the coming of the salvation that is ready to be revealed in the last time" (1 Pet 1:4–5). The completion of salvation for both the living and the dead takes place at the return of Jesus, when he establishes his kingdom, sits in judgment of the wicked, and thereafter unveils the new heaven and new earth. The interim time is one of patient endurance, faithfulness, and pursuit of holiness. It requires a disposition, which Jude describes as "building yourselves up in your most holy faith and praying in the Holy Spirit, keep yourselves in God's love as you wait for the mercy of our Lord Jesus Christ to bring you to eternal life" (Jude 20–21).

The Salvation Story

It is helpful to remember that the Bible uses a wide variety of images to describe salvation, often in one dense space like Psalms 51:1–4, 103:1–10, and Romans 5:1–11 where authors pile up one image after another to describe God's rescuing work in all of its glorious array. Among the images are redemption, reconciliation, rescue, renewal, cleansing, forgiveness, justification, adoption, pacification, eternal life, and even deification. The Apostles' Creed regards "forgiveness of sins" as a convenient head term to encompass the whole package of salvation. Luke seems to regard "forgiveness of sins" as a shorthand reference to the gospel message (Luke 1:77; 7:37–50; 11:4; 24:47; Acts 2:38; 5:31; 10:43; 13:38; 26:18), while Paul prefers the key terms of "justification" (Rom 4:25; 5:1, 18; 8:30) or "reconciliation" (Rom 5:11; 2 Cor 5:18–21).

I am inclined to think that no single image for salvation really has the capacity to explain everything about salvation. We will always need a host of adjectives and adverbs to describe the meaning of salvation. It takes a few moments to describe what we are saved from, what we are saved to, and whom we are saved by. Yet all of the diverse images point to the same reality—that God, instead of wiping out rebels, wipes out our sins. He wipes them out with the blood of his beloved Son.[2] Thereafter, his people can be forgiven, justified, reconciled, or whatever image we think fit to describe it.

---

2. See D. A. Carson, *The God Who Is There: Finding Your Place in God's Story* (Grand Rapids: Baker, 2010), 27–42.

Together we come to worship God, not as a judge waiting to condemn us but as our Savior who loves us. The forgiven family meets to rejoice in the God who saves his people from the penalty of sin (justification), the power of sin (transformation), and even the presence of sin (glorification).

The true meaning of salvation, when understood in its scope of past, present, and future and in light of the diverse array of biblical images used for it, is more than the rescue of the sinner's soul and more than fire insurance against hell. Salvation, biblically conceived and theologically explored, is holistic and includes the whole person comprised of body, heart, mind, and soul. David Bentley Hart bemoans the "rather feeble and formal way many Christians have habitually thought of [salvation] at various periods in the Church's history: as some sort of forensic exoneration accompanied by a ticket of entry into an Elysian aftermath of sun-soaked meadows and old friends."[3] In Scripture, salvation can mean deliverance from enemies, physical danger, death, disability, demonic powers, illness, impurity, poverty, injustice, social exclusion, false accusation, shame, and of course sin and its consequences before God. Undoubtedly what lies behind the misery and mortality of the human condition is sin, a power that corrupts us as much as it kills us. Sin affects everything around us—the physical world as much as our spiritual state; everything is fallen and in decay. Salvation is deliverance from all that is fallen in us and around us. If the Old Testament prophets and the ministry of Jesus teach us anything, it is that God profoundly cares about the life of his covenant people and all people in general even ahead of a final judgment. Scripture affirms God's desire to save us in our future eternal state as much as it affirms God's desire to save us in our current physical state. If we take into account the *whole* biblical witness, it yields a *holistic* understanding of salvation.

---

3. David Bentley Hart, "The Lively God of Robert Jenson," *First Things* 156 (2005): 15.

World without End

There was once a dear old lady named Meryl. At her funeral, as many relatives and friends were paying their respects, everyone who drew near the open casket came away feeling a little confused. Meryl was lying there holding a fork in her hand. Gradually the guests took their seats, and when the burial service began the minister stood up and addressed the congregation of mourners.

"Dear friends," he said, "thank you for coming, but before we begin our service I'm sure you are all wondering why our dear sister Meryl lies in state holding a fork. Well, I have to tell you that Meryl's final request was to be buried with a fork in her hand. I have done a number of funerals in my time and received all sorts of requests from people about how they would like their funeral to be conducted. Meryl's request was certainly one of the strangest requests I have heard. When I asked her why, she explained, 'When I was a little girl, my grandmother would take me to church, and after the service there would always be a selection of cakes and desserts. Often I would eat a piece of cake and then put my fork and plate away. But sometimes my grandmother would come up and tell me to keep my fork because the best desserts were yet to come. The reason I want to be buried holding a fork is because, just as my grandmother told me, I believe that the best is still yet to come.' And that, my dear friends, is why Meryl asked to be buried holding a fork. The best for her was yet to come, though I believe that for her it has come!"

Meryl's story is a wonderful reminder that Christian faith is forward-looking and rests upon God's promise that his people will enjoy life everlasting. This is why Paul wrote to Titus about "the hope of eternal life" (Titus 1:2; 3:7). It is this hope that gives us courage, purpose, and a belief that no matter what trials and travesties we face in this life, that in the end, all shall be well. Without this hope Christians would be a pitiable people (1 Cor 15:19). Yet we take it on faith that where Christ is, there his people shall one day be as well (Phil 1:23), that Christ has prepared a place for us (John 14:2–3), that we will be "at home with the Lord" (2 Cor 5:8) in a place where John tells us, "There will be no more death or mourning or crying or pain, for the old order of things has passed away" (Rev 21:4). Such a blessed future is the blessed hope of Christians.

This is what the Apostles' Creed means when it refers to "the resurrection of the body, and the life everlasting." However, this requires some unpacking since much of what people think of our future life with Christ owes more to caricatured images of heaven in cartoons, movies, medieval art, and greeting cards than to the biblical portrait of the afterlife. What I want to do is briefly set out our blessed hope as it relates to heaven, the resurrection of the dead, and the new creation.

Heaven on My Mind

To begin with we should note that in biblical language, *heaven* refers to the cosmological world above and beyond earth (Gen 1:1; Matt 5:18). Heaven is the abode of God (Deut 4:39; Matt 6:9) and the place from whence Jesus will be revealed at the end of history (1 Thess 1:10; 4:16; 2 Thess 1:7). Heaven is the divine command center from which the Almighty orders the cosmos and abounds in divine splendor. It is interesting that when John of Patmos was granted a vision of heaven, it is like he's summoned to view a place that is a cross between a military headquarters and the throne room of a monarch. It's a mixture of an operations room planning the conquest of evil, combined with worship that abounds in symbols, metaphors, and visions which language stretches to adequately describe (Rev 4–5).[4]

We also associate heaven with hope and blessing in the here and now. Heaven is the place of our treasure (Matt 6:19–20; 19:21), our citizenship (Phil 3:20), our inheritance (1 Pet 1:4–5), and where our hope is laid up (Col 1:5). That does not mean, though, that we have to go to heaven in order to get them any more than we have to actually crawl into the fridge to get the beer kept cold for us.[5] We already enjoy many heavenly blessings in the present time as joyous anticipations of the life that is to come. The church's

---

4. G. B. Caird, *A Commentary on the Revelation of St. John the Divine* (London: A. & C. Black, 1966), 60–61.

5. N. T. Wright, *The Resurrection of the Son of God*, Christian Origins and the Question of God 3 (London: SPCK, 2003), 368; idem, *Surprised by Hope: Rethinking Heaven, the Resurrection, and the Mission of the Church* (New York: HarperOne), 151–52.

earthly life is like looking through a glass darkly into our future eternal life. Heaven is not all about clouds, angels, and elevator music. Heaven is the seat of God's throne and the source of the hope that we currently possess here on earth.

Heaven is also the place where believers go upon death. It is where we receive our "heavenly dwelling" (2 Cor 5:1–4) and go to be with Christ, "which is better by far" (Phil 1:23). For our departed saints, as Sunday school children rightly sing, "Heaven is a wonderful place filled with glory and grace," because one is transported into the presence of the Lord Jesus Christ. We must remember that heaven is not a dreamlike holiday resort, where we spend our time playing harps and challenging angels to volleyball contests. If we listen to the biblical witness, we learn that heaven is a place of both longing for the future state (Rev 6:10–11) and a place of worship (Rev 7:13–17). Heaven is not our final home and from all accounts looks like a rather busy place. The heavenly state can be likened to being wrapped in a blanket of joy, but still anticipating through worship the full blessings yet to come in the new creation. Heaven is a glorious interlude before the end but is not our final destination. That is because heaven is a temporary abode until the resurrection of the dead and the arrival of the new creation. Heaven is a waiting place for people who belong in the new heaven and the new earth. I invite you to read Revelation 21–22 and to ponder the glorious picture of a new Jerusalem coming down from heaven to earth. Though God made heaven and earth, he intends in the end to remake both and to join them together forever.[6] So although heaven might be a rewarding and blessed state for departed saints to be with Christ, it is certainly not the final state. The final state we long for is not heaven but the renovation of heaven and earth and the joining of the two together. We will live for eternity, not as disembodied spirits floating around like leaves caught in the wind but in glorified human bodies enjoying God's new creation. For believers, heaven is life after death, but resurrection is life *after* life *after* death.[7] Or, as N. T. Wright puts it, "Heaven is important, but it is not the end of the world."[8]

---

6. Wright, *Surprised by Hope*, 19.
7. Wright, *Surprised by Hope*, 148.
8. Wright, *Surprised by Hope*, 52.

What the Ending Looks Like:
Resurrection and Recompense

In addition, the end will begin with the return of Jesus, who will usher in the resurrection of the dead and the final judgment. Paul gives us a brief picture of the end at the return of Jesus. He writes, "For the Lord himself will come down from heaven, with a loud command, with the voice of the archangel and with the trumpet call of God, and the dead in Christ will rise first. After that, we who are still alive and are left will be caught up together with them in the clouds to meet the Lord in the air. And so we will be with the Lord forever" (1 Thess 4:16–17). Paul's primary point is pastoral—assuring his readers that those who have died will not miss out on the resurrection. When Jesus returns, the Spirit will raise those still living and those who have already passed away, bringing life and infusing glory into their bodies. And how we wish Paul said more about it! I will resist the temptation to delve into debates about tribulations, raptures, and a millennium and focus instead on the main thing: at the return of Jesus there is a resurrection of the dead.

God will raise the dead in the same way that he raised Jesus (Rom 8:11; 1 Cor 6:14). The nature of this resurrection body is such that "the body that is sown is perishable, it is raised imperishable; it is sown in dishonor, it is raised in glory; it is sown in weakness, it is raised in power" (1 Cor 15:42–43). Resurrection shows that our future life entails the redemption *of* our bodies, not redemption *from* our bodies (Rom 8:23). What this future resurrection body is like, we do not know for sure. It is a physical, glorified, and immortal body that cannot succumb to death and decay.[9] I find it interesting that biochemists inform us that during a seven-year cycle the molecular composition of our bodies is completely changed. But in spite of the permanent state of mutation in which we exist, our personal identity is maintained, and we are the same personal and psychological entity that we have always been. The same is undoubtedly true about our future resurrection bodies; they are remade, but we remain the same person.[10] Going further than that, perhaps

---

9. See Murray J. Harris, *Raised Immortal: Resurrection and Immortality in the New Testament* (Grand Rapids: Eerdmans, 1985), 98–171.
10. Harris, *Raised Immortal*, 126.

the best we can do is follow the godly imagination of C. S. Lewis who said that our future bodies will be more real, more substantial, and perhaps even more human than our present ones.[11]

What I suggest you take away from this is that Christians do not believe in the immortality of the soul but in the resurrection of the body. Although the soul or spirit may depart to be with the Lord upon death, it is only an interim state. The state after that, life *after* life after death, is resurrection! Thus we need to bring our congregations back to the language of resurrection and new creation to underscore the embodied and physical nature of our future hope. A lot rides on getting this right. The difference is between the pagan idea of escaping creation and the Christian idea of God renewing creation. As Michael Horton declares, "The pagan idea of the immortality of the soul and the Christian doctrine of the gift of everlasting life issue in radically different worldviews."[12]

It is not only believers who are resurrected but also unbelievers, the wicked, to face a resurrection unto judgment. Daniel announced that "multitudes who sleep in the dust of the earth will awake: some to everlasting life, others to shame and everlasting contempt" (Dan 12:2). According to the Gospel of John, Jesus taught that "a time is coming when all who are in their graves will hear his voice and come out—those who have done what is good will rise to live, and those who have done what is evil will rise to be condemned" (John 5:28–29). The fact that Jesus warned that one's body could be thrown into hell shows that the final judgment is an embodied punishment (Matt 5:29–30). Hell is elsewhere described as the "fiery abyss" where the wicked go after the general resurrection (Mark 9:43). For the wicked and disobedient, hell is "eternal fire," "eternal punishment" (Matt 25:41, 46), and outer darkness (Matt 8:12). In Revelation, the final place of the wicked is expressed as a "shaft of the Abyss" or bottomless pit (Rev 9:1–2, 11), a place of "torment" (Rev 14:10–11), a "second death" (Rev 21:8), and a lake of "burning sulfur" (Rev 14:10; 19:20; 20:10; 21:8).

Of course the themes of final judgment, hell, and eternal separation from God have always been theologically controversial. Many have sought

---

11. C. S. Lewis, *The Great Divorce* (London: Macmillan, 1946), 87.
12. Michael Horton, *The Christian Faith* (Grand Rapids: Zondervan, 2011), 908.

to soften the severity of divine recompense by envisaging hell as merely metaphorical or perhaps temporary, or by teaching that maybe the unrighteous are annihilated rather than tormented forever. Yet if we get beyond the cultural stereotypes of hell as some kind of subterranean cavern where cadavers are reanimated to experience the enduring torment of being perpetually prodded by devils with pitch forks, we can regard hell as more like a cosmic Hague where the inhumanity of humanity is given fitting recompense for choosing evil and rebellion over the love and mercy of God. Perhaps we could say that hell will be that dimension of the future reality that quarantines evil, much like the last traces of smallpox are locked in a secured laboratory so that it can never escape. I suspect that those in hell will mourn their bitter state, but they will still rage against the one that put them there. What is more, some might still prefer in the end to languish in hell than to serve in heaven, for in hell they still may be able to savor and enjoy their defiance against God. Hell is the place for creatures who have rejected God's revelation of himself in both nature and in the gospel, who refuse to bow the knee to the one true Lord, and who would rather live in darkness than in the light that exposes them as wicked. I surmise, following N. T. Wright, that persons who have entered into a posthuman state become what they worship—greed, lust, power—and cease to reflect the divine image in any meaningful sense. They arrive at a state beyond hope and beyond pity. Hell, then, is the eternal and punitive quarantining of a humanity that has ceased to be human.[13]

The Marriage of Heaven and Earth

It is vital that we remember that our ultimate hope is not heaven but dwelling forever in the new heaven and new earth. The Bible's best kept secret according to J. Richard Middleton is that it teaches a "holistic vision of God's intent to renew or redeem creation" (Matt 19:28; Acts 3:21).[14] Heaven and earth are changed into the new creation. Heaven does not swallow up earth and earth does not simply absorb heaven. The earth is transfigured

---

13. Wright, *Surprised by Hope*, 182–83.

14. J. Richard Middleton, *A New Heaven and a New Earth: Reclaiming Biblical Eschatology* (Grand Rapids: Baker, 2014), 24.

into a heavenly plane of existence and the dividing line between heaven and earth is obliterated. Heaven becomes earthly and earth becomes heavenly. While our hope is stored up in heaven (Col 1:5), it does not consist of heaven; rather, as Peter writes, "We are looking forward to a new heaven and a new earth, where righteousness dwells" (2 Pet 3:13).

Eternal life will be terrestrial life lived in the glorious space of the new creation; this is the "life everlasting" that the Apostles' Creed summons us to believe. We first read about a new heaven and a new earth in Isaiah 65–66. Those who remain faithful to the one true God will forget their "past troubles" when the Lord brings his new world into being (65:16). Immediately following, Isaiah reports God's promise: "See, I will create new heavens and a new earth. The former things will not be remembered, nor will they come to mind. But be glad and rejoice forever in what I will create, for I will create Jerusalem to be a delight and its people a joy. I will rejoice over Jerusalem and take delight in my people; the sound of weeping and of crying will be heard in it no more" (65:17–19). The picture that Isaiah gives to us consists of the absolute and inscrutable reign of the Lord who sovereignly renews the cosmos, and this new place is characterized by intense and irrepressible joy. The new creation will give people an everlasting life that is contrasted with the judgment of those who rebelled against God (66:22–24).

In Revelation 21, John first describes the final state as a new heaven and new earth (v. 1), and then moves to describe a new Jerusalem (vv. 2, 10–21). This is not a two-staged revelation of the end through a new heaven and new earth followed by a new Jerusalem; these images portray one and the same new creation. The vision represents a merging of the new heaven and new earth from Isaiah 65–66 with the new temple imagery from Ezekiel 40–48 in order to display the transcendent abode of God and God's people at the very end. In Revelation 21:1–22:5 we see a convergence of the scriptural themes of new covenant, new temple, new Israel, new Jerusalem, and new creation. It depicts the one reality of God's intimate and glorious presence with his redeemed and renewed people.[15] In our resurrection bodies we will

---

15. Greg K. Beale, *Revelation*, NIGTC (Grand Rapids: Eerdmans, 1999), 173.

do in the new creation what Adam and Eve were supposed to do in Eden—reign over God's world and enjoy God forever!

The Apostles' Creed reminds us that Christian hope is for life, an eternal life that can never end or fade. It is a hope that takes us through heaven, into resurrection, and then to dwelling forever in the new creation. God's new world ahead of us is our inheritance and our home. This is not something to file away in your head under "afterlife" next to your mental compartment for "religious stuff" or "funeral arrangements." The terrestrial life of the new creation of the future radically shapes our attempt in the present to fill earth with the life of heaven.

The Story Complete

The story of our faith, as the Apostles' Creed teaches us, is this: we believe in God, the Father almighty, from whom the Son is eternally begotten and from whom the Spirit proceeds, one God in three persons. God the Father, with the Son and the Spirit acting like his hands, is the creator of heaven and earth. Humanity was created to rule over God's creation but fell into transgression and corruption. God's saving plan and promise was to rescue this world, and this rescue began with the call of Abraham and with his covenant with Israel, through whom the promised deliverer would come. It is in the midst of Israel that Jesus was conceived by the power of the Holy Spirit and born of the Virgin Mary. His mission was to bring Israel's story to its climax and to dethrone the evil that tyrannized the world. His gospel of the kingdom drew together the nucleus of a renewed Israel among his followers, who would carry God's purposes forward to the ends of the earth. After Jesus came to Jerusalem for one fateful visit, he suffered under the injustice of Pontius Pilate, was crucified, died, and was buried. Jesus's death was an atonement for sins, his resurrection on the third day was the start of the new creation, and his ascension into heaven marked the beginning of a new divine order over the world. The church now has the duty of living in the power of the Holy Spirit to declare the forgiveness of sins and the restoration of all things. We do this until the glorious day when Jesus returns from heaven to put the world to rights, to judge the living and the dead, to rescue his people, and to bring them into the new heaven and new earth. The goal of our hope is not a disembodied bliss in heaven but rather the resurrection of the body and life everlasting in God's new world. This is the Christian story, the church's story, the story we live by, the story which gets our "amen." This is the story we sing about and proclaim until such a time when "God's dwelling place is now among the people, and he will dwell with them. They will be his people, and God himself will be with them and be their God" (Rev 21:3).

Recommended Reading

Bird, Michael F. "The Intermediate State: What Happens When You Die?" and "The Final State: Heaven, Hell, and New Creation." Pages 309–39 in *Evangelical Theology: A Biblical and Systematic Introduction*. Grand Rapids: Zondervan, 2013.

Colijn, Brenda B. *Images of Salvation in the New Testament*. Downers Grove, IL: InterVarsity Press, 2010.

Peterson, Robert A. *Salvation Accomplished by the Son: The Work of Christ*. Wheaton: Crossway, 2012.

Stanley, Alan. *Salvation Is More Complicated Than You Think: A Study on the Teachings of Jesus*. Colorado Springs: Authentic, 2007.

Thiselton, Anthony C. *The Last Things: A New Approach*. London: SPCK, 2012.

EARLY TEXTS *and* TRADITIONS ASSOCIATED WITH *the* APOSTLES' CREED

The genetic origins of the Apostles' Creed probably go back to the late second-century Roman church, who developed creedal formulas for catechizing new converts and as part of the confession of faith made by baptismal candidates at their baptism. This creedal tradition spread and developed with several variations until it crystallized into the received form of the Apostles' Creed in the Middle Ages.[1]

The Interrogatory Creed of Hippolytus (ca. 215)

Πιστεύεις εἰς θεόν πατέρα παντοκράτορα;	Do you believe in God the Father Almighty?
Πιστεύεις εἰς Χριστὸν Ἰησοῦν, τὸν υἱὸν τοῦ θεοῦ, τὸν γεννηθέντα διὰ πνεύματος ἁγίου ἐκ Μαρίας τῆς παρθένου, τὸν σταυρωθέντα ἐπὶ Ποντίου Πιλάτου καὶ ἀποθανόντα, καὶ ἀναστάντα τῇ τρίτῃ ἡμέρᾳ ζῶντα ἐκ νεκρῶν, καὶ ἀνελθόντα εἰς τοὺς οὐρανού, καὶ καθίσαντα ἐκ δεξιῶν τοῦ πατρός, ἐρχόμενον κρῖναι ζῶντας καὶ νεκρούς;	Do you believe in Christ Jesus, the Son of God, begotten through the Holy Spirit, from the Virgin Mary, who was crucified under Pontius Pilate, died and rose up on the third day alive from the dead, and ascended into heaven, and is seated at the right hand of the Father, and will come to judge the living and the dead?
Πιστεύεις εἰς τὸ πνεῦμα τὸ ἅγιον ἐν τῇ ἁγίᾳ ἐκκλησίᾳ;[2]	Do you believe in the Holy Spirit and the holy church?

---

1. Unless otherwise noted, English translations in what follows are the author's own.
2. Johannes Quasten, *Patrology*, 4 vols. (Utrecht: Spectrum, 1950; repr., Allen, TX: Christian Classics, 1995), 2:191–92.

The Creed of Marcellus (ca. 340)

Πιστεύω εἰς θεὸν [πατέρα], παντοκράτορα·	I believe in God the Father Almighty,
καὶ εἰς Χριστὸν Ἰησοῦν, τὸν υἱὸν αὐτοῦ τὸν μονογενῆ, τὸν κύριον ἡμῶν,	and in Christ Jesus, his only-begotten Son, our Lord,
τὸν γεννηθέντα ἐκ πνεύματος ἁγίου καὶ Μαρίας τῆς παρθένου,	who was begotten by the Holy Spirit and the Virgin Mary,
τὸν ἐπὶ Ποντίου Πιλάτου, σταυρωθέντα, καὶ ταφέντα,	who was crucified under Pontius Pilate and buried,
καὶ τῇ τρίτῃ ἡμέρᾳ ἀναστάντα ἐκ τῶν νεκρῶν,	on the third day he rose from the dead,
ἀναβάντα εἰς τοὺς οὐρανούς,	ascended into heaven,
καὶ καθήμενον ἐν δεξιᾷ τοῦ πατρός, ὅθεν ἔρχεται κρίνειν ζῶντας καὶ νεκρούς·	is seated at the right hand of the Father, from whence he will come to judge the living and the dead.
καὶ εἰς τὸ ἅγιον πνεῦμα,	And I believe in the Holy Spirit,
ἁγίαν ἐκκλησίαν,	the holy church,
ἄφεσιν ἁμαρτιῶν,	the forgiveness of sins,
σαρκὸς ἀνάστασιν,	the resurrection of the body,
ζωὴν αἰώνιον.[3]	and eternal life.

The Aquileian Creed according to Rufinus (ca. 404)

Credo in Deo Patre omnipotente [invisibili et impassibili]	I believe in God the Father Almighty, invisible and impassible,
Et in Jesu Christo, unico Filio ejus, Domino nostro; qui natus est de Spiritu Sancto ex Maria virgine; crucifixus sub Pontio Pilato, et sepultus; [descendit in inferna]; tertia die resurrexit a mortuis;	and in Jesus Christ, his only Son, our Lord, who was born of the Holy Spirit from the Virgin Mary, crucified under Pontius Pilate and buried, he descended to hell, and on the third day rose from the dead,
ascendit in cælos;	He ascended to heaven,
sedet ad dexteram Patris;	He sits at the right hand of the Father,
inde venturus est judicare vivos et mortuos.	from whence he will come to judge the living and the dead,
Et in Spiritu Sancto; sanctam ecclesiam; remissionem peccatorum; [hujus] carnis resurrectionem.[4]	and in the Holy Spirit, the holy church, the remission of sins, and the resurrection of the body.

---

3. Phillip Schaff, *The Creeds of Christendom*, 3 vols. (Grand Rapids: Baker, 1984), 2:47–48.

4. Schaff, *Creeds of Christendom*, 2:49.

The Old Roman Creed according to Rufinus (ca. 404)

Credo in Deum Patrem omnipotentem.	I believe in God the Father Almighty,
Et in Jesum Christum, Filium ejus unicum, Dominum nostrum;	and in Jesus Christ, his only Son, our Lord,
qui natus est de Spiritu Sancto et Maria virgine;	who was born of the Holy Spirit and the Virgin Mary,
sub Pontio Pilato crucifixus, et sepultus; tertia die resurrexit a mortuis;	who was crucified under Pontius Pilate and buried, and on the third day rose from the dead,
ascendit in cælum,	He ascended to heaven,
sedet ad dexteram Patris;	He sits at the right hand of the Father,
inde venturus judicare vivos et mortuos.	from whence he will come to judge the living and the dead,
Et in Spiritum Sanctum; Sanctam Ecclesiam; remissionem peccatorum; carnis resurrectionem.[5]	and in the Holy Spirit, the holy church, the remission of sins, and the resurrection of the body.

The Received Text of the Apostles' Creed (ca. 700)

Credo in Deum Patrem omnipotentem;	I believe in God the Father Almighty,
Creatorem cæli et terræ.	Maker of heaven and earth:
Et in Jesum Christum, Filium ejus unicum, Dominum nostrum;	And in Jesus Christ his only Son our Lord,
qui conceptus est de Spiritu Sancto,	Who was conceived by the Holy Ghost,
natus ex Maria virgine;	Born of the Virgin Mary,
passus sub Pontio Pilato,	Suffered under Pontius Pilate,
crucifixus, mortuus, et sepultus;	Was crucified, dead, and buried:
descendit ad inferna;	He descended into hell;
tertia die resurrexit a mortuis;	The third day he rose again from the dead;
ascendit ad cælos;	He ascended into heaven,
sedet ad dexteram Dei Patris omnipotentis;	And sitteth on the right hand of God the Father Almighty;

---

5. Schaff, *Creeds of Christendom*, 2:47.

The Received Text of the Apostles' Creed (ca. 700) [continued]

inde venturus (est) judicare vivos et mortuos.	From thence he shall come to judge the quick and the dead.
Credo in Spiritum Sanctum;	I believe in the Holy Ghost;
sanctam ecclesiam catholicam;	The holy Catholick Church;
sanctorum communionem;	The Communion of Saints;
remissionem peccatorum;	The Forgiveness of sins;
carnis resurrectionem;	The Resurrection of the body,
vitam æternam.	And the Life everlasting.
Amen.[6]	Amen.

The Apostles' Creed Today

Πιστεύω εἰς θεὸν πατέρα, παντοκράτορα, ποιητὴν οὐρανοῦ καὶ γῆς.	*Credo in Deum Patrem omnipotentem, Creatorem caeli et terrae.*	I believe in God, the Father almighty, creator of heaven and earth.
Καὶ (εἰς) Ἰησοῦν Χριστὸν, υἱὸν αὐτοῦ τὸν μονογενῆ, τὸν κύριον ἡμῶν,	*Et in Iesum Christum, Filium Eius unicum, Dominum nostrum,*	I believe in Jesus Christ, his only Son, our Lord,
τὸν συλληφθέντα ἐκ πνεύματος ἁγίου,	*qui conceptus est de Spiritu Sancto,*	who was conceived by the Holy Spirit,
γεννηθέντα ἐκ Μαρίας τῆς παρθένου,	*natus ex Maria Virgine,*	born of the Virgin Mary,
παθόντα ἐπὶ Ποντίου Πιλάτου,	*passus sub Pontio Pilato,*	suffered under Pontius Pilate,
σταυρωθέντα, θανόντα, καὶ ταφέντα,	*crucifixus, mortuus, et sepultus,*	was crucified, died, and was buried;
κατελθόντα εἰς τὰ κατώτατα,	*descendit ad inferos,*	he descended to the dead.
τῇ τρίτῃ ἡμέρᾳ ἀναστάντα ἀπὸ τῶν νεκρῶν,	*tertia die resurrexit a mortuis,*	On the third day he rose again;
ἀνελθόντα εἰς τοὺς οὐρανούς,	*ascendit ad caelos,*	he ascended into heaven,
καθεζόμενον ἐν δεξιᾷ θεοῦ πατρὸς παντοδυνάμου,	*sedet ad dexteram Patris omnipotentis,*	he is seated at the right hand of the Father,

---

6. Schaff, *Creeds of Christendom*, 2:45.

The Apostles' Creed Today [continued]

ἐκεῖθεν ἐρχόμενον κρῖναι ζῶντας καὶ νεκρούς.	*inde venturus est iudicare vivos et mortuos.*	and he will come to judge the living and the dead.
Πιστεύω εἰς τὸ πνεῦμα τὸ ἅγιον,	*Credo in Spiritum Sanctum,*	I believe in the Holy Spirit,
ἁγίαν καθολικὴν ἐκκλησίαν,	*sanctam Ecclesiam catholicam,*	the holy catholic Church,
ἁγίων κοινωνίαν,	*sanctorum communionem,*	the communion of saints,
ἄφεσιν ἁμαρτιῶν,	*remissionem peccatorum,*	the forgiveness of sins,
σαρκὸς ἀνάστασιν,	*carnis resurrectionem,*	the resurrection of the body,
ζωὴν αἰώνιον.	*vitam aeternam.*	and the life everlasting.
Ἀμήν.[7]	*Amen.*[8]	Amen.[9]

See further J. N. D. Kelly, *Early Christian Creeds*, 3rd ed. (London: Continuum, 2006) and Jaroslav Pelikan, *Credo: Historical and Theological Guide to Creeds and Confessions of the Faith in the Christian Tradition* (New Haven: Yale University Press, 2003).

---

7. Not normally used in Greek and Eastern Orthodox churches.

8. *Catechismus Catholicae Ecclesiae* (Vatican City: Libreria Editrice Vaticana, 1997).

9. *Common Worship: Services and Prayers for the Church of England* (London: Church House, 2000), 43.

SCRIPTURE INDEX

Romans

1 Corinthians

SUBJECT INDEX

AUTHOR INDEX